Christina Rossetti Revisited

Twayne's English Authors Series

Herbert Sussman, Editor

Northeastern University

TEAS 517

THE ROSSETTI FAMILY, PHOTOGRAPHED BY CHARLES LUTWIDGE
DODGSON (LEWIS CARROLL), 7 OCTOBER 1863.
Reproduced courtesy of the National Portrait Gallery, London.

Christina Rossetti Revisited

Sharon Smulders

Mount Royal College

Twayne Publishers
An Imprint of Simon & Schuster Macmillan
New York

Prentice Hall International
London • Mexico City • New Delhi • Singapore • Sydney • Toronto

Twayne's English Authors Series No. 517

Christina Rossetti Revisited
Sharon Smulders

Twayne Publishers
An Imprint of Simon & Schuster Macmillan
1633 Broadway
New York, NY 10019

Library of Congress Cataloging-in-Publication Data

Smulders, Sharon.
    Christina Rossetti revisited / Sharon Smulders.
        p. cm. — (Twayne's English authors series ; no. 517)
    Includes bibliographical references and index.
    ISBN 0-8057-7050-X
    1. Rossetti, Christina Georgina, 1830–1894—Criticism and interpretation. 2.
Women and literature—England—History—19th century. I. Title. II. Series:
Twayne's English authors series ; TEAS 517.
PR5238.S68   1996
821'.8—dc20   95-40019
                                                                                            CIP

The paper used in this publication meets the minimum requirements of American
National Standard for Information Sciences—Permanence of Paper for Printed Library
Materials, ANSI Z39.48-1984.∞ ™

10 9 8 7 6 5 4 3 2 1

Printed in the United States of America

For my parents

Contents

Preface

This study, in accordance with the objectives of the series, provides a critical introduction to the life and works of Christina Rossetti. Like many Victorians, Rossetti was a prolific writer. Inaugurating her career with *Verses,* privately printed in 1847, she published five further volumes of poetry that, in turn, provided material for two collected editions of her work. At her death, however, nearly a third of her lyrics remained either unpublished or uncollected. In addition to well over a thousand poems, she also produced six volumes of devotional prose, two collections of fiction, and the juvenile novella *Maude: Prose and Verse,* which appeared posthumously in 1897. But despite the volume and variety of her work, Rossetti's reputation rests largely on "Goblin Market" and a few short, melancholy lyrics.

Examining Rossetti's efforts to privilege unique and obscure points of view in her writing, this study focuses on her versatility as a writer. Interested in fostering and sustaining possibilities for feminine self-expression, Rossetti engages in a range of formal experiments in prose as well as verse and frequently resists or dislocates established generic conventions to achieve her ends. Because her attitudes to the social, religious, and esthetic issues of her day inform the thematic and formal preoccupations of her work, this study begins with an overview of her life as a Victorian woman. The next four chapters provide a chronological survey of the major works of the Rossetti canon. Beginning with a discussion of *Maude,* Chapter 2 moves to a consideration of *Goblin Market and Other Poems* in light of Rossetti's association with the Pre-Raphaelite Brotherhood. Chapter 3 then examines the poet's relationship with her brother, Dante Gabriel Rossetti, and her negotiation of his influence in *The Prince's Progress and Other Poems.* After her first two volumes of verse, Rossetti entered a phase of heightened formal diversification. The work produced during this period—*Commonplace and Other Short Stories, Sing-Song,* and *Speaking Likenesses*—forms the subject matter for Chapter 4. Rossetti's interest in the situation of the Victorian woman, clearly evident in her short stories and nursery rhymes, becomes muted in her later writing. Chapter 5 thus deals with the intensification of spiritual concerns in the sonnet sequences published in her final volumes of verse. Circumventing the tensions between gender and genre that drive her earlier writing, Rossetti accommodates the voice of feminine experience to the imperatives of Christian self-realization at the end of her life. Though her work repeats key themes and motifs, her oeuvre shows a refinement of strategies aimed at exploring the fullest range of forms available to the woman writer. The Conclusion considers how Rossetti's reputation has changed in the last century.

Over the past 15 years, developments in critical theory have helped to give a new breadth and depth to Rossetti scholarship. My attempt to reassess Rossetti's achievement on the basis of her fiction as well as her poetry builds on the insights provided by such research. I wish to thank Ina Ferris and Keith Wilson for stimulating my interest in Victorian literature and Geoffrey Hemstedt and Norman Vance for guiding my first efforts to understand Rossetti. I also wish to thank Herbert Sussman whose criticism and encouragement have been of inestimable value in the completion of this project. Finally, I am grateful to the National Portrait Gallery, London, for permission to reproduce Charles Dodgson's photograph of the Rossetti family as the frontispiece to this book.

Chronology

1830   Christina Rossetti is born 5 December at 38 Charlotte Street, Portland Place, London, the youngest child of Frances (Polidori) and Gabriele Rossetti.

1839   Family moves to 50 Charlotte Street.

1843–1847   Deterioration of father's health and family fortunes precipitates adolescent crisis. First signs of chronic invalidism and intense religiosity appear.

1847   *Verses* (privately printed by grandfather, Gaetano Polidori).

1848   Denied formal membership in newly formed Pre-Raphaelite Brotherhood (PRB). Makes publishing debut with two poems in the *Athenaeum*. Plans to marry James Collinson. Models for brother Dante Gabriel's painting *The Girlhood of Mary Virgin* (exhibited 1849).

1849   Models for Dante Gabriel's painting *Ecce Ancilla Domini!* (exhibited 1850).

1850   Contributes seven poems to the *Germ*. Finishes *Maude: Prose and Verse* (published posthumously in 1897). Breaks off engagement to Collinson.

1851   Family moves to 38 Arlington Street, Mornington Crescent. Assists with mother's day school.

1852   Spends brief period in Staffordshire as a governess.

1853   Moves with parents to Frome, Somerset. Helps mother establish another day school. The PRB is virtually defunct.

1854   Family reunites at 45 Upper Albany Street, London. Father dies. Applies unsuccessfully to serve as a nurse in the Crimea.

1855   Takes last temporary post as a governess.

1859   Works with reformed prostitutes as an associate of St. Mary Magdalene's, Highgate.

1861   Makes first tour abroad, to France.

1862   *Goblin Market and Other Poems*. Deepening friendship with Charles Bagot Cayley.

1864   Suffers from severe pulmonary ailment feared to be tuberculosis. Convalesces at Hastings (from December 1864 to April 1865).

1865   Makes second tour abroad, to Switzerland and Italy.

1866   *The Prince's Progress and Other Poems*. Refuses Cayley's offer of marriage.

1867   Family moves to 56 Euston Square.

1870   *Commonplace and Other Short Stories*.

1871   Graves' disease diagnosed.

1872   *Sing-Song: A Nursery Rhyme Book*.

1874   *Speaking Likenesses. Annus Domini: A Prayer for Each Day of the Year*.

1875   *Goblin Market, The Prince's Progress, and Other Poems* (first collected edition).

1876   Leaves household of brother William Michael to live with mother and aunts, Eliza and Charlotte Polidori, at 30 Torrington Square. Sister Maria Francesca dies.

1879   *Seek and Find: A Double Series of Short Studies of the Benedicite*.

1881   *A Pageant and Other Poems. Called to be Saints: The Minor Festivals Devotionally Studied*.

1882   Brother Dante Gabriel dies.

1883   *Letter and Spirit: Notes on the Commandments*.

1885   *Time Flies: A Reading Diary*.

1886   Mother dies.

1890   *Poems* (second collected edition).

1892   *The Face of the Deep: A Devotional Commentary on the Apocalypse*. Undergoes operation to arrest breast cancer.

1893   *Verses* (reprinted from *Called to be Saints, Time Flies, The Face of the Deep*).

1894 Dies 29 December.

1896 *New Poems, Hitherto Unpublished or Uncollected,* edited by William Michael Rossetti.

1904 *The Poetical Works of Christina Georgina Rossetti,* edited by William Michael Rossetti.

Chapter One
Reading the Life

On the day following her sixtieth birthday, Christina Rossetti enclosed a complete symbolist autobiography in a letter to her surviving brother. In this letter she not only consigned to him "for contempt and cremation" the photograph that she called "the *idiotic I*" but spoke pointedly of two other selves: "I am feeling at 60," she assured William, "very much as I did at 59!! though not quite as relieved and exhilarated by the circumstance as when at 30 I gazed in the looking-glass, and discerned no marked change from 29."[1] Tagging these self-assessments to the photographic evidence of herself at age 46, Rossetti discreetly chronicles a history of emotional and physical change that encompasses the exhilaration of youth, the vacancy of middle age, and the moderate relief of old age. Challenging William to destroy proof of "the *idiotic I*," she goes on to suggest, moreover, an opening for comparison with the poet who lived, in some ways, a mirror existence. Her exact contemporary, Emily Dickinson "*had* (for she is dead)," as Rossetti says emphatically, "a wonderful Blakean gift, but therewithal a startling recklessness of poetic ways and means" (*FL,* 176–77). This assessment, coming from a writer who herself often shows "a startling recklessness of poetic ways and means," is doubly surprising inasmuch as the text she possessed presents a Dickinson carefully edited for Victorian consumption and hardly recognizable to modern readers. Ironically, the texts of Rossetti's life and verse would also be carefully rewritten by her editor. That editor was, of course, her brother William.

After his sister's death, William was initially reluctant to prepare the expected biography because, as he confided to Mackenzie Bell, her outer life possessed "scarcely any *events*" and "her inner life was one of religious devoutness."[2] For *The Poetical Works of Christina Georgina Rossetti,* he nevertheless deemed a memoir of her "hushed life-drama" a necessary prelude to the verse.[3] In the memoir he reiterates that his sister's life "did not consist of incidents: in few things, external; in all its deeper currents, internal" (*PW,* lviii). Intrigued, Rossetti's biographers have returned, subsequently and unfailingly, to the portrait of the poet that emerges from the memoir.[4] In most twentieth-century studies she appears as an

1

intensely personal and utterly spontaneous writer whose work demonstrates her character as a woman disappointed in love, an invalid preoc-
cupied with her own frail mortality, and a pious, rather unworldly
recluse. Yielding to the attractions of myth, Rossetti's biographers thus
arrive at a sentimental parody of the life. But religious though she certainly was, she was far from naive about what she called "our world of
brick and mortar."[5] Sick as she often was, she was also resilient and used
"the privileges & immunities" of "semi-invalidism" to travel and to
write.[6] Unmarried though she remained, she chose her life, and if her
choices involved some heartache, they also provided a good deal of personal and esthetic satisfaction. Finally, confessional as her verse seems, it
reveals less of the person Rossetti was than of the many personas she
expressly created for her readership.

An Anglo-Italian Girlhood

Rossetti was born into a family of uneasily reconciled contradiction. Her
father, a scion of the Abruzzi proletariat, was a gifted improvisational
poet devoted to constitutional reform in his native Italy. After the fall of
the Bonapartiste regime, he fled Naples to escape the enmity of the rein-
stated Bourbons. Arriving in London in 1824, Gabriele Rossetti eventually met and married Frances Lavinia Polidori. After their marriage, the
couple settled at 38 Charlotte Street, Portland Place, and had four children in as many years: Maria Francesca in February 1827, Gabriel
Charles Dante (afterwards Dante Gabriel) in May 1828, William
Michael in September 1829, and Christina Georgina in December 1830.
Rossetti's Christian names uniquely embody the contradictions of her
parentage: as a reminder of her father's politics, she took her first name
from Princess Christina Bonaparte; as a reminder of her mother's
respectable English connections, she took her second name from
Georgina (daughter of Sir Patrick) Macgregor. From her father, Rossetti
received not only a name but an appreciation for Dante. "Perhaps," she
observed in 1892, "it is enough to be half an Italian, but certainly it is
enough to be a Rossetti, to render Dante a fascinating centre of thought"
(*FL*, 184). Writing among other things two essays on Dante, she was,
however, the last of her siblings to be "sucked into the Dantesque vor-
tex" (*FL*, 188).[7]
   While Rossetti's father bequeathed to her a love of chess as well as
Dante, her mother's legacy was one of whist and strong-mindedness
tempered by religious pietism. In fact, the household as a whole, albeit

neither conventionally Victorian nor securely middle class, took its tenor from Frances Rossetti. Moreover, it owed its peculiar blend of Italian and English elements to a pattern matrilineally established. Rossetti's maternal grandfather, like her father, belonged nominally to the Roman Catholic Church, taught Italian, and occupied himself with literary matters. On the other hand, her grandmother, the former Anna Maria Pierce, was an Englishwoman of staunch Anglican conviction. By way of compromise between the two national heritages, the Polidoris raised their sons as Roman Catholics and their daughters as Anglicans. But whereas genteel conformity distinguished Rossetti's mother and aunts, her uncles' eccentricities ran the gamut from Philip Polidori's benign mental incompetence through the self-styled Henry Polydore's marital and professional failures to the suicidal Byronism of Dr. John Polidori, author of *The Vampyre* (1819).

Although all the Rossetti children were baptized within the Anglican communion, gender also dictated their religious differences. Beginning their attendance at Christ Church, Albany Street, sometime after 1843, the Rossettis came under the influence of Tractarianism—the precursor to Anglo-Catholicism—in the person of Rev. William Dodsworth. Although his successor and Rossetti's lasting friend, Rev. (later Canon) H. W. Burrows, wrote the preface for her first devotional work, *Annus Domini,* the lingering effects of Dodsworth's fiery premillennial sermons reach their apogee in the last of her works, *The Face of the Deep.*[8] But despite his influence, Rossetti did not follow him to the Roman Catholic Church in 1850. In fact, while her brothers became agnostics, she and her sister remained devout Anglo-Catholics to the end of their lives.

If, as William attests, "all the four children were treated alike," this treatment certainly did not persist beyond 1836.[9] In that year, the family moved to larger accommodations at 50 Charlotte Street and Gabriel, followed by William in 1837, began to attend a preparatory day school for boys. From this school, both went to King's College, where their father held a professorship in Italian. By contrast, the girls' education stayed wholly in the hands of their mother, who had, previous to her marriage, served as a governess to the Macgregor family. Indeed, like their mother before them, all four Polidori sisters—Margaret, Frances, Charlotte, and Eliza—received educations suitable to prepare them as governesses. The only occupation with a modicum of middle-class respectability open to Victorian women, governessing was, as William once said, "the family vocation" (W. Rossetti 1906, 1:39), but it was not a vocation for which Rossetti had any fondness. After a few brief stints as a governess, she took her last post toward the end of 1855. Falling sick, she confessed herself delighted to find that she was "really unfit . . . for miscellaneous governessing *en permanence*" (*FL*, 24). Many years later she described herself to Algernon Swinburne as an "escaped governess," adding "wherefore I ought to feel for my 'sisters-who-should-have-been'" (quoted in Jones, 21). Her phrasing ("ought to" instead of "do") is enlightening. That her relief at escape, even so long after the event, clouds an otherwise characteristic attempt at sympathy with a different feminine point of view suggests just how onerous Rossetti found her experience of the family vocation.

While she was yet preparing for this calling, 1843 ushered in a change of fortune for the family. When blindness began to succeed bronchial problems, her father relinquished his position at King's College. Always narrowly constrained, family circumstances became dire in 1844. Taking matters into her own hands, Frances Rossetti advertised for private pupils and dispatched Maria to her first posting as a governess. The situation improved marginally in 1845 when William, at 15, began his career with the civil service. During the difficult years between 1843 and 1848, the youngest of the Rossettis was also the one most often at home with an ailing father and a mother who, notwithstanding her almost proverbial composure, was harassed by financial concerns. In this environment, the factors contributing to the elusive malady (tentatively diagnosed as angina pectoris) that then afflicted Rossetti are not hard to find: the financial insolvency threatening familial solidarity; physiological changes overtaking a pubescent girl; cultural prescriptions affecting a Victorian woman; medical practices predisposing female patients to chronic invalidism; climactic conditions prevailing in a British urban center; and the religious enthusiasms sweeping a nation.[10] Organic or not, Rossetti's illness released her temporarily from the obligations of family support and allowed her to travel almost annually to England's south coast. Moreover, like Elizabeth Barrett Browning and Emily Brontë, she used an invalid's exemption from social duties to nurture her art.

Five years after she had composed her first verses to her mother, Rossetti possessed enough material to merit her grandfather's indulgence. Of the *Verses* printed on his private press in 1847, her mother records that she "scrupulously rejected all assistance in her rhyming efforts, under the impression that in that case they would not be her own" (quoted in Packer, 17). Though later involved in several cooperative endeavors, Rossetti remained a scrupulously independent writer. This independence did not, however, come easily. For just as her younger brother took control of her posthumous reputation, her elder brother exercised fraternal rights over her professional development.

The Pre-Raphaelite Brotherhood

While the other Rossettis struggled to keep the family afloat, Gabriel had gone from King's College to Sass's Academy to train as a painter. "He therefore cost something," William remembered, "and earned nothing" (W. Rossetti 1906, 1:39). A student at the Royal Academy since 1846, Gabriel began to move out in his own direction in 1848 and drew in his wake the family interests. Now in addition to Italian exiles, another group of colorful and flamboyant individuals frequented the Rossetti household. But instead of elders, these were peers infused with the idealisms of youth; and instead of expatriates, these were Englishmen. Though the interests of the emerging group were primarily literary and artistic, they were also political and religious. In fact, the group's rubric facilitated an unlikely and highly volatile combination of Chartist radicalism and Anglo-Catholic pietism. Comprised of the Rossetti brothers, William Holman Hunt, James Collinson, John Everett Millais, Frederick George Stephens, and Thomas Woolner, the Pre-Raphaelite Brotherhood (PRB) and its short-lived literary magazine, the *Germ,* were natural successors to the family collective that had in 1843 produced *Hodge Podge* and the *Illustrated Scrapbook.* As for Rossetti, she may have been a Pre-Raphaelite, but she was not part of the Brotherhood: she was a poet, but not a painter; she was an Anglo-Catholic, but never a Chartist; she was young, but she was female. And as its nomenclature suggests, the PRB did not, like the Rossetti family, incorporate sexual difference.

In August 1848, while Rossetti and her youngest brother were at Brighton writing sonnets, her eldest brother and Hunt had taken a studio together, read Richard Monckton Milnes's *Life and Letters of John Keats,* and begun hosting literary meetings. Shortly thereafter, an exclusive club, composed of the Rossetti brothers, Hunt, and Collinson, agreed to meet for discussion of poems each would write. Convinced that his sister's superior literary gifts would be an asset to the group, Gabriel proposed her membership, but he met protest from Hunt. Withdrawing her name, he explained that he "never meant that she should attend the meetings," for "it would be impossible to persuade her, as it would bring her to a pitch of nervousness infinitely beyond Collinson's."[11] On the contrary, "I merely intended," he told Hunt, "that she should entrust her productions to my reading; but must give up the idea, as I find she objects to this also, under the impression that it would seem like display, I believe,—a sort of thing she abhors" (D. G. Rossetti 1965, 1:45). Because she readily submitted several poems to the *Athenaeum,* however, two of which—"Death's Chill Between" and "Heart's Chill Between"— appeared in October of 1848, her objection seems manufactured, whether by herself or Gabriel, for other reasons as well. Indeed, when the PRB succeeded the abortive club, Rossetti shared their enthusiasms enough not only to contribute seven poems to the *Germ* but also to contemplate marriage with one of their number.

Rossetti knew Collinson, then a convert to Roman Catholicism, as a former communicant at Christ Church as well as a member of the PRB. Though she refused his initial proposal, she agreed to marry him upon his reversion to the Church of England. Gabriel supported the engagement "with," said William later, "perhaps too headlong a wish to serve the interests of a 'Praeraphaelite Brother'" (W. Rossetti 1906, 1:72). Certainly, the arrangement savors of a feudal alliance intended to formalize the bonds of masculine kinship, but the proposed marriage also offered Rossetti a way to integrate her aesthetic aspirations with more conventional feminine expectations. The engagement was not, however, without its difficulties. Embarrassed by "talk of *beaus,*" she did not, for instance, find her visit to the Collinson family at Pleasley Hill altogether pleasant and so, as she told William, "knit lace with a perseverance completely foreign to my nature" (*FL,* 6). Exiled within a "foreign" world of feminine interests, she missed the stimulation of writing sonnets in concert with her brothers and implored them for news of the PRB. But even as she discovered that her engagement put her beyond the fraternal pale, she used the intelligence to advantage for *Maude,* a novella that explores the vocational opportunities open to women and examines the concept of sisterhood.

Although William later blamed Collinson for destroying his sister's "peace of mind on the very threshold of womanly life" and for years following (*PW,* lii), *Maude* suggests she had serious reservations about the idea of marriage before breaking off her engagement. Returning to London, she nevertheless felt that Mary Collinson's wish to discontinue their correspondence because of the "unpromising" nature of "her brother's affairs" was "extraordinary" (*FL,* 10). It was also prescient, for Collinson returned to Roman Catholicism in the spring of 1850, precipitating the termination of the engagement and eventually of his association with the PRB. Adamant about Collinson's love for Rossetti, her brother was less willing to "say that she was in love with Collinson" (W. Rossetti 1906, 1:73). Yet long afterwards she retained a fondness for him, submitting his poem "The Child Jesus" as a candidate for inclusion in *The Poets' Bible,* edited by Rev. W. Garrett Horder, and publishing one of his sonnets—a gift she had committed to memory—under the entry for 24 January in *Time Flies.* Moreover, in the affair's immediate aftermath, she risked her mother's displeasure to petition William for news of Collinson's health as well as his progress on his painting *St. Elizabeth.* Begun in 1849 and first exhibited in 1851, the painting was based on Charles Kingsley's *The Saint's Tragedy,* which Collinson had brought to Rossetti's attention. In 1850 and 1852 she also addressed the subject in two poems, "St. Elizabeth" and "St. Elizabeth of Hungary." Paradoxically, the inspiration of affianced concern bore fruit in the theme of St. Elizabeth's devout self-denial.

While Rossetti's engagement pursued its tremulous course, plans for the group's literary magazine crystallized. At first she refused to be associated with the project because it included "among its contributors a 'rabid chartist,' and one 'who thinks nothing but politics' and 'the negation of religion.' Your plan," she concluded, "is far too *Blissful* for my taste" (*FL,* 7). The withdrawal of William North, the "rabid chartist," and the irreligious Bliss from the magazine neutralized her objections. Now the magazine would, she said, "have more prospect of success" (*FL,* 10). Apparently, others shared her concerns about the kind of contributions suitable to publication. On 6 November 1849 the PRB decided to exclude from the magazine's first number any material "referring to politics or religion."[12] Divisiveness persisted, however. Indeed, even the question of a title for the prospective magazine proved difficult. In this crisis Rossetti readily abandoned her own "overwhelming business"—"nothing more important than needle-work and such like" (*FL,* 11)—to become Gabriel's unofficial secretary. Writing to William, she described the contributions secured thus far and urged him as the PRB's official secretary to contact F. G. Stephens again about the title. "Several," she writes, "are thinking of calling it the P.R.B. Journal" (*FL,* 12). Finally, in December, the group agreed upon the *Germ,* but after two numbers again altered the title to *Art and Poetry: Being Thoughts Towards Nature.* Winning special praise from Coventry Patmore, another PRB outsider, Rossetti's verse— "Dream-Land," "An End," "A Pause of Thought," "Song" ("Oh! roses for the flush of youth"), "A Testimony," "Repining," and "Sweet Death"— appears in three of the journal's four numbers.

Rossetti's connection to the PRB fostered her artistic inclinations as well as her literary interests. When she went to Staffordshire to tutor the daughters of Swynfen Jervis (a Shakespearean scholar and family friend) in conversational Italian, Gabriel wrote to ask for some of her drawings, cautioning her to "take care however not to rival the Sid, but keep within respectful limits" (D. G. Rossetti 1965, 1:108). The Sid was Elizabeth Siddall—Gabriel's model, his pupil, and later his wife. Stinting in his estimate of his sister's art, he offered greater encouragement of her verse, which he promoted among the Howitts and others of his growing acquaintance. In 1854 three of her poems appeared in gift books under Mary Howitt's editorship: "The Rose" in Aikin's *Pictorial Calendar of the Seasons,* "The Trees' Counselling" in *Midsummer Flowers,* and "Twilight Calm" in the *Düsseldorf Artist's Album.*

In the meantime, the press of necessity was yet upon the Rossettis. Early in 1851 the family had moved to 38 Arlington Street, Mornington Crescent, where Rossetti assisted her mother in the day school they established. Achieving dismal success with the Arlington Street venture, she and her parents moved in 1853 to Frome, Somerset, to set up another school. Although she could no longer take drawing lessons from Ford Madox Brown at his school in Camden Town, she continued to sketch as well as write during the year-long interlude at Frome. About her recent verse, Gabriel found much to praise. Of her chances as a painter, he was rather less sanguine. For unlike Barbara Leigh Smith (later Bodichon) who occasionally wore "breeches . . . in the sacred name of pigment," she found "art interfere[d] with the legitimate exercise of anguish" (D. G. Rossetti 1965, 1:163).

While Rossetti continued to draw in later years, she was never able to integrate this interest within her professional career: her illustrations for *Sing-Song* yielded to Arthur Hughes's, and her wall-paper designs failed to interest the firm of Morris, Marshall, Faulkner & Co. As a model, however, her face shaped early Pre-Raphaelite iconography. The subject of her brother's first oil, a portrait dated 1847, she also figures as the Virgin in *The Girlhood of Mary Virgin* (exhibited 1849) and *Ecce Ancilla Domini!* (exhibited 1850). Moreover, she sat for Hunt's studies of Christ's face in *The Light of the World* (completed 1854). In these works she embodies the religious ideal that gave to early Pre-Raphaelitism its incandescence. Attempting "something more probable and at the same time less commonplace" with the Virgin in *The Girlhood,* Gabriel sought "to interest the members of a Christian community" (D. G. Rossetti 1965, 1:48). Later, he told Stephens that the painting "was a symbol of female excellence. The Virgin being taken at its highest type. It was not," he continued, "her *Childhood* but *Girlhood*."[13] Also symbolizing "female excellence," the Virgin of *Ecce Ancilla Domini!* was, according to George Boyce, "full of intense thought and awakened and growing religious awe, almost my ideal of a woman's head."[14] In retrospect, Gabriel called this painting "the ancestor of all the *white* pictures which have since become so numerous—but," he noted, "there was an ideal motive for the whiteness."[15] Ironically, insofar as apocryphal readings of Rossetti draw implicitly on her brother's pictorial symbolism, she has never entirely escaped the "ideal motive" for what are, in Gabriel's final analysis, avant-garde experiments in the use of composition and coloration to advance a religious program.

In 1853 Gabriel's white painting "lost its familiar name of *The Ancilla,*—the mottoes having been altered from Latin to English to guard against the imputation of 'popery'" (Fredeman, ed., 99). The revisions, done with an eye to the painting's commercial viability, respond to the marketplace realities responsible, in part, for the dispersal of the PRB. Still at Frome, Rossetti devised two witty lyrics for the group's epitaph: "The two Rossettis (brothers they)" and "The P.R.B. is in its decadence." About the same time, William received a promotion allowing him to reunite the family, all but Gabriel, at 45 Upper Albany Street. Shortly after the move Gabriele Rossetti died. But while William and fate had conspired to deliver Christina at once from teaching and nursing duties, she wanted employment. In 1854 she applied to accompany Aunt Eliza, recently freed by the deaths of the elder Polidoris, to Scutari, where Florence Nightingale had established a hospital to care for casualties of the Crimean War. Disqualified from Nightingale's nursing service on the basis of her youth, Rossetti explored other means to self-fulfillment in the years to follow.

Sororal Competition and Cooperation

Elizabeth Siddall, the subject of numerous pencil sketches and watercolors executed during the 1850s, succeeded Christina Rossetti as Gabriel's type of female excellence. Upon his sister's return from Frome, he was eager to bring the two women together. Hoping to promote both his protégée's artistic career and his sister's poetic career, he planned to make their first meeting the opening for a joint volume. The scheme came to nothing. Instead, a "coldness" developed between Rossetti and her brother because she and Siddall, being thrust into unwanted competition, did "not agree. She works at worsted ever," wrote Ford Madox Brown of Rossetti in September 1855, "and talks sparingly."[16] But although Rossetti used the drudgery of needlework to escape conversation, she not only understood Siddall's trials as a model but also respected her abilities as a poet and a painter. In 1865, she acknowledged her late sister-in-law's poetic skill by proposing that Siddall's verse grace her forthcoming volume. Interestingly, Rossetti esteemed in the other woman's poems the very qualities that distinguish her own. Of course, her work probably provided the model. Dropping the pose she took as the leading poet of melancholy, she even made jest of the resemblance: "Talk of my bogieism," she said to Gabriel, "is it not by comparison jovial?"[17] Admiring the "cool bitter sarcasm" of "Dead Love," she exclaimed of Siddall's other lyrics, "How full of beauty they are, but how painful" (W. Rossetti, ed., 1903, 76). Despite the beauty of Siddall's verse, she judged her poems as "almost too hopelessly sad for publication *en masse*" (W. Rossetti, ed., 1903, 78).

Although Rossetti did not publish anything with Siddall either before or after her death in 1862, she used the 1850s to hone her craft. Indeed, she had a high estimation of her powers. To William Aytoun, editor of *Blackwood's Magazine,* she wrote, "My love for what is good in the works of others teaches one that there is something above the despicable in mine; that poetry is with me, not a mechanism, but an impulse and a reality; and that I know my aims in writing to be pure, and directed to that which is true and right."[18] But except for a few poems published with *Once a Week* in 1859, her verse received little notice from the Victorian literary establishment.[19] Then, at the beginning of 1861, Gabriel again set to furthering her career, approaching his patron John Ruskin and, when that failed, considering either Elizabeth Gaskell or William Allingham as likely to advance her cause with W. M. Thackeray, editor of *Cornhill Magazine.* The break, however, came with Alexander Macmillan. After one evening spent in his company, Gabriel informed her that Macmillan "has been congratulated by some of his contributors on having got a poet at last in your person" (D. G. Rossetti 1965, 2:389). In February 1861 Rossetti made her debut in *Macmillan's Magazine* with "Up-Hill," the "lively little Song of the Tomb" that had charmed the publisher at first reading (D. G. Rossetti 1965, 2:390). Even more impressed by "Goblin Market," Macmillan read it aloud to a workingmen's society at Cambridge and arranged for its appearance as the opening attraction of her first published volume of verse, *Goblin Market and Other Poems,* released in March 1862.

Far from complacent in her success, Rossetti recognized that publication necessarily involved commercial competition. Jean Ingelow, the so-called lost Pre-Raphaelite, posed the first challenge to her new celebrity. Reading the initial reviews of Ingelow's *Poems* of 1863, Rossetti believed she "would be a formidable rival to most men, and to any woman" (Packer, ed., 19). When *Poems* went into its eighth edition the following year, she drolly remarked that it had lent to her "complexion a becoming green tinge" (W. Rossetti, ed., 1903, 70). Ingelow's *Poems* also whet Rossetti's curiosity, however. "I want," she told Dora Greenwell, "to know who she is, what she is like, where she lives" (quoted in Bell, 161). She had not long to find out, for shortly after receiving a copy of Ingelow's work from Anne Gilchrist (the Blake biographer and later Whitman apologist), she met her formidable rival. The acquaintance prospered and Ingelow tendered an introduction for Rossetti to Roberts Brothers, Boston, who became her American publishers in 1866. As female contemporaries, Ingelow and Rossetti—along with Dora Greenwell—inevitably invited comparative assessment. Published at the end of the century, an article on the three poets gives perhaps the clearest, certainly the quaintest, indication of the anxiety caused by the idea of literary competition among women. Moreover, such anxiety affected the writers as well as the readers of women's poetry. Rather than discussing their verse, "A Poetic Trio" prints the letters that the three women wrote on the occasion of a "great sewing competition" when Ingelow challenged Rossetti to provide "proof that she can do hemming and sewing."[20] But Rossetti, while she thanked Greenwell for her present of a workbag, chose to ignore the dare. Having escaped a contest with Siddall through working "at worsted," she now refused to engage in a rivalry so domesticated.

Rossetti's friendship with Greenwell, an essayist as well as a poet, began with their meeting in Newcastle in 1858. Interested in such issues as the plight of "Our Single Women," the other writer possessed what Rossetti called "large-mindedness" (*FL,* 51). In 1875 Greenwell appealed to Rossetti's own capacity for large-mindedness when she drew her friend's attention to "the horror of vivisection" in all its "revolting magnitude" (*FL,* 51). Although William afterwards maintained that his sister "had no politics" (*PW,* lxx), she became a committed antivivisectionist and fielded petitions for this cause as well as the Minors' Protection Bill, which aimed to curb child prostitution by raising the age of consent for girls to 16 from 13. Moreover, her political sympathies often make their way into her verse. While "In the Round Tower at

Jhansi, June 8, 1857" offers her sentimentalized response to the India
Mutiny, "Counterblast on Penny Trumpet" (buried at the end of the
Poetical Works) records her admiration of John Bright, who opposed
British expansion into North Africa and consequently resigned from
William Gladstone's ministry following the bombardment of Alexandria
in 1882. Indeed, the violence of this imperial venture prompted her to
remark that she would "willingly . . . *incur* Income Tax for the sake of *not*
murdering Egyptians or any one else" (*FL,* 120).

Rossetti respected Bright because he would not sacrifice his moral
convictions to the expediencies of party politics. Also driven by conscience, her own politics are difficult to disentangle from her religious
convictions. In addition to reviving ritual as an integral aspect of worship, the Anglo-Catholic movement fostered the growth of sisterhoods
and encouraged women, particularly single women of the middle and
upper classes, to engage in practical service to the impoverished, the
sick, and the disenfranchised.[21] Implicitly challenging the ideal of feminine fulfillment that Coventry Patmore had popularized in his epic of
conjugal devotion, *The Angel in the House* (1854–62), these women found
self-worth in religious work that was also social work. Rossetti's sister,
Maria, worked at one time for the Young Women's Friendly Society,
directed by "the Honourable" Mrs. Chambers under the auspices of
Christ Church. While this society catered to the needs of servant girls,
another of Chambers's concerns was an institution for the reclamation of
"fallen women," later superseded by the Diocesan Penitentiary, St. Mary
Magdalene's, Highgate, where Rossetti worked as a lay sister during the
1860s.[22] Writing in the summer of 1860, Letitia Scott describes Rossetti
in the modified habit of an associate: "the dress . . . is very simple, ele-
gant even; black with hanging sleeves, a muslin cap with lace edging
quite becoming to her with the veil."[23] The understated elegance of the
habit aside, Rossetti's occupation brought her into contact with unmarried mothers of the working class—whether prostitutes, servants, or
seamstresses—who led lifestyles vastly different from her own.

The concerns addressed by the Anglican sisterhoods are also those
Rossetti raises in much of the verse composed in the 1850s and 1860s.
Meeting opposition from Gabriel, she stood by the publication of these
poems even as she assented to his "opinion of the unavoidable and
indeed much-to-be-desired unreality of women's work on many social
matters."[24] "The Lowest Room," an examination of the meaninglessness
of women's existence, especially irritated her brother and provoked him
to attribute its strong-mindedness to a variety of influences, including

Jean Ingelow, Adelaide Procter, and Isa Craig. With Rossetti, these three women belonged to the Portfolio Society, a satellite of the Langham Place circle. Under the leadership of Barbara Bodichon and Bessie Parkes, the ladies of Langham Place set out to serve women's interests in the areas of employment and education. Though limited, Rossetti's involvement in the literary and artistic activities of the group testifies to her interest in contemporary debates on the Woman Question. A corresponding member of the Portfolio Society, she submitted two poems, "'Behold, I Stand at the Door and Knock'" and "Gone Before," to the *English Woman's Journal,* a periodical established by Bodichon and Parkes in 1858.[25] Another Langham Place associate was Emily Faithfull, the woman behind the Victoria Press, run for and by women. In 1863 Rossetti contributed three poems to Faithfull publications. "Dream-Love" appeared in *A Welcome: Original Contributions in Poetry and Prose*; "A Royal Princess" in *Poems: An Offering to Lancashire*; and "L.E.L." in the *Victoria Magazine*. As for "The Lowest Room," eventually published in *Macmillan's,* Rossetti acknowledged the justice of "the Isa and Adelaide taunt" (Troxell, ed., 142) but denied any resemblance to Ingelow's work, since "as to date, it *was* written," she said, "before Miss J[ean] I[ngelow] misled me any-whither" (*FL,* 55).

Gabriel attributed the strong-mindedness of "The Lowest Room" to one other source: Elizabeth Barrett Browning. Though Barrett Browning ended her career with *Last Poems,* which appeared posthumously in 1862, she was to be Rossetti's most formidable poetic rival. To stave off potential comparisons between herself and her late contemporary, she relied upon a noncompetitive strategy she refined in her dealings with Gabriel: to insist on her difference and, not infrequently, her inferiority. For instance, when asked to abandon her "one-stringed lyre" for something approximating the elder woman's "many-sidedness," she said bluntly, if somewhat disingenuously, "It is not in me, and therefore will never come out of me, to turn to politics or philanthropy with Mrs. Browning" (*FL,* 31). Admiring such "many-sidedness," she later disclaimed the suggestion that she was the greater poet of the two: "I doubt whether the woman is born, or for many a long day, if ever, will be born, who will balance not to say outweigh Mrs. Browning" (quoted in Bell, 93). But despite critical efforts to yoke the two women as rivals, Barrett Browning was more important to Rossetti as a poetic precursor than she was as a contemporary competitor. Taking her epigraph for "L.E.L." from "L.E.L.'s Last Question," she tacitly traced her lineage as a female poet back through Barrett Browning's oeuvre to their common ancestor, Letitia Landon. Moreover, publishing "L.E.L." with Faithfull, she openly proclaimed her association with women of both the present and the past. Fittingly, younger poets such as the Irish Katherine Tynan and the Jewish Amy Levy, both estranged from the Victorian mainstream by their foreignness as well as their femaleness, would find in Rossetti the model she had found in Barrett Browning.[26]

Middle Age: "So Different, and Yet So Vividly the Same"

As early as 1863 Rossetti entertained the thought of issuing a second volume of verse, but she hesitated, as she later said, to "rush before the public with an immature volume" (W. Rossetti, ed., 1903, 50). Willing to wait for "a sufficiency of quality as well as quantity," she remarked ghoulishly, "If meanwhile my things become *remains,* that need be no bugbear to scare me into premature publicity" (W. Rossetti, ed., 1903, 50). By December of 1864 her health had deteriorated so alarmingly that her doctors advised a move to Hastings, a seaside town much frequented by consumptives. Living here until April of 1865, she worked against the "fear lest by infinite delay" her next volume would, in fact, be one of remains (W. Rossetti, ed., 1903, 74). Her sojourn at Hastings was enormously productive, for on her return to London she had virtually completed work on the volume. Much recovered, she then accompanied William and her mother to the Continent. In 1861 she had visited France, but this second trip, partly memorialized in "Later Life," took her through Switzerland to Italy.

During the period between the publication of her first and second volumes of verse, she became closely attached to Charles Cayley, a scholar who had once been her father's pupil. William judged Cayley to be "a personage of higher type" than Collinson (*PW,* liii), but the outcome was very much the same, for Rossetti declined his proposal. A realist rather than a romantic in daily life, she had "nothing," she told her brother, "but mere feeling to offer"; and although she "might be selfish enough to wish that [money] were the only bar," she saw other impediments too (*FL,* 29). Rossetti probably based her refusal, as William speculates, on the perception of something "wofully defective" in Cayley's faith (*PW,* liii). Yet several other reasons exist for her decision, and her brother, by so reducing them to the singular (and conjectural) one of religion, manifestly simplifies her motivations and options. For while William associates marriage with feminine fulfillment in typically Victorian fashion, she could not reconcile the loss of personal freedom, especially in the area of religious belief, with that prospect of marital happiness. As her devotional writings suggest, Rossetti felt that she must as a wife relinquish to her husband the relative independence of mind she enjoyed as a sister.[27] She had, supposedly, her mother's experience of happy compromise as an example to the contrary, but the tranquil serenity that William ascribes to his parents' marriage seems suspect given their religious differences, much less their financial difficulties. While Frances Rossetti tolerated her husband's apostasy during his lifetime, all her frustrated resistance appears in one act after his death: she burned his scholarly work *Mistero dell' Amor Platonico*.[28] Rather than marriage, therefore, her daughter chose friendship. In 1866 Rossetti appreciated the position of a wife far differently from the way she had in 1848: marriage, though it had promised more freedom to the girl of 17, augered less autonomy for the woman of 35.

Beyond these considerations lie other reasons for Rossetti's chosen independence. Owing to an uncertainty as to whether Cayley proposed in 1864—when she was quite ill—or 1866, Georgina Battiscombe plausibly suggests, for example, that her health influenced her decision (Battiscombe, 122). This reason also holds well beyond 1864, however, for Dr. William Jenner apparently did not reprieve Rossetti from a diagnosis of tuberculosis until 7 February 1868 (see W. Rossetti, ed., 1903, 297–98). A marriage to Cayley was, moreover, financially impracticable. When William graciously offered to provide a marital subsistence, Rossetti refused. As a single woman, she found her economic dependence on her brother galling and later devised a plan to reimburse him through her will. Meticulously precise, she calculated her "debt to him at (say) £100 a year for 20 years" (*FL*, 125)—that is, for the interval between her father's death and her brother's marriage. In such light, William's well-meant proposal promised to increase a financial obligation that she felt she could only remit through her death. She would have been gratified to learn that the royalties he later received for her work were substantial and, in fact, "always about double" those received for Gabriel's (W. Rossetti 1990, 600n4). She was always, as she once told her publisher, "happy to attain fame (!) and guineas" through her verse (Packer, ed., 23).

During the course of these personal deliberations, *The Prince's Progress and Other Poems* finally made its long-awaited appearance in the spring of 1866. Rossetti received her copy while she, in company with W. B. and Letitia Scott, was visiting Alice Boyd at Penkill Castle. Making a second visit to Penkill in 1869, Rossetti enjoyed a warm friendship with Boyd and later invited her to illustrate *Sing-Song*. The several mischances experienced by *Sing-Song* before its publication in 1872 led, however, to a change in illustrators. Finishing the *Sing-Song* manuscript early in 1870, Rossetti was also in the process of changing publishers. At the instigation of Gabriel and, to a lesser extent, William, she left Macmillan for F. S. Ellis, who published *Commonplace and Other Short Stories* in 1870. In this year Gabriel also published with Ellis his first volume of original *Poems*. During the preparation of this volume, he asked his sister to read his verse just as she had asked him to read hers. One tantalizing glimpse of Rossetti suggests her thoughts on at least some of his work: "Gabriel writes me he has done the best he has yet accomplished in the *Eden Bower*," W. B. Scott told William, "and that it drove Maria and Christina out of the room" (W. Rossetti, ed., 1903, 470). Notwithstanding either her reservations or the Fleshly School debacle, *Poems* was a publishing success. On the other hand, the comparative failure of *Commonplace and Other Short Stories* prompted Rossetti to release Ellis from his obligation to *Sing-Song*. Only with the publication in 1874 of *Speaking Likenesses* did she return to her original publisher. In the following year, Macmillan issued the collected edition of her verse, *Goblin Market, The Prince's Progress, and Other Poems*. Prompted by Gabriel's criticism of the volume, she belatedly admitted some possible errors of judgment. "The whole subject of youthful poems grows anxious in middle age, or may at some moments appear so," she said by way of excuse: "One is so different, and yet so vividly the same" (*FL*, 55).

Publishing no fewer than five books between 1870 and 1875, Rossetti was also sick much of this time. During 1870 she fell victim to a prostrating lassitude, succeeded by other symptoms including heart palpitations, goiter, and hair and weight loss. She was, as William recorded in his diary, "a total wreck" (*FL*, 208). Finally, in 1871, her doctors diagnosed her condition as exophthalmic bronchocele, better known as Graves' disease. In 1872 she spent time recuperating in Sussex. In typically two-sided fashion, she wrote to William of her improvement: "*Pro* you will find me fatter; *contra* of a fearful brownness" (*FL*, 38). Meanwhile, Gabriel suffered a near fatal collapse and eventually went into retreat at Kelmscott (the country house that he shared with William Morris). Visiting him there in 1873, Rossetti and her mother received the news that William and Lucy Madox Brown had become engaged.

The announced marriage, warmly welcomed by the Rossetti women, had various effects. Acting on a long-standing desire, Maria entered her novitiate at All Saints Sisterhood in 1873, taking her full vows the year before her death in 1876. Despite her activities as a lay sister, Rossetti had no wish to pursue a religious profession: "It was my dear Sister, not I," she later wrote to a correspondent, "who felt drawn to the noble vocation *I* have never attempted to fulfil" (quoted in Bell, 121). Although she and her mother initially remained with William and his new bride at 56 Euston Square, the house they had taken in 1867, the arrangement was far from satisfactory. Lucy Brown had been a tractable pupil when the Rossetti women undertook her tuition in the mid-1850s. Lucy Rossetti, however, was the free-thinking mistress of her husband's household and an artist in her own right. Conflict was inevitable. Finally, Rossetti and her mother decamped, moving with Charlotte and Eliza Polidori to 30 Torrington Square in 1876. Despite their differences, Rossetti strove to sympathize with Lucy's point of view. Assuring Gabriel that "of course we part friends," she revealingly added, "I am evidently unpleasing to Lucy, and, could we exchange personalities, I have no doubt I should then feel with her feelings" (*FL,* 57). This ability to feel from other points of view was what made Rossetti such a fine poet.

"Later Life": "The Poetry of Impulse" and "the Prose of Calculation"

Sympathy in antipathy characterized many of Rossetti's friendships. In 1878 Augusta Webster published a pamphlet on the *Parliamentary Franchise for Women Ratepayers*. Forwarding a copy to Rossetti, she began "a courteous tilt in the strong-minded woman lists" (*FL,* 97). Despite her opposition to the suffrage campaign, Rossetti's correspondence with Webster, a dramatic poet whose work she highly esteemed, again shows her capacity for large-mindedness. Briefly taking her adversary's position, she criticized the timidity of the suffragists' demands and proposed that all women, married as well as single, should receive the right to vote and to run for a seat in Parliament. Nevertheless, she argued against the franchise because "men should continue the exclusive national legislators, so long as they do continue the exclusive soldier-representatives of the nation" (quoted in Bell, 112). In so dismissing women's right to vote on the grounds of women's inability (or, in her case, unwillingness) to fight, she implicitly takes a position against making women responsible for the legislation of martial policies. Her pacifism was, however, not the only bar to her feminism. As "a humble orthodox [Chris]tian," she could not, as she said, "aim at 'women's rights'" for two reasons: first, the

Bible and the priesthood suggested to her the divine ordinance of male privilege "in this world"; second, contemporary "social movements [did not] tend on the whole to uphold [Chris]tianity" (quoted in Bell, 112). Making her position public in 1889, Rossetti submitted her name to "A Woman's Protest against Female Suffrage," a petition published in the August issue of the *Nineteenth-Century*.

During her final years Rossetti strove increasingly to fulfil the role of an orthodox Christian in literature as well as life. With the publication of *Annus Domini* in 1874, she had inaugurated her career as a writer of devotional prose, and she gave increased attention to this pursuit in the years following the move to Torrington Square. Indeed, the sheer voluminousness of the resulting work suggests that she considered her religious prose an important, if separate, part of her literary vocation. "To my regret," she lamented nonetheless, "the poetry of impulse has been succeeded by the prose of calculation" (quoted in Bell, 128). At biannual intervals between 1879 and 1885, she brought out four works with the Society for Promoting Christian Knowledge (SPCK): *Seek and Find, Called to Be Saints, Letter and Spirit,* and *Time Flies*. Then, in 1892, she published the last of her sacred meditations, *The Face of the Deep*. In her devotional prose, her calculation bridged monetary, moral, and esthetic considerations. On the one hand, she wrote these works for the income and, for example, sold the copyright of *Seek and Find* for the modest sum of £40. On the other, she intended them to be of interest and instruction to her public. Even if such work might, as Gabriel feared, damage her popularity as a poet, she avowed herself "glad to throw my grain of dust into the religious scale" (*FL*, 92). For these writings, moreover, she carefully cultivated a meditative prose style. Speaking of *Seek and Find,* she told her brother, "I flatter myself some of it is that prose which I fancy our Italian half inclines us to indite" (*FL*, 80). Indeed, though opposed in spirit, her devotional studies resemble nothing so much as her father's anticlerical researches in the attention given exegetical minutiae.

Of these works, *Time Flies* and *The Face of the Deep* are perhaps the most significant. Like *Annus Domini, Time Flies* provides a calendar of daily readings closely tied to the liturgical year, but it substitutes brief essays and occasional poems for the earlier prayers. Because *Time Flies* also includes a number of personal anecdotes, striking for their perception and originality, Rossetti's first biographer says "it may almost be called a kind of spiritual autobiography" (Bell, 304). Bell's qualification ("almost") is important to bear in mind, for Rossetti not only selectively allegorizes her experience but shapes it to the pattern of seasonal and liturgical moments that comprises her moral universe. Less doctrinal than homiletic in orientation, *Time Flies* submits anecdote to the intentions of parable. As for *The Face of the Deep*, it marks Rossetti's apotheosis as a devotional writer. By far the most ambitious of her later works, it undertakes to render the Book of Revelation accessible through reflective rather than interpretative intercession. Despite its difficulties, the book contains interesting asides on contemporary concerns as well as glosses on the apocalyptic text.

Except for *Letter and Spirit* and *Seek and Find*, Rossetti's devotional works all contain examples of her verse. When an otherwise laudatory review of *The Face of the Deep* criticized some of her lyrics, she was affronted. "I am surprised," she declared, "to see the suggestion that (perhaps as a devout self-denial) I forebore to make my verse as good as I could: neither as praise nor as blame do I deserve the imputation" (*FL*, 189). Convinced of the merit of her SPCK lyrics, she collected them for *Verses*. The appearance of *Verses* in 1893 signified, however, the end of her association with the SPCK. Discovering soon after that the group had issued a pamphlet in favor of vivisection, Rossetti revoked her subscription to its publications and returned all revenues received for *The Face of the Deep*.

Aside from *Verses*, Rossetti produced one other volume of poems after 1875. Published in 1881, *A Pageant and Other Poems* differs from her earlier work in several ways. First, the volume is not obviously divided into separate categories of secular and devotional verse according to the plan first suggested by Gabriel in 1861. Second, it contains much work of a dark philosophical complexion and includes some of her most ambitious verse—"Monna Innominata," "Later Life," "An Old-World Thicket." At about this time, Rossetti's perceptions of herself as a poet also register a change. Always the ironist, she increasingly points to the disparity between her private and public selves. On the appearance of *A Pageant and Other Poems*, she wrote to Gabriel: "Considering that I was 'old and cold and grey' so many years ago, it is (as you suggest) no wonder that nowadays I am 'so shrunk and sere.'—If only my figure would shrink somewhat!" (*FL*, 95). Distinguishing her very substantial person from the fictional persona projected in her verse, she nonchalantly observes that "a fat poetess is incongruous especially when seated by the grave of buried hope" (*FL*, 95). In these later years, moreover, she frequently used her reputation as an improvisational poet as a defense against writing improvisational poetry. Insisting that she wrote only "at the mercy of impulse," she was unperturbed by its absence. "At 61," she told one correspondent, "one can neither wish nor expect to be as impulsive as at 16" (quoted in Bell, 130). As *A Pageant and Other Poems* suggests, however, she had abandoned the impulsive for the meditative mode more than 10 years earlier.

A Pageant and Other Poems differs from Rossetti's first two volumes in one other respect: her familiar critic did not vet the manuscript. Of late years, Gabriel could neither give nor receive disinterested poetic advice. When Rossetti commended his responsible "use of an influential talent" in "The White Ship," he peevishly accused her of trying to incite "envy and spite" (*FL*, 89). His jealousy was, if only in its admission, a symptom of his dependence on chloral. While he jokingly told her that "Sonnets mean Insomnia" (D. G. Rossetti 1967, 4:1838), insomnia actually meant more chloral, and more chloral meant severe depression. During his convalescence at the coastal village of Hunter's Forestall in 1877, Rossetti used chess as a tactic to revive her brother's spirits—a fact less celebrated than her renunciation of the game on the grounds of the pleasure she took in winning. Although Gabriel eventually rallied, depression again overtook him toward the end of 1881. Recommending to him the solace of confession, she also defended him against William's exasperated impatience. "It is trying to have to do with him at times," she admitted, "but what must it be TO BE himself" and to suffer from "wrecked health at least in some measure, nerves which appear to falsify facts, and most anxious money-matters?" (*FL*, 106). Having wrestled with many of the same demons and come to terms with what it was to be herself, she had rare compassion for the brother who so often played luminous night to her dark day.

The death of Gabriel in 1882 was a prelude to others: Frances Rossetti in 1886, Charlotte Polidori in 1890, and Eliza Polidori in 1893. Except for William, Rossetti had survived her whole family. After her mother's death she considered for a time moving to Rochester, where Canon Burrows then lived, and taking a house large enough to accommodate visits from William's family. He, however, was suspicious that she would then attempt "to proselytize the kids" (W. Rossetti 1990, 490). In the event, she did not move; but what William called their "entirely hostile" (W. Rossetti 1990, 639) opinions on religion sometimes strained their relationship in these final years. In 1883, when her infant nephew was at the point of death, she asked to baptize him and, receiving permission, performed the service herself. Writing a few years later, she cautiously urged Lucy to reconsider the matter for the other four children: "Baptism (where attainable) is the sole door I know of whereby entrance is promised into the happiness which eye has not seen nor ear heard neither hath heart of man conceived" (*FL,* 164). Faltering slightly over her own attachment to the here and now, she continued, "I now live so much in the other world—or at least I ought to do so, having my chief Treasure there—that please do not take offence at what I say" (*FL,* 164).

That other world grew inexorably near when Rossetti, suffering from breast cancer, underwent a radical mastectomy on 25 May 1892. Although the prognosis was initially favorable, her doctors again detected the cancer in the early part of 1893. Notwithstanding her pain, she could still laugh at herself. "I am," she told William, "such an exceptional phenomenon" (*FL,* 195). Finally, on 29 December 1894, she died at the age of 64. At the end, the opiates administered to alleviate her physical pain sorely intensified her spiritual anguish. William, seeing his sister's faith become the instrument of her torture, could not forgive her God. In death as in life, she remained for him "an exceptional phenomenon."[29]

Chapter Two

First Fruits: From *Maude* to *Goblin Market and Other Poems*

In the spring of 1851 the entrenched conservatism of the Royal Academy seemed poised to crush the PRB. At this point the art critic John Ruskin provided an eloquent defense of the group's efforts. Having not only legitimized but also popularized Pre-Raphaelite painting, Ruskin seemed likely to appreciate the merits of Pre-Raphaelite verse. But after reading a manuscript of Rossetti's poems early in 1861, he proclaimed them virtually unpublishable. "They are full of beauty and power," he admitted, but "so full are they of quaintnesses and offences" that "no publisher . . . would take them" (W. Rossetti, ed., 1899, 258). Measuring "Goblin Market" against the epics of Homer, Dante, and Virgil, he was especially appalled by its metrical irregularity and told her brother that she "should exercise herself in the severest commonplace of metre until she can write as the public like. Then," he continued, "if she puts in her observation and passion all will become precious. But she must have the Form first" (W. Rossetti, ed., 1899, 259). Fortunately, while some other early reviewers also expressed a distaste for the "new-fangled shape or shapelessness" of Rossetti's verse, Ruskin did not speak for the public taste.[1] In fact, *Goblin Market and Other Poems* so thoroughly demonstrated "in essence and form the individuality of the writer" that the critic for the *Athenaeum* compared reading the volume to "passing from a picture gallery, with its well-feigned semblance of nature, to the real nature out-of-doors."[2] Ruskin's misgivings notwithstanding, the formal novelty that distinguished Rossetti's work won her the praise of her contemporaries and eventually established her as "the queen of the Preraphaelite school."[3] She was, as Algernon Swinburne observed later, "the Jael who led their host to victory."[4]

Rossetti is, however, a strange figure to preside over the Pre-Raphaelite host. Luxuriating in vivid color and detailed abundance, her poetry exemplifies many Pre-Raphaelite qualities: it captures the poignancy of heartfelt truths, celebrates the beauty of nature, and indulges a conscious medievalism. In addition, she challenges in her work the conventions of an established poetic tradition much as the PRB challenges in its paintings the prescriptive standards of the Royal Academy. But because the PRB was jealous of its masculine privilege, the group accorded her only a marginal status. Turning her exclusion to advantage, she examines in her first works, *Maude: Prose and Verse* and *Goblin Market and Other Poems,* alternatives to the Pre-Raphaelite ideal of fraternity. In her exploration of sororal models of esthetic, social, and religious activity, Rossetti encodes her resistance to Pre-Raphaelitism—the very movement she later led to victory—and endeavors to overcome the discontinuities of her experience as a poet, a woman, and a Christian.

In Search of "Unity of Purpose" in *Maude*

Finished in 1850, *Maude: Prose and Verse* failed to interest the *Germ*'s first publishers, Aylott and Jones, and so lay "*perdu* in a drawer, several removes from undergoing a revise" (*FL,* 17), until Rossetti's brother effected its appearance in 1897. Deeming the work interesting "if not for the writing's own sake, then for the writer's," William claimed in his preface that he felt "no qualms in giving publicity to *Maude*."[5] Nevertheless, his qualms about the novella's literary merit prompted him not only to underline its autobiographical significance but to appeal doubly to readers' indulgence of the prose and discretion of the verse. William's apology aside, *Maude*'s importance lies less in its psychological curiosity than its daring as an experiment across genres.[6] While its heroine's "writing-book was neither Common-Place Book, Album, Scrap-Book nor Diary" but "a compound of all these" (*MPV,* 30), *Maude* is also a compound work that marks out, as its title suggests, Rossetti's twin objectives as a writer accomplished in prose and verse. Exploiting the ironies facilitated by the work's generic anomaly, Rossetti plays her narrator's wittily acid prose against her heroine's often (but not always) morbidly sentimental verse. To refine and contain these tensions, she relies on sophisticated tripartite harmonies affecting theme, character, and structure. Consequently, "whatever other merit it lacks," *Maude* "possesses," as Rossetti wrote of its poetic climax, "unity of purpose in a high degree" (*FL,* 6).

Rossetti wrote much of *Maude* at Pleasley Hill, where, in her double exile from London and the PRB, she sought to reconcile her ambitions in love and art. From her acquaintances among the Collinsons, she derived some of the names for her characters. Although William identifies Alicia and Priscilla Townsend as the originals for Maude's cousins, the unpoetic Mary Clifton, seems modeled, at least in part, after Mary Collinson, who did not "appreciate" with her future sister-in-law "the sweet prettiness of 'As I lay a-thinkinge'" (*FL*, 9). Likewise, the heroine's name, Maude Foster, recalls Rosanna Foster, whom Rossetti met in September of 1849. On the other hand, Rosanna Hunt, a minor character in the novella, may derive her name equally from Rosanna Foster and William Holman Hunt. Similarly, two other characters, Jane and Alice Deverell, bear the same surname as Walter Deverell, a PRB associate. But while Rossetti feminizes and marginalizes certain Pre-Raphaelite names, she yet excludes men from *Maude* as rigorously as the PRB excluded women. Exploring the idea of sorority rather than fraternity, she not only investigates the vocational choices open to women but concentrates specifically on possible alternatives to marriage. Accordingly, *Maude* is a künstlerroman that provides a portrait of the artist as a young woman, but it is also a bildungsroman that chronicles the progress of four girls toward maturity. Despite Magdalen Ellis's later appearance as a Sister of Mercy, however, adult independence effectively eradicates sororal interdependence. Thus, although three of the girls successfully achieve womanhood, the novella ends with the separation of all four.

Proliferating in triadic arrangements, *Maude* traces a complete movement from girlhood through adolescence into womanhood. The novella's three parts, each further subdivided into another three parts, chart this growth as a pattern of increasing restriction for the four girls. Part 1, the childhood phase of *Maude,* takes place in the country and in the summer. Set more than a year later in town, part 2 focuses on the period of Advent and culminates on Christmas Eve. Finally, part 3 moves forward from June into July, a temporal advance that takes the novella full circle to its beginning two years earlier. The narrative fails, however, to accomplish a like return to the countryside and so suggests the irretrievability of childhood freedom. Since, as the narrator states at the outset, the purpose of the tale is to "enable . . . readers to form their own estimate of Maude's character" (*MPV,* 31), the central sections of each part treat the heroine's individual performance at three different social gatherings. Becoming progressively more alienated from her female peers, Maude first amuses the company at Mary's fifteenth birthday party, then refuses to perform a similar service at Mrs. Strawdy's tea party, and finally fails—albeit through force of circumstance rather than will—to take part in Mary's marriage. Then, to close each of the novella's three parts, Rossetti concentrates on Maude's attempts to formulate resolutions aimed at the achievement of personal integrity. The unity of purpose that distinguishes the novella, however, is precisely what its heroine lacks. Ultimately escaping the demands of relationship in death, Maude leaves her cousin Agnes to impose a meaningful shape on her life as well as her art.

Cousinhood serves as the basis for Maude's first experience of sisterhood. Although the novella opens with the Foster family, an attenuated urban household composed only of mother and daughter, it rapidly moves to accommodate Maude's country cousins, Agnes and Mary, who belong to a large family comprised of two parents and eight children. Born within a year of each other, the three girls are all 15. But whereas the dark-haired and pale-skinned Maude is not, as her mother fears, "quite well" (*MPV,* 29), her cousins are "well-grown and well-made, with fair hair, blue eyes and fresh complexions" (*MPV,* 31). The two sisters' external resemblance does not, however, predicate internal resemblance. Consequently, even though both sisters differ from their cousin, "a strong contrast" (*MPV,* 32) develops between Mary and Maude. Indeed, while Agnes crowns Maude with a wreath into which she has placed "a surreptitious sprig of bay" (*MPV,* 33) in ambiguous tribute to her cousin's skill as a poet, Mary later crowns herself with the flower of bridal purity, "seringa (the English orange-blossom)" (*MPV,* 57). In these symbolic coronations, Rossetti situates marriage as a socially authorized option available to women, but she undermines the validity of this choice by making Mary the least sympathetic of the novella's characters.

The cousins' differences clearly emerge at Mary's birthday party when Maude, asked to direct the amusements, proposes to play a game of *bouts-rimés.* According to her, this game "is very easy. Some one gives rhymes . . . and then every one fills them up as they think fit" (*MPV,* 35). In fact, Maude's sonnet, originally written for just such a competition, took Rossetti seven minutes to complete.[7] Often playing the game with her brothers in 1848, she uses *bouts-rimés* in the novella to establish an esthetic kinship between Maude, Magdalen, and Agnes. Together, the three girls form a Pre-Raphaelite sisterhood. Although they write sonnets to the same rhymes, their productions are very different in both form and content. As such, they testify to the individuality of their putative authors. While the novella includes four other sonnets as evidence of "the variety of Maude's compositions" (*MPV,* 72), these *bouts-rimés* sonnets not only testify to Rossetti's technical virtuosity but symbolize the way the girls choose to fulfill their lives "as they think fit" given a common pattern of limitation. Mary, who eventually chooses the conventional form of feminine fulfillment, provides the rhymes (and so dictates the pattern of restriction) to those who later choose alternatives to marriage. Not surprisingly, none of the *bouts-rimés* that the girls write fits the parameters of the amatory sonnet. Agnes, as her sonnet makes clear, does not covet the role of poet:

> Would that I were a turnip white,
> Or raven black,
> Or miserable hack
>   Dragging a cab from left to right;
>   Or would I were the showman of a sight,
> Or weary donkey with a laden back,
> Or racer in a sack,
>   Or freezing traveller on an Alpine height;
> Or would I were straw catching as I drown,
>   (A wretched landsman I who cannot swim,)
>   Or watching a lone vessel sink,
>   Rather than writing: I would change my pink
> Gauze for a hideous yellow satin gown
>   With deep-cut scolloped edges and a rim. (*MPV,* 36–37)

Wittily arrhythmic, the poem has, like the hideous gown, deeply scalloped edges. The formal deficiencies of Agnes's sonnet, however, argue less her ineptitude as a poet than her humor and her refusal to conform to the prescribed rhythm of either verse or life. Oddly, given her final inability to fit feminine stereotypes, Maude tells Agnes "that my sympathy with your sorrows would have been greater, had they been expressed in metre" (*MPV,* 36). Despite this reproof, Agnes lives her life, as she writes her sonnet, with "heroic equanimity" (*MPV,* 36) and without the common meter.

Revealing clear poetic skill, Magdalen's sonnet foreshadows her later role in the novella when, as a nun, she engages in such duties as "teaching children, or attending the sick, or making poor things" (*MPV,* 43). A supernatural rather than a religious sisterhood, the "good fairies" of her sonnet "foster embryo life" and maintain their independence of the masculine secular world: "Without much work to do for king or hack," they are nonetheless busy "training," "sweeping," "binding," "bringing," "fishing," "teaching," "dyeing," and "wrapping" all manner of "embryo life" (*MPV,* 36). As her catalog of verbals suggests, Magdalen's fulfillment exists in action. Interestingly, the contrast between Magdalen's and Maude's sonnets brings out the full irony of the heroine's last name. Far from fostering life, Maude takes "poetical licence" to create "a very odd sonnet" in which she writes, "If all the world were water fit to drown / There are some whom you would not teach to swim" (*MPV,* 37). Because her sonnet is formally correct, Maude's license is not so much poetical as social, for she publishes a "Lynch-law" (*MPV,* 41) on those "fit to drown." Isolating the "woman in a great-coat like a sack / Towering above her sex with horrid height" and "Certain old ladies dressed in girlish pink" (*MPV,* 37), Maude castigates female misfits in particular and seems curiously unconscious of the anomaly of her own existence. In the end, however, her poetic aspirations are as unbecoming to adult femininity as the girlish garb worn by certain old ladies.

Adolescence fractures the sisterhood established in part 1. When the cousins join Maude in London a year later, Mary informs her "that poor Magdalen has done with Albums and such like" and "entered on her noviciate in the Sisterhood of Mercy established near our house" (*MPV,* 43). The differences between the cousins become apparent once more as Maude substitutes the adjective "happy" for the one Mary has chosen. Acknowledging that she is not "fit or inclined for such a life," she tells her cousin, "I can perceive that those are very happy who are" (*MPV,* 43). But while Maude later puts this sympathetic perception to work in "Three Nuns," Magdalen's decision to have "done with Albums and such like" dissolves their poetic kinship. Moreover, a sorority founded on blood kinship is also impossible for Rossetti's heroine. Sickness, seemingly an inevitable effect of urbanity, prevents Mary and Agnes from accompanying Maude to Mrs. Strawdy's tea party, where she encounters a series of "contrarieties" (*MPV,* 48). First, she meets the three Mowbray sisters, who function as a mirror for the three cousins. Laboring to find some commonality with Annie and Caroline, she abandons her attempts before "Sophy, whose countenance," writes Rossetti in delightfully alliterative prose, "promised more cake than conversation" (*MPV,* 48). With the arrival of the Savages, Maude's contrarieties culminate. As their name suggests, the Savages are, notwithstanding their pretensions to culture, female barbarians. Maude, well aware of "the absurdity of her position" (*MPV,* 49), finds herself "attacked on either hand with questions concerning her verses" (*MPV,* 48). In the view of the assembled company, "she was so young, so much admired, and, poor thing, looked so delicate. It was quite affecting to think of her lying awake at night meditating those sweet verses—('I sleep like a top,' Maude put in drily,)—which so delighted her friends, and would so charm the public, if only Miss Foster could be induced to publish" (*MPV,* 49). Far from being so induced, Maude refuses to consent even to a recitation of her verse.

Significantly, this central section of the novella contains no verse. Having avowed herself "sick of display and poetry and acting" while yet in the country (*MPV,* 41), Maude now suffers from a "divided heart" (*MPV,* 54). From the start, she has been "one who without telling lies was determined not to tell the truth" (*MPV,* 29), but her attempts to negotiate a compromise between truth and art become vexed in adolescence. Although poetry allows her to act out or (dis)play a number of fictive roles, her "discerning public" (*MPV,* 35) speculates about the personal motivation for such "broken-hearted" verse (*MPV,* 31). Subject to the same kind of prying curiosity, Rossetti understandably banned her brothers from circulating verse "which the most imaginative person could construe into love personals" or the "outpourings of a wounded spirit" (quoted in Battiscombe, 54). By so forcing an equivalence between poetic and personal sincerity, Maude's readers—both condemnatory and commendatory—trivialize her imaginative endeavors: either she is "quite affecting to think of . . . lying awake at night," or she is "affected" and writes "foolishly about things she could not possibly understand" (*MPV,* 31).

Although Maude "drily" tries to correct the Savages, she is, as Rossetti's parenthetical aside suggests, signally unsuccessful. Conversely, Agnes's insistence on the sincerity of her verse does not assuage her feeling that she is "such a hypocrite" (*MPV,* 52), for she is, by vocation, one who pretends. Maude's inability to sustain poetic play without also engaging in vain display precipitates, therefore, a crisis as much of religious as of esthetic faith. This crisis of faith allows Rossetti to explore and resolve the contradiction between art and religion that threatened to destroy her career before it had properly begun. Initially, her heroine views beauty and belief as equal and exclusive in their claims. While Maude's first inclination to renounce poetry takes shape the day after Mary's birthday, her decision to refuse the Eucharist and "never to Communicate again" (*MPV,* 53) occurs on the eve of Christ's nativity. Continuing to write in solitude, she retreats doubly from public forms of relation. In one of the many ironies that characterize *Maude,* part 2 closes with a carol performed by a company of singers outside the heroine's window. She falls asleep alone within in her small, warm bedroom, but outside in the cold lies the warmth of Christian fellowship.

Maude's resolution is, of course, untenable. Restricted as her world is to the private sphere of influence, it is also public in its demands to social and religious activity. Desiring neither to become a "poor thing" for her readers' delectation nor to "profane Holy Things" (*MPV,* 52), she is rather romantic in her recusancy. Finally, in a double disclosure to her spiritual advisor, Mr. Paulson, and to the novella's arbiter of feminine conduct, Agnes, Maude acknowledges her presumption. As she repents, the novella's narrative fissures. Externalizing the heroine's internal conflict, Rossetti turns to the epistolary mode and so turns over to Agnes and Maude the storyteller's responsibility. At the beginning of part 3, therefore, Agnes writes of Mary's forthcoming marriage and Magdalen's recent profession into a religious order. Both events leave Agnes excluded: Mary gives her whole attention to her fiancé, and Magdalen invites no friends to her ceremonial induction into the sisterhood. When Agnes later meets Magdalen, she can neither see the face nor penetrate the thoughts behind the veil. Agnes, by so communicating her growing sense of isolation, appeals to Maude for sisterhood.

Although Maude responds physically to her cousin's request to "come without delay" (*MPV,* 57), an accident overturns her cab and prevents her from leaving London. In her letter, however, she rejects Agnes's plea and, instead, responds poetically to Magdalen's "fancy" of her as "very different, as pale Sister Maude" (*MPV,* 58). In some ways, the resulting poem, "Three Nuns," is as odd as Maude's *bouts-rimés* sonnet, for in lieu of "an Epithalamium for our fair fiancée" (*MPV,* 60), she composes an elegy on Magdalen's entry into the convent. This poem represents, however, an appropriate climax to various choral efforts in *Maude.* Like the other lyrics interspersed throughout the novella, it allows different voices to intercede in the same narrative. A three-part harmony authored by Maude, "Three Nuns" most closely resembles the three *bouts-rimés* sonnets written by three separate authors and the Christmas song performed in full and separate chorus by glad carolers. Furthermore, it also recalls Maude's "She sat and sang alway." Placed at the end of part 1 and later published (with two other poems from *Maude*) in *Goblin Market and Other Poems,* this poetic duet integrates first- and third-person points of view to achieve a holistic harmony. Opposed as song is to sorrow, hope to memory, up to down, day to night, the two women described in "She sat and sang alway" occupy the same physical locale but embody different psychic conditions.

In "Three Nuns," on the other hand, Maude alternates between monody and polyphony to forge unity of purpose from disparate experience.

Giving each woman a separate voice, she unites them through the mottoes: "Put together they form a most exquisite little song which the Nuns sing in Italy" (*MPV,* 60). Furthermore, this Italian hymn authorizes each nun's private disclosure of her dissatisfaction with worldly constraints by translating it into a communal devotional exercise. Indeed, for all three nuns, the convent is at once a shelter from the world and a metonym for it. The first, having escaped "the troublesome / Noise of life," "would be dumb" (*MPV,* 61). Finding esthetic relief in birdsong, she seeks to prolong the pleasure:

> Sing a little longer yet:
>   Soon the matins will begin;
> And I must turn back again
> To that aching worse than pain
> I must bear and not complain. (*MPV,* 62)

The second nun, suffering from unrequited desire, puts her passion into prayer:

> My voice rose in the sacred choir,
>   The choir of Nuns; do you condemn
>   Even if, when kneeling among them,
> Faith, zeal and love kindled a fire
> And I prayed for his happiness
> Who knew not? was my error this? (*MPV,* 64)

While her sisters seek death's release from pain, the third nun looks forward to heaven's reward as Christ's bride. For the first two nuns, death is an end. For the last, it is a beginning. But even as Rossetti distinguishes between true and false vocations, the sisterhood of "Three Nuns" and of *Maude* inheres in women's common desire for freedom.

The motifs of song and sisterhood in "Three Nuns" testify to Rossetti's interest in the issue of poetry as a vocation for women. Describing her method of writing poetry and of imagining truth as it is not or as it might be, Maude offers an explanation of the poem: "The first Nun," she tells Agnes, "no one can suspect of being myself, partly because my hair is far from yellow and I do not wear curls; partly because I never did anything half so good as profess. The second might be Mary, had she mistaken her vocation. The third is Magdalen" (*MPV,* 60). While Magdalen, like the third nun, has a true religious vocation, Mary's true calling is marriage and Maude's is poetry. Unlike Magdalen and Mary, Maude cannot achieve adult fulfillment. Unable to reconcile the contradiction between poethood and womanhood, she is locked, like the first nun, into a childhood dream. As for Agnes, she has no apparent vocation. When pressed by Maude to "change with Sister Magdalen, with Mary, or with me," she replies, "You must even put up with me as I am" (*MPV,* 69). As rigorously individual as the others, she refuses her cousin's alternatives. Nevertheless, her death imminent, Maude attempts to change roles with Agnes by using her yellow hair for the alter ego created in the first of "Three Nuns." Moreover, she installs Agnes as her literary executor and as her mother's good foster-daughter. But telling her to "destroy what I evidently never intended to be seen" (*MPV,* 71), Maude puts her work into the hands of a sympathetic friend who does not understand her.

For Agnes, her cousin's life is one with that "locked book she never opened: but . . . placed in Maude's coffin, with all its records of folly, sin, vanity; and, she humbly trusted, of true penitence also" (*MPV,* 72). Among sundry other lyrics, she finds many "mere fragments, many half-effaced pencil scrawls, some written on torn backs of letters, and some full of incomprehensible abbreviations" (*MPV,* 72). Sifting through an already fractional (albeit inscrutably "full") opus, she radically abridges the oeuvre to three lyrics and destroys most of Maude's poetic remains in order to save what is, from her point of view, the best of her cousin. As her choice of three poems on the theme of resurrection suggests, she chooses to save the orthodox Christian in Maude. In some ways prophetic of William's posthumous revision of his sister, Agnes's selected edition of her cousin is, to say the least, economical with the truth.

Because Agnes, according to Sandra Gilbert and Susan Gubar, operates as the heroine's "superego-like" nemesis, "the moral of this story is that the Maude in Christina Rossetti—the ambitious, competitive, self-absorbed and self-assertive poet—must die, and be replaced by either the wife, the nun, or, most likely, the kindly useful spinster."[8] The poet in Rossetti did not, however, die with Maude. Moreover, Agnes's unworldly ambitions are far more radical than Maude's worldly ones. Apart from her cousin's poems, Agnes retrieves one other token of remembrance, a lock of hair that she places with the like received from Magdalen. These two personal mementoes become for her a kind of devotional fetish, for "gazing on them, [she] would long and pray for the hastening of that eternal morning, which shall reunite in God those who in Him, or for His Sake, have parted here" (*MPV,* 75). Positing her own unity of purpose in the mystical union of one-in-three persons, Agnes contemplates not so much Christian fellowship as an empyrean sisterhood composed of herself, Maude, and Magdalen. Agnes, whose name alludes to *agnus dei* (lamb of God), is a revisionist. Less punishingly superego-like than restoratively Christ-like, her revision of Maude pales beside her revision of patriarchal symbology to accommodate a corresponding female trinity.

While Rossetti disavowed Mariolatry, her Anglican orthodoxy yet embraces a mysticism that ratifies feminine independence in this world and envisions feminine interdependence in the next. Reconstituting the sisterhood of "Three Nuns" in Agnes's heavenly vision, she not only includes and unites single women but tacitly excludes the married woman. The moral of *Maude,* therefore, has less to do with Rossetti's renunciation of art than with the consolations of religious belief. Nonetheless, Maude's failure to achieve independence and survive as a writer explains the novella's worldly pessimism, its unworldly optimism, and its peculiar pathos. That Rossetti assimilated the ideal of feminine interdependence to her purpose as a writer explains the thematic, formal, and linguistic preoccupations of *Goblin Market and Other Poems.*

Kinship and Kindness in "Goblin Market"

Organizing the key themes of the 1862 volume, "Goblin Market" rewrites *Maude* in its return to Rossetti's formative experience among brothers as well as sisters. In fact, her two eldest siblings defined the nature of this experience: Maria was, according to William, childhood's "inspiriting Muse in a pinafore"; Gabriel, "a familiar spirit—familiar but fiery, and not lightly to be rebelled against" (W. Rossetti 1906, 1:19).[9] In tribute to her doubly inspiring sibling muses, Rossetti not only dedicated the manuscript to her "dear only sister" but later acknowledged the assistance of her brother's "suggestive wit and revising hand" in the volume's preparation.[10] So central is the interplay between brothers and sisters in "Goblin Market" that Ellen Moers describes the poem as a Gothic fantasy "derived from the nightside of the Victorian nursery—a world where childish cruelty and childish sexuality come to the fore."[11] By the time of the poem's composition in 1859, however, Rossetti's association with the PRB had confirmed that the relations between men and women were as fraught by cruelty as those between boys and girls.

Consequently, her exploration of kinship and kindness in "Goblin Market" takes the PRB for its "overriding frame of reference."[12]

Although the PRB's invitation to self-fulfillment would be as spurious as the goblins', it initially offered Rossetti some means of pursuing her esthetic goals. While Maude's "little copies of verses were handed about and admired" (*MPV,* 31), Rossetti's lyrics appeared in the *Germ* and circulated among the group's members. J. E. Millais, for instance, sent a copy of her *Verses* to Mrs. Thomas Combe, wife of a High Church patron, in 1851. Moreover, he expedited her introduction to *Once a Week* in 1859 by illustrating "Maude Clare." Under the aegis of the PRB, Rossetti's verse also served as her first introduction to a very specific female audience. Trying out the language of surfeit and appetite she would use in "Goblin Market," she teased William about his visit to her prospective in-laws in 1848: "You probably not only *profusely banqueted* but surfeited," she said, "your victims with my *poetry*" (*FL,* 3). Wishing to gauge her acceptability to the Collinson women, she not only asked William to fit appropriate adjectives ("*prim*" or "kind-hearted" or "*alarming*") to her fiancé's mother and sister but commissioned "a detailed account" of his sister-in-law (*FL,* 3–4). But just as the PRB's offer to introduce Rossetti to the Victorian reading public virtually collapsed in the *Germ,* its offer to incorporate her through marriage within a new familial alliance disintegrated with the end of her engagement in 1850. Nearly a decade later, she had yet to find a readership receptive to her verse. Fittingly, when success arrived in 1862, it took its register from a poem that not only explores the fulfillments, illusory and otherwise, of sisterhood and brotherhood, but creates its own audience.

Providing a literary banquet in excess of *Verses* or the *Germ* poems, "Goblin Market" examines the individual's search for communal identity. As an experiment in form and language, however, it constantly tests the truth of certain idioms of inclusion against their fraudulence. While Laura and Lizzie first sit "Crouching close together" (l. 36), the goblins speak with a single "voice like voice of doves / Cooing all together" (ll. 77–78). "Brother with queer brother" and "Brother with sly brother" (ll. 94, 96), they act together to constitute a freemasonry, like the PRB, complete with secret signs and occult knowledge. On the other hand, Laura and Lizzie's names suggest their kinship. While the alliterative initial consonants yoke Laura and Lizzie, the doubling combinations of internal vowel sounds (neutral and diphthong arrangements of *a* versus *i*) render their distinction and recall the pseudonym Ellen Alleyn "invented" by Rossetti's brother to assimilate her to the *Germ* (Fredeman, ed., 47). Nevertheless, Rossetti refrains from clearly establishing the girls' sisterhood until after the first encounter with the goblins. Then, Laura, using the appellative "sister" to "hush" Lizzie (l. 164), virtually silences the claims of feminine kinship in her obsession with the goblin fruits. These fruits, impossibly "All ripe together / In summer weather" (ll. 15–16), not only exist themselves in a form of alliance but promise to forge a community of interest between brothers and sisters. Indeed, just as Rossetti's 1853 sonnet, "The P.R.B. is in its decadence," associates the image of "luscious fruit [that] must fall when over ripe" with "the consummated P.R.B." (ll. 13, 14), "Goblin Market" draws an insoluble connection between the goblins and their wares. But far from allowing Laura to join the twilight brotherhood, the fruits subjugate her to the group's power, ratify its exclusivity, and threaten to destroy her relationship with Lizzie. Consequently, while "Goblin Market" opens with the double attractions of the fruits and the goblins, it increasingly articulates a considered resistance to masculine control, however benevolent sounding. Observing that the goblins "sounded kind" (l. 79), Rossetti describes the fruits as "Sweet to tongue and sound to eye" (l. 30). The verbal play on the homonymic "sound" is critical to understanding the limits of inclusion in "Goblin Market." Sounding the same, homonyms confuse difference—in this case, the crucial difference between what is wholesome or trustworthy and what is heard or seen to be so.

Although Rossetti writes in *Time Flies* that puns rarely "profit" wisdom since they "are a frivolous crew likely to misbehave unless kept within strict bounds," her puns on "sound" and "kind" exploit the doubleness of language in order to expose goblin—and masculine—duplicity.[13] Thus, as Lizzie discovers, the goblins are not kind but "fiery, and," as William observed of his brother, "not lightly to be rebelled against." Neither generically nor behaviorially kind, they subscribe to a profit motive inimical to wisdom and, instead, retail their promises by way of a "customary cry" (l. 231).[14] Again punning, the poet conflates the two meanings of "customary" to link goblin habits and goblin commerce. Initially allowed free play in the text, such puns contribute, like the goblins, to a sheer surfeit of possible meaning. But while "Goblin Market" is seemingly as capricious of meaning as it is of rhyme and rhythm, its author implicitly asks her readers to profit wisely from the very indifference to nice semantic distinctions that leads to Laura's downfall. Having profited from her own folly, Laura finally acts as the poet's agent by giving this tale of "wicked, quaint fruit-merchant men" (l. 553) its "right

moral reading."[15] To begin, however, readers must make their own deter-
minations.

Part of a sensuous assault launched not so much at the sisters (who
enter the poem later) as at readers, the fruits confound all manner of
sound differences. Beginning with "Apples and quinces" (l. 5), the
poem's first catalog provides the fruitful plurality of kind and amount
suited to a postlapsarian world.[16] Indeed, while the sisters' temptations
double on Eve's temptation, the fruits multiply outrageously. If the first
fruit of goblin as well as satanic temptation is the allusive apple, the second (the quince) and the twenty-first (the pear) belong to the apple
genus. On the other hand, "crab-apples" and "pine-apples," also mentioned, are nominal rather than actual apples. The aural resemblance
among the fruits conspires to eradicate the distinctions among the items
the goblins sell. At the same time, the loading of nouns either in
hyphenated formulations (*crab-apples* or *pine-apples*) or through compound adjectives ("Bloom-down-cheeked peaches, / Swart-headed mulberries, / Wild free-born cranberries" [ll. 9–11]) suggests not so much
difference as excess. In addition to apples, cherries, dates, figs, currants,
and grapes, the initial catalog also includes three kinds of citrus fruit
(lemons, oranges, citrons), four of the plum genus (apricots, bullaces,
damsons, greengages), and nine kinds of berry (raspberries, mulberries,
cranberries, dewberries, blackberries, strawberries, bilberries, gooseber-
ries, barberries). Such lush profusion, as much linguistic as otherwise,
propagates the illusion that the goblins' fruits are, as Lizzie later says,
"both choice and many" (l. 149). Such typically Pre-Raphaelite abundance, however, obscures the true issue of choice: to buy or not to buy.

Impervious to latitudinal or seasonal differences affecting their ripening, the fruits come together in "Goblin Market" from outside the text.
Their precise origins remaining mysterious, they derive from "that
unknown orchard" (l. 135). Again testing readers' cognitive abilities, this
phrase (in which the demonstrative "that" wars with the adjective
"unknown") claims simultaneously to know and not to know from
whence the fruits derive. In fact, the mystery of their provenance is part
of their dangerous allure. Initially, this mystery inspires caution. "We
must not look at goblin men," Laura says imperatively, "We must not
buy their fruits" (ll. 42–43). Shifting from statement to question, she
wonders, "Who knows upon what soil they fed / Their hungry thirsty
roots?" (ll. 44–45). Then, moving from question to speculative assertion,
she says, "How fair the vine must grow / Whose grapes are so luscious; /
How warm the wind must blow / Thro' those fruit bushes" (ll. 60–63).

"Curious Laura" (l. 69) has, as such subtle shifts in phrasing suggest, forgotten caution. After tasting the fruits, she returns to the problem of their source; but since, for her as for Milton's Eve, desire impairs reason, she relies on the fruits' initial effects to authenticate her assumptions about their causality. "Odorous indeed must be the mead / Whereon they grow," she tells Lizzie, "and pure the wave they drink / With lilies at the brink, / And sugar-sweet their sap" (ll. 180–84). As heedless of consequences as of causes, Laura makes her own appeal to her sister's sensual and intellectual desires: "You cannot think," she says pointedly, "what figs / My teeth have met in" (ll. 173–74).

If the question of the fruits' origins remains open, the question of their effects—"How should it cloy with length of use?" (l. 133)—finds a resounding answer in the physical and spiritual decline that follows on Laura's rational decline. Foolish "to choose such part / Of soul-consuming care" (ll. 511–12), she begins to follow Jeanie, another of the goblins' victims, to the grave. Like the speaker of "An Apple-Gathering," who forfeits marriage because she has prematurely "plucked pink blossoms from mine apple tree" (l. 1), Jeanie dies "for joys brides hope to have" (l. 314). Since Jeanie's experience suggests that the fruits represent carnal as well as esoteric knowledge, it is no small coincidence that her name resembles that of the sleeping prostitute in Gabriel's "Jenny" or that Rossetti checked the proofs for *Goblin Market and Other Poems* while staying at "an institution . . . for the reclamation and protection of women leading a vicious life" (*FL*, 26).[17] For "sweet-tooth Laura" (l. 115), however, the pleasure that the goblins purvey is as much esthetic as it is either sexual or intellectual.

After Laura's orgy, the goblins deprive her of further gratification by withholding both the fruits and "the fruit-call" (l. 243). Giving Rossetti's verse technique its cue in the poem, the goblin brotherhood speaks "In tones as smooth as honey" (l. 108). In fact, their "iterated jingle / Of sugar-baited words" (ll. 233–34) aptly describes the sensuous appeal of poetry that is "Sweet to tongue" when spoken and "sound to eye" when read. Gorging on both metaphoric and actual fruits of verse, Laura "sucked and sucked and sucked the more" (l. 134) and "sucked until her lips were sore" (l. 136). But whereas the goblins' "customary cry" ("Come buy, come buy") represents their command of consumption, Rossetti reduces their "iterated jingle" to one iterated word ("sucked") to delineate Laura in the thrall of consumption. When she realizes that she can no longer hear their cry, she "turned as cold as stone" (l. 253) and "Her tree of life drooped from the root" (l. 260). The comparison of

Laura's coldness to an inorganic stone not only foreshadows her kernel-stone's fate but recalls Jeanie's cold sterility. As Lizzie reminds her sister, Jeanie "fell with the first snow" (l. 157), and "no grass will grow" (l. 158) upon her grave.

Nevertheless, Laura's possession of the kernel-stone suggests that she has the capacity to reproduce her first pleasurable experience:

> One day remembering her kernel-stone
> She set it by a wall that faced the south;
> Dewed it with tears, hoped for a root,
> Watched for a waxing shoot,
> But there came none;
> It never saw the sun,
> It never felt the trickling moisture run:
> While with sunk eyes and faded mouth
> She dreamed of melons, as a traveller sees
> False waves in desert drouth
> With shade of leaf-crowned trees,
> And burns the thirstier in the sandful breeze. (ll. 281–92)

In this savage parable of the PRB's *Germ*—the seed that failed after four numbers—Rossetti recounts Laura's unsuccessful attempt to "root" a barren kernel-stone and to substitute her *Thoughts towards Nature* for "Her tree of life." In so doing, she turns her brother's advice to abandon her own poetic "'dreamings'" for "any rendering either of narrative or sentiment from real abundant Nature" (D. G. Rossetti 1965, 1:162) into an indictment of the rootlessness of Pre-Raphaelite principle. For while the *Germ*'s prospectus identifies "a rigid adherence to the simplicity of Nature" as Pre-Raphaelitism's one goal and while Ruskin claims "minute" fidelity to nature as its "one truth," Laura's dream of melons hints at the paltriness, not to mention the falseness, of this ideal.[18] Later overturned "Like a wind-uprooted tree" (l. 517), her desire is no more than, as the brilliant metaphor suggests, a desert mirage. As for the kernel-stone, it only fosters "an absent dream" (l. 211) precisely because, originating from nowhere, it can originate nothing. Notably, when the goblins disappear, "Not leaving root or stone or shoot" (l. 441), they take with them the means both to verify their existence and to reproduce their wares. But Laura, having once told Lizzie of "Pellucid grapes without one seed" (l. 179), overlooks the transparent sterility of the beauty she admires.

While Laura suffers from emptiness after having eaten her "fill" (l. 165) of goblin fruits, Lizzie's intellectual and emotional fullness arms her against temptation. "Full of wise upbraidings" (l. 142), she chastens Laura. "Mindful of Jeanie" (l. 364), she speaks to the goblins. She is not, however, perfect. For while Laura "chose to linger" (l. 69), she chose to "thrust a dimpled finger / In each ear, shut eyes" (ll. 67–68), and abandon her sister. Leaving Laura vulnerable to goblin persuasions, she begins decidedly prim, but her "kind heart" (l. 461) awakens to her sister's suffering. Consequently, inasmuch as Laura is "the moral begetter of Lizzie," both sisters "share equally in the moral outcome of the poem's events."[19] Indeed, Lizzie's attempt to plant daisies on Jeanie's grave suggests the degree to which she must grow before she is able to respond effectively to her sister's dilemma. Her childish effort to restore to the dead girl the innocence and hope emblematized by the daisies that "never blow" (l. 161) is futile precisely because it is too late. Significantly, the "thought of Jeanie in her grave" (l. 312) finally inspires her to delay no longer on Laura's behalf.

Fully alive to the peril of trading with the goblins, Lizzie brings "a silver penny in her purse" (l. 324), stipulates the terms of monetary exchange, and refuses to part with "a precious golden lock" (l. 126) or eat freely at the goblins' expense. Enraged, the goblins pull "her hair out by the roots" (l. 404) and push "their fruits / Against her mouth to make her eat" (ll. 406–407). Tearing and soiling her clothes, pinching and bruising her body, they effect forcibly the exchange that Laura participated in willingly. Their actions are tantamount to rape, but Lizzie, though outwardly defiled, remains inwardly untouched by the effects of male sexual violence:

> White and golden Lizzie stood,
> Like a lily in a flood,—
> Like a rock of blue-veined stone
> Lashed by tides obstreperously,—
>
> . . . .
>
> Like a fruit-crowned orange-tree
> White with blossoms honey-sweet
> Sore beset by wasp and bee,—

Like a royal virgin town
Topped with gilded dome and spire
Close beleaguered by a fleet
Mad to tug her standard down. (ll. 408–21)

As pure as a lily and as strong as a rock, Lizzie emerges as a victor rather than a victim. Moreover, the extended analogies of the tree and the town, both besieged, magnify her heroism and diminish the goblin threat.

In some respects, the account of Lizzie's struggle with the goblins recalls Rossetti's relationship with her brothers. Making fun of her "modest but not the less definite self-regard," William "once told her jocularly . . . that 'she would soon become so polite it would be impossible to live with her'" (*PW,* lx). Lizzie, too, is polite. Though "called . . . proud, / Cross-grained, uncivil" (ll. 394–95), she addresses the goblins as "Good folk" (l. 363), thanks them for their hospitality, and respectfully insists on holding to the business at hand. The goblins, on the other hand, are extremely discourteous. But if Rossetti's description of their abusiveness owes something to the "fraternal stone-throwing" that her verse received from Gabriel (quoted in Battiscombe, 161), she was clearly able to give as good as she got. Exposing the goblins' kind-sounding ruse, Lizzie causes them to vanish even more irradicably than had the PRB in 1853. Vanquishing them, she profits from the encounter. Returning to Laura, she "heard her penny jingle / Bouncing in her purse, / Its bounce was music to her ear" (ll. 452–54). Silencing and replacing the goblins' "iterated jingle," Lizzie's saved penny plainly symbolizes her moral and esthetic power.

Returning home, Lizzie announces, "Eat me, drink me, love me; / Laura, make much of me" (ll. 471–72). While Lizzie, in parody of Eucharistic communion, offers herself as a banquet for her sister's feasting, Laura shows her worthiness of redemption insofar as she understands the price of her sister's heroism.[20] Furthermore, the "Tears [that] once again / Refreshed her shrunken eyes, / Dropping like rain / After long sultry drouth" (ll. 487–90), hint at her possession of the inner resources necessary to survive the poem's final reenactment of feast, fall, and fast. After her sister's nighttime vigil, Laura awakens "as from a dream" (l. 537). "Her breath" is, moreover, "as sweet as May" (l. 541). As she reawakens, "the first birds" (l. 530) sing, "early reapers" (l. 531) walk to work among "golden sheaves" (l. 532), "the morning winds" (l.

534) blow, and "new buds with new day" (l. 535) unfold. While Rossetti stresses nature's dawn and Laura's spring, she locates these renewals within the autumnal moment of ripening sheaves. Associated with diurnal and seasonal moments of transition, Laura escapes the twin threats of unnatural winter waste and unnatural summer excess. These markers of temporal change accede to time's swift movement as "Days, weeks, months, years" (l. 543) pass. Eliding time, Rossetti also elides the sisters' transformation into wives and mothers. Even as the children demonstrate both sisters' generative capacity, Laura emerges as the type of the artist. In fact, the story Laura tells her immature auditors in the poem's concluding half-frame is also a version of the story that the reader has already received. Mentioning "the haunted glen" (l. 552) and "wicked, quaint fruit-merchant men," she regales the children with the tale "of her early prime, / Those pleasant days long gone / Of not-returning time" (ll. 549–51). Clearly, she does not simply relate her childhood experience but converts it into a fiction for children. The author of her own experience, albeit in retrospect, she also authors herself and so achieves another victory over the goblins. Nevertheless, as inspiriting muses, Laura's sister and (goblin) brothers are necessary to the creation of her tale: the goblins provide an experience to which Lizzie brings a kind heart and, thus, new purpose. Redeeming her encounter with wickedness to kind-hearted purpose, Laura shapes the narrative to the theme of sisterhood and provides, like Agnes in *Maude,* meaningful closure to experience. As a result, her story is not only pleasant in the telling but safe and instructive.

While Rossetti constructs Laura as the tale-teller, "Goblin Market" ends with a communal rather than an individual voice. Told to "cling together" (l. 561), the children speak together:

> "For there is no friend like a sister
> In calm or stormy weather;
> To cheer one on the tedious way,
> To fetch one if one goes astray,
> To lift one if one totters down,
> To strengthen whilst one stands." (ll. 562–67)

As the "iterated jingle" of "one" suggests, sisterhood facilitates the achievement of a communal identity. Notwithstanding Rossetti's grammatical erasure of sexual difference, the poem ends, as Dorothy Mermin

"Golden head by golden head"

D. G. ROSSETTI'S TITLE-PAGE ILLUSTRATION FOR *GOBLIN MARKET AND OTHER POEMS* (LONDON: MACMILLAN, 1862).

argues, with a vision of "female potency and exclusively female happiness" in a world "without men."[21] Whereas brotherhood excludes women at the poem's beginning, sisterhood pushes husbands and fathers into the margins of the poem's conclusion. Because the textual ellipsis obscures the secret of the sisters' maternal productivity, the children's origins are seemingly as mysterious as the origins of the goblins' fruits. Though "Goblin Market" generally frustrates the determination of cause to effect, however, the children and the tale result (as well as follow) from the sisters' experience with goblin men.

The monologic point of view that Rossetti finally imposes on "Goblin Market" receives two challenges in the volume to which it lends its name. On the one hand, Rossetti's experiments with point of view in the volume disturb the prerogatives of sisterhood in the title poem; on the other, her brother's pictorial complements to the text critically revise the reading Laura gives to her experience.[22] Indeed, insofar as Rossetti relinquished her authority over the poem to Gabriel, the rivalry between brother and sister that partly inspired "Goblin Market" continues into the finished volume. At the same time, her authorization of the illustrations also represents a gesture—a kind one at that—to inclusiveness that contrasts the poem's two forms of exclusiveness. The illustrations slyly pervert the principle of collective incorporation, however. For the title page, Gabriel prepared a pictorial gloss on the line "Golden head by golden head" (l. 184) and so opened the volume at the moment when Laura and Lizzie are enfolded in each other's arms. Unlike the many sisters "joining hands to little hands" (l. 560) at the poem's end, these sisters are, as the illustration shows, not hand in hand. Moreover, while their bodies form together one sphere, another circle, presumably Laura's dream, shows the goblin men descending the nighttime slope that Lizzie climbs in the other illustration. In so doing, Rossetti's fraternal illustrator intrudes the goblin presence into the poem at a point that focuses on sororal union.

Dilating on Rossetti's concern with balance, the illustrations abound in pictorial asymmetries and excesses. Thus, for the frontispiece, Lizzie moves into the background. As her outstretched arm and bound hair indicate, she is balanced and restrained. In the crowded foreground, toothy rodents (one beckoning to the retreating Lizzie) and sharp-beaked birds train sidelong glances at the hapless Laura, who looks down at the golden curl she clips. Cut very short, this lock of hair not only sensuously drapes about the "cat-faced" (l. 109) goblin's neck, but suggestively mirrors his snakelike tail. Gabriel enlarges this suggestion of menace, moreover, by enlarging the goblins. They are manifestly not "little men" (l. 55) but large beasts. Since, in a private act of correction, Rossetti painted "very slim agile" goblins into her copy of the first edition (*PW,* 460), her later tribute to her brother's revising hand seems expressly ironic.[23] Gabriel took other liberties, however. For example, his interest in Laura's interactions with the goblins in both blocks undermines the privilege Rossetti gives to sisterhood. While "Goblin Market" valorizes independent choice as well as sororal activity, its illustrations focus on women's dependence on men. As a result, the illustrations for "Goblin Market" demonstrate the contingency of meaning to point of view in a way that enlightens the intertextual dynamic of *Goblin Market and Other Poems* as a whole.

"*Buy from us with @ golden curl*"

D. G. ROSSETTI'S FRONTISPIECE FOR *GOBLIN MARKET AND OTHER POEMS* (LONDON: MACMILLAN, 1862).

Sisters and Selves: Relating Estrangement

The concept of relation, as it affects both the state of being and the act of telling, gives to *Goblin Market and Other Poems* its purposive unity. At the same time, various lyrics within the volume deviate from the thematic imperatives of the title poem and submit to ironic revision the moral that Laura draws from her experience: "There is no friend like a sister." A "capacious trope" for the fullest range of feminine experience, sisterhood offers, in Helena Michie's words, "a protecting framework . . . within which female sexuality can be explored and reabsorbed within the teleology of family."[24] Rossetti's conflation of sexual, social, and religious identities within this flexible trope contributes to the dynamic, often confrontational tensions of the 1862 volume. Moving from sororal friendship in "Goblin Market" through enmity in such ballads as "Maude Clare" and "Noble Sisters" to "old familiar love" in "The Convent Threshold" (l. 148), she experiments with different formal shapes to contain the varieties of feminine experience. Indeed, because much of her verse is, as William Rossetti observes, "more in the nature of dialogue or speech than of narration," it possesses a "quasi-narrative" or generically indeterminate quality.[25] The privilege that Rossetti gives to speech, becoming thus a function of poetic form, derives from her belief that "the voice is inseparable from the person to whom it belongs" (TF, 30). In *Goblin Market and Other Poems* the telling voice becomes the means, then, to inscribe feminine subjectivity and to discriminate the priorities of selfhood from those of sisterhood. In this light, the different points of view represented by successive lyrics contribute to an open colloquy on the formal and thematic concerns raised in the title poem.

A dialogue poem in the ballad tradition, "Noble Sisters" issues an early challenge to the moral concluding "Goblin Market." Like many of Rossetti's quasi-narrative lyrics, this poem makes love the inspiration for hateful utterance in a way that corrupts the possibilities for meaningful relation. Although the title posits nobility and sisterhood as grounds for self-sameness between the two speakers, both terms erode during the course of their debate and render their nominative address ("sister") highly ironic. Gradually unfolding the tale of a secret suitor, the first four stanzas chart increasing animosity between the two women. Calling her sister twice "dear" (l. 2) and later "fair and tall" (l. 14), the first speaker meets like response from the other who calls her "sister dove" (l. 11) and "highborn sister" (l. 21). While affection subtly modulates to hauteur between the two groups of adjectives, the appellative of "sister" disappears in the central stanza and reappears unadorned by descriptive terms in the final two stanzas. By this time, sisterhood no longer adequately defines the women's relationship.

The first stanza establishes the relative roles the sisters take in the ensuing discussion. Beginning in polite inquiry, the first sister has eight lines of dialogue to her respondent's four lines. As the interrogative mode suggests, however, she cedes her verbal advantage to the second sister who, for all her succinctness, holds the power of knowledge over the other. Betraying the urgency of her desire with each question, the first sister asks the other whether she has seen any of her lover's envoys—a falcon, a hound, a page—and finally whether she has met the man himself. The three envoys ratify the lover's mastery. The falcon, a noble bird, wears "jingling bells about her neck" (l. 5); the hound, "a silken leash about his neck" (l. 17); the page, "eaglets broidered on his cap, / And eaglets on his glove" (ll. 29–30). Marked as a strong man's possessions, they carry tokens of his embassy. Although the first sister has no certain knowledge, she speculates that the first "may have been a ribbon, / Or it may have been a ring" (ll. 7–8); the second, "A chain of gold and silver links, / Or a letter writ to me" (ll. 19–20); the third, "some pledge of love" (l. 32). Leaving off the uncertainty of the alternatives suggested by the iterated "or," she is certain, however, that her lover has "Come home across the desolate sea" (l. 41) to plight his troth. Even more certainly, she asserts, "in his heart my heart is locked, / And in his life my life" (ll. 43–44). Although the words used and the tokens imagined make love a matter of ownership, the speaker welcomes the metaphoric "chain of gold and silver links" that promises to bind her to her suitor.

Acting as her sister's keeper, the other repels the threat the lover thus represents. Insisting that "for your love, my sister dove, / I 'frayed the thief away" (ll. 11–12), she suggests that the falcon and, by extension, its master are come not only to rob them but to destroy them, for the falcon and dove are incompatible. Likewise, her other responses express solicitous care of her sister. Finally, when she meets the man, she rebuffs him utterly: "Her husband loves her much, / And yet she loves him more" (ll. 47–48). Repeating the word "lie" four times in the final stanza (ll. 49, 50, 54), the first sister not only substitutes assertion for interrogation but effectively charges the second with a lie in each of her four previous responses. In so doing, she also accuses the other of murdering truth as well as love. But while the second sister has, in turning the suitor away, "stabbed him with a lie" (l. 54) and so played Cain to his Abel, she condemns her interlocutor to the exile's curse of "sorrow" (l. 58) and "shame" (l. 59).

Arguing that the "wicked sister" tells lies to conceal her jealousy, Helena Michie believes that Rossetti eventually yields control of the poem to the "wounded sister."[26] Similarly, for Dolores Rosenblum, the poet authenticates the experience of the "betrayed woman" and renders the "outwardly legitimized" sister "inwardly inauthentic."[27] But Rossetti is far more impartial than these critics suggest. Although the poem invites readers to judge the respective claims of the two speakers, the poet refrains from choosing sides. She does not clarify whether the so-called wicked sister wants marriage for herself or wants to maintain, albeit vainly, the bonds of sorority by frustrating the other's marriage. Nor does she clarify whether the second sister has, in fact, lied. The surreptitious nature of the lover's suit should cast doubt on the benevolence of his intention. For instance, each of his envoys arrives before dawn rather than in the light of day. Moreover, as the first sister admits, he is an exile and has but "Come home across the desolate sea" (l. 41). Even her final speech, asserting as it does the primacy of her love for him, does not answer to the existence of a husband. Thus, while the first defends the lover's claims, the form of suggestion in the poem does little to disestablish the other's counterclaim that the suitor is not noble, but "nameless" (l. 45). As Rossetti's manipulation of point of view suggests, truth is relative in "Noble Sisters." Because subterfuge characterizes the speech of both sisters, this poem, even more than "Goblin Market," corrodes singular readings and its only certainty lies with the violent breach that comes when, in the final turn of debate, they articulate their new allegiances—the first to the "nameless" lover, the second to "our father's name" (l. 59).

Variations of the paradigm Rossetti works with in "Noble Sisters" recur in "Love from the North," "Maude Clare," and "Sister Maude." The last of these takes the theme of sororal betrayal to its climax. Recollecting, like "Maude Clare," the title of Rossetti's juvenile novella, *Maude,* "Sister Maude" rewrites "Noble Sisters" as a monologue. An informer "Who lurked to spy and peer" (l. 4), Maude resembles the second of "Noble Sisters," but she stands accused of an actual rather than a metaphoric murder. Charged with a criminality that likewise severs the bonds of relationship, she has no voice and, therefore, no defense. Instead, she becomes the recipient of the speaker's curse: "Sister Maude, oh sister Maude, / Bide *you* with death and sin" (ll. 21–22). Dwelling ironically on their intimacy of relation in the twice-iterated "sister," this emphatic curse foists upon Maude the nameless speaker's own experience—love's "shame" (l. 1) and death's sorrow—and so reverses the final thrust of "Noble Sisters."

In both "Noble Sisters" and "Sister Maude," the imperatives of heterosexual desire destroy sisterhood. But while the male lover's intrusion translates sorority into hostility, Rossetti yet excludes his point of view.

In "Maude Clare," she accommodates, albeit marginally, this third perspective. Although Thomas, the bridegroom, looks "pale with inward strife" (l. 13), he has already chosen Nell over Maude Clare. In so reconstituting the volume's relational paradigm, Rossetti polarizes wife against lover rather than sister against sister. Shifting the paradigm again in "Love from the North," she similarly poises the balance between two suitors, but she opposes these alternatives as male rather than female. Like Thomas, the female speaker of "Love from the North" suffers from inward strife. Having enthralled her soft southern lover, however, she wavers before, not after, the point of marriage: "I pacing balanced," she recalls, "in my thoughts: / 'It's quite too late to think of nay'" (ll. 11–12). The balance of the poem, shifting here from the speaker's unvoiced to voiced thoughts, shifts further to accommodate the strong northern lover's "nay" (l. 16). Enthralled in her turn by this alternative, she is bound, like the first of "Noble Sisters," to her suitor "With links of love" (l. 30). Accordingly, she has "neither heart nor power / Nor will nor wish to say him nay" (ll. 31–32). As this final series of negative conjunctions suggests, Rossetti's concern is, in part, with the loss of female self-possession. But the critique of love implied in her use of the language of power and possession is muted. The ambivalent phrasings used to close the poem notwithstanding, the speaker has resolved her inward strife. By contrast, marriage does not confer closure of emotion in "Maude Clare."

Despite the centrality of Thomas's choice in "Maude Clare," the poem's drama inheres less in his internal conflict than in the external conflict between two women. Reducing the manuscript poem to nearly a quarter of its length for publication, Rossetti excised large portions of narrative to focus more closely on the speech of the two women and to reveal, much as she does in "Noble Sisters," the ignobility of their passions. As in the other ballads, the spoken revelation of intense inner feeling, however spiked with hatred, makes these women dynamic and attractive. Of course, Maude Clare dominates the poem verbally. While the inward strife of the weak-willed Thomas accedes to faltering speech, her scorn issues in powerful words. To him, she gives her "half of the golden chain" (l. 21) that he wore during their courtship and her "half of the faded leaves" (l. 25) that they gathered together. To Nell, she says, "Take my share of a fickle heart, / Mine of a paltry love" (ll. 37–38). Hitherto silent, Nell has, however, the last word in the contest. In the poem's closing speech, she insists on her own emotional power: "I'll love him till he loves me best, / Me best of all, Maude Clare" (ll. 47–48).

While Maude Clare focuses on Thomas's infidelity, Nell implies a betrayal on her rival's part. But if Maude Clare compromises her integrity by publishing her indictment after the marriage, Nell similarly besmirches her love for Thomas by taking up the other woman's challenge. For both, the speech of accusation is also the speech of betrayal.

In "The Convent Threshold" and "From House to Home" Rossetti relies on the form of the monologue to integrate the warring alternatives that characterize the foregoing poems on sisters and lovers. Easing the transition into her devotional verse, "The Convent Threshold" not only looks forward in the volume to "From House to Home," but looks backward, outside the volume, to "Three Nuns." Choosing to become a religious sister rather than a carnal lover, the novice of "The Convent Threshold" takes the veil in order to achieve undivided selfhood. As a result, the violence directed outward in the other sister poems moves inward in "The Convent Threshold." While the male lover beckons the speaker of "From House to Home" to "Come home, O love, from banishment" (l. 75), the novice implores her unrepentant lover to "Kneel, wrestle, knock, do violence, pray" (l. 48). For her, as for the ballad heroines, erotic love has done violence to the bonds of kinship: "There's blood between us, love, my love," she says, "There's father's blood, there's brother's blood; / And blood's a bar I cannot pass" (ll. 1–3). Consequently, her "lily feet are soiled with mud, / With scarlet mud which tells a tale / Of hope that was, of guilt that was" (ll. 7–9), and because the past determines the future, "Of love that shall not yet avail" (l. 10). But as "yet" suggests, the novice defers, not denies, love's availing power. Partly in reparation for the double violence of patricide and fratricide, she must "do violence" to her immediate desire to guarantee its ultimate fulfillment.

Because desire denied turns inward upon the self, repression provides, as John Kucich argues, a profoundly "autoerotic foundation for the nineteenth-century subject."[28] Thus the speaker of "From House to Home" must, like the novice, "do battle, suffer, and attain" (l. 142) in order to come home not so much to the departed lover as to her neglected soul. Precipitated by his abandonment, her sense of self-division accounts for the poem's opening double riddle: her "first" experience of love, "like a dream thro' summer heat" (l. 1), reveals "a tissue of hugged lies" (l. 9); her "second," "like a tedious numbing swoon" (l. 2), constitutes the first's "ruin fraught with pain" (l. 10). But describing her "first" as a "pleasure-place" (l. 6), an "earthly paradise" (l. 7), a "castle . . . of white transparent glass" (l. 13), and a "pleasaunce" (l. 17), the speaker carefully labels and sensuously describes the experience she exposes as "fair delusion" (l. 11). Even though this pleasure-place in which frogs and toads "propagate in peace" (l. 34) yields to painful ruin, Rossetti provides an authorized reconstruction in the "vision of a woman, where / Night and new morning strive for domination" (ll. 117–18). Watching this struggle waged on the threshold of being, the desirous speaker discovers that she is desirable to herself, for as the poem's conclusion makes clear, the woman is her soul. By so eroticizing spiritual devotion in place of sexual desire, Rossetti's religious lyrics eroticize the achievement of self-hood. "Incomparably pale, and almost fair, / And sad beyond expression" (ll. 119–20), the visionary woman inhabits "inner ground that budded flowers" (l. 126) while the speaker occupies "the outer barren ground" (l. 125). Reversing the momentum of the speaker's initial experience, the second part of her vision moves from "measureless sorrow" (l. 135) to immeasurable joy: "The lost in night, in day was found again; / The fallen are lifted up" (ll. 195–96). This revelation, integrating the speaker's inner and outer awareness of self, marks the victory of new morning over the dark night of the soul.

Like "From House to Home," "The Convent Threshold" also uses the passage of night into day to trace the process of the novice's self-regeneration. In fact, her final dream reprises and reverses the bipartite experience of the speaker in transit "From House to Home." While the first part includes a nightmare vision of satanic intoxication, the second hypostatizes sexual union as a "tissue of hugged lies," recalls the blood bar that separates the novice from her lover, and brings the poem's physical and psychic violence to a new pitch. In these dreams the novice resembles the nightgown-clad women of such Pre-Raphaelite canvases as *Ecce Ancilla Domini!* (for which Rossetti modeled) and *The Awakening Conscience*. In these paintings the woman's awakening to religious or moral purpose provides erotic spectacle, but the novice, having dreamed of reddened sheets, awakens to discover "frozen blood . . . on the sill / Where stifling in my struggle I lay" (ll. 135–36). The heat of sexual and murderous passions abated, the resulting chill gives over to the vision of the lovers' reunion in heaven: "There we shall meet as once we met / And love with old familiar love" (ll. 147–48). Because Rossetti's last words erase the distinctions between platonic and erotic love, the poem's conclusion, with its invocation of a new beginning that is also old, is rife with paradox. The echo of Gabriel's poem "The Blessed Damozel" is particularly unsettling since Rossetti's speaker, having become a religious sister, casts her lover into the role of a brother. But although "The

Convent Threshold" opens with the bloody suggestion of parricide and ends with the incestuous one of "old familiar love," the poem charmed its Victorian readership. Alice Meynell observes, for example, that this work contains "more passion than . . . any other poem written by a woman" but "never breaks into the relief of violence."[29]

"The Convent Threshold" transgresses categories of relationship to reconcile desire and devotion. In the monologue, Rossetti uses a form that permits her speaker's sustained self-realization and that, therefore, allows the novice to transcend the experience of love described in the poet's other quasi-narrative lyrics. For the ballad heroines, romantic love implies its opposite. Breeding hostility and division, it dissolves the bonds of familial alliance without necessarily providing any compensatory satisfaction. Indeed, even when Rossetti envisions a consummation, she subtly erodes its fulfillment by revealing that the language of love renders women powerless. Thus, gaining erotic fulfilment, the speaker of "Love from the North" gainsays what is, from the perspective of the devotional poems, far more valuable: a sense of self. In "The Convent Threshold," on the other hand, the novice's choice of vocation, taking "old familiar love" as its end, allows Rossetti not only to unify the female speaker's sexual and spiritual aspirations but also to amplify, intensify, and ironize Laura's sense that "there is no friend like a sister." Renouncing the power of heterosexual desire, the novice effectively befriends the beloved. A religious sister, she moves into a community of women whose self-devotion authorizes their autonomy from men. As the bridge between "Goblin Market" and "From House to Home," "The Convent Threshold" thus represents a climax in the volume's progression from secular to religious concerns, from sisters to selves, and from fragmented to integrated awareness.

Dreams and Death: Estranging Awareness

As "Goblin Market," "The Convent Threshold," and "From House to Home" suggest, the dream is another key motif in the 1862 volume. While the dream as a literary device goes back through the romantics to the medieval *Roman de la Rose* and Dante's *Divina Commedia,* Rossetti's use of the visionary mode links her to other *Germ* contributors, most notably her brother Gabriel. Indeed, for Ruskin's workingman correspondent, Thomas Dixon, reading the *Germ* "produce[d] on the mind . . . a vague and dreamy sensation, approaching as it were the Mystic Land of a Bygone Age" (W. Rossetti, ed., 1899, 221). Besides Gabriel's poems

"The Blessed Damozel" and "My Sister's Sleep," the *Germ* contains Scott's "Morning Sleep," Deverell's "The Sight Beyond," and Rossetti's own "Dream-Land." Republishing "Dream-Land" along with five of six other *Germ* poems in *Goblin Market and Other Poems,* she establishes a continuity between the earlier joint concern and her later individual success that, on the one hand, identifies her with other Pre-Raphaelite dreamers and, on the other, allows her to bring an outsider's critical perspective to Pre-Raphaelite dreaming.

Rossetti's dream lyrics explore alternative modes of consciousness. In so doing, they place point of view in strangely unlocalized temporal and spatial settings. "Dream-Land" concerns, for instance, a woman who "sleeps a charmèd sleep" (l. 3) and who "seek[s] where shadows are / Her pleasant lot" (ll. 7–8). Because Rossetti treats death as "a secret between-time" that is "liberated from both life and afterlife, both regret and expectation," she seems "profoundly indifferent to both love and faith."[30] Thus, while the element of enchantment and the reference to "sunless rivers" (l. 1) recall "Kubla Khan," "Dream-Land" is far gentler and, in some ways, far odder than Samuel Taylor Coleridge's poem. Positioned in a world between two modes of being and feeling, the dead dreamer not only "sees" (l. 14) and "hears" (l. 15) aspects of the physical world, but she "cannot see" (l. 21) and "cannot feel" (l. 23) the effects of physical change represented in "the grain / Ripening on hill and plain" (ll. 21–22). Neither entirely sensible nor insensible to the world, she rests "Upon a mossy shore" (l. 26) and so occupies a liminal landscape of "perfect peace" (l. 32) that is neither here nor hereafter.

For Rossetti, to die is, as Hamlet says, "perchance to dream." While other lyrics in *Goblin Market and Other Poems* associate death with zones of transitional awareness, however, not all are quite so endued with perfect peace. In "At Home," for example, the dead speaker's spirit returns "To seek the much frequented house" (l. 2). Retracing Alfred, Lord Tennyson's return to the house of mourning in the seventh lyric of *In Memoriam,* Rossetti points out that death makes no impression on the living, for her speaker finds a scene of revelry upon which her shadow "cast[s] / No chill" (ll. 25–26). When the speaker discovers, after having "passed the door" (l. 3), that she has doubly "passed away" (ll. 22 and 30) from life and love, she "passe[s] from the familiar room" (l. 29). While pastness also distinguishes her use of tense, her friends speak of what "shall be" (ll. 10 and 15) on the morrow. Estranged by death, the speaker's point of view not only defamiliarizes this familiar scene, but drives home the ironic pun on "familiar": this phantom consciousness has clearly not answered a summons to return. Again bespeaking inti-macy as estrangement, Rossetti turns from life as past to future as death in the "Song," "When I am dead, my dearest" (l. 1), and so writes into the present tense the phrase that opens "At Home": "When I was dead, my spirit turned" (l. 1). In this dirge, moreover, she turns from the "I all-forgotten" (l. 27) of "At Home" to the would-be forgotten "me" (l. 2). Indeed, by the poem's second line, the grammatical object "me" buries the lyric subject. Composed of two perfectly balanced stanzas, this "Song" pauses between the certainty of each part's opening imperatives and the uncertainty of each part's closing conditional options. But while Rossetti once more explores an indeterminate terrain, death's promise of restful "dreaming through the twilight / That doth not rise nor set" (ll. 13–14) argues an indifference to whether buried consciousness remem-bers or forgets earthly experience.

In *Goblin Market and Other Poems* Rossetti's approach to dreams, like her approach to sisterhood, is highly variable. While it represents a pre-ferred state of posthumous awareness, the dream also symbolizes a deluded state of vital awareness. Looking back to union "long ago" (l. 18) and looking forward to union "in Paradise" (l. 8), the speaker of "Echo" dreams in order to recapture a lost lover and to fill another empty between-time. Although the poem's proliferating verbal echoes linguistically achieve the desired echo of past and future experience, its erotic luxuriousness serves to reinscribe rather than satiate desire. As the poem's title and the reference to "sunlight on a stream" (l. 4) suggest, the dream that the speaker would reecho "Pulse for pulse, breath for breath" (l. 16) has no substance. As a result, the desired consummation is as vain of realization as the spirit's return in "At Home" or Laura's dream in "Goblin Market." As both the poems "Fata Morgana" and "Mirage" demonstrate, the dream offers only illusive fulfillments. In "Fata Morgana" the titular allusion to the fairy enchantress of Arthurian legend emphasizes the seductive nature of delusion. Thus, even as the vision of the "blue-eyed phantom far before" (l. 1) inspires delight, the pursuing consciousness eventually capitulates to sorrow since this image remains ever "so far before" (l. 10). Coming to a like realization in "Mirage," Rossetti's awakened speaker observes, "Life, and the world, and mine own self, are changed / For a dream's sake" (ll. 11–12). Radically transformed, the subject experiences self as other—not as new, but as "Exceeding comfortless, and worn, and old" (l. 3).

Treating the dream as a now-and-then symbol for death's restful sleep and life's restless desire, Rossetti takes a third approach in the coy grotesquerie of "My Dream." A tale of sibling rivalry, monstrous self-indulgence, and autocratic excess, "My Dream" is truly "curious" (l. 1). From "out of myriad pregnant waves" (l. 6) emerges a brood of crocodiles. Out of these rises one to dominion over "His punier brethren" (l. 21), thereby becoming "lord and master of his kin" (l. 23). Sacrificing his own "brethren" to his "execrable appetite" (l. 25) for power, the cannibal crocodile defies the "binding law" (l. 27) of kinship. Falling asleep, the crocodile "dwindled to the common size" (l. 36). When a "wingèd vessel" (l. 38) approaches, he awakens as a "prudent crocodile" (l. 47), "shed appropriate tears and wrung his hands" (l. 48). Having told this tale, the speaker refuses—as Rossetti herself did for "Goblin Market" (see *PW,* 459)—to "answer . . . / For meaning" and will only "echo, What?" (ll. 49–50). She even refrains from explaining the crocodile's "prudent" parody of remorse—after all, he only sheds crocodile tears. Nevertheless, if the dream contains "sifted truth" (l. 2), it must mean something.

Seriousness of thought and style, maintains Matthew Arnold in "The Study of Poetry," distinguishes verse of the highest value. Although Arnoldian precepts clearly do not hold for Rossetti's playful "anti-style," they do explain the rather humorless attitude taken by some critics of "My Dream."[31] One early reviewer, calling the poem "the very choicest balderdash," exclaims, "We would give the world to see [it] translated into some foreign language, we have such an intense eagerness to understand it" (Rudd, 843). More recently, Thomas Burnett Swann guesses that the poem's biblical symbolism holds the key to its meaning and suggests that the dream seeks to admonish readers to repentance. But while he goes on to assert that "My Dream" "is not a good poem," the fault lies less with Rossetti's masterpiece than his egregious misreading of it.[32] Instead, the key to "My Dream" lies with the poet's stylistic indirections. In other words, the poem's meaning is subject to readers' appreciation of its form.

Insofar as the speaker pantomimes the crocodile's actions, "My Dream" symbolizes, like "Goblin Market," the process of its own creation. While the crocodile prudently recants his fattening indulgence once he awakens to expediency, the speaker stands outside of her dream to relate its sifted truth in mingled tones of command and apology. First, she imperiously enjoins the reader's close attention in the poem's opening lines: "Hear now a curious dream I dreamed last night, / Each word whereof is weighed and sifted truth" (ll. 1–2). After one sentence recounting the dream's beginning, however, she becomes diffident. This diffidence allows Rossetti to preserve, much as she does in "Winter: My Secret," "the very possibility of integrity and truth in speech" (McGann 1980, 246). Fearing that even the "closest friend would deem the facts untrue" (l. 10), she suggests that the rest "were wisely left untold" (l. 11). Inasmuch as poetic or dream facts inspire skepticism because they are not demonstrably facts, Rossetti returns to her preoccupation with truth in *Maude* as well as in numerous lyrics in *Goblin Market and Other Poems*. Indeed, she went so far as to write "not a real dream" beside "My Dream" in her own copy of the 1875 edition (*PW,* 479). Yet as she observes elsewhere, "Fabrications, blunders, even lies, frequently contain some grain of truth: and though life at the longest cannot be enough for us to sift all, one occasionally may repay the sifting" (*TF,* 78).

The speaker, having hinted at the difference between sifted truth and everyday reality, then opens to the reader the option of continuing: "If you will, why, hear it to the end" (l. 12). But if she respects her auditors' volition in hearing, she appeals powerfully to their crocodilian appetite for curiosity. The dream, born in the pregnant depths of the mind, then yields to the empire of one idea embodied in the ravenous crocodile that feeds on the rest to its self-exaltation. In this respect, "My Dream" encodes the activities of the Pre-Raphaelite imagination much as "Kubla Khan" describes the processes of the romantic imagination. Rossetti does more than symbolize the Pre-Raphaelite creative process, however. She launches a tongue-in-cheek attack on it. So whereas the dream tells of unbridled authority and its abuse, her method of telling wryly relinquishes the task of explication to readers. By inviting readers to participate in the construction of meaning in "My Dream," she opposes the egocentrism of the masculine imagination, epitomized in the crocodile, and makes reciprocity the key to feminine creativity.

Of course, the crocodile fraternity, like the goblin brotherhood, suggests closer brethren than even the PRB. Apparently, Rossetti's brothers appreciated the joke at their expense, for they gave her a drawing of crocodiles in 1864. When Gabriel proposed to give her another, however, she demurred. Writing herself into the picture he had already sent, she explained her position: "I am so happy in my nest of crocodiles that I beg you will on no account purchase the Prudent to lord it over them: indeed amongst their number, by a careful study of expression, one may detect latent greatness, and point out the predominant tail of the future" (W. Rossetti, ed., 1903, 68–69). In so refusing the second drawing, she was also refusing Gabriel's efforts "to lord it over" her and to dictate "the predominant tail of the future." Although she had cut him down "to the common size" in the dozing crocodile, he yet posed a threat to her autonomy as a poet. Indeed, since she was then writing "The Prince's Progress" under his close supervision, her caution was itself most prudent.

Chapter Three

Conciliation, Circumvention, and Rebellion: *The Prince's Progress and Other Poems*

Rossetti was, according to her brother William, a spontaneous poet who rarely meditated her subjects or revised her writing and who never, "in the course of her work, invited any hint, counsel, or co-operation" (*PW,* lxix). During the course of her work on *The Prince's Progress and Other Poems,* published in 1866, she had frequent occasion to rue the counsel and cooperation that she had solicited from her brother Gabriel. Acting as her illustrator, editor, and agent, Gabriel provided designs for the title poem, made suggestions affecting the form and content of individual lyrics as well as their collective arrangement within the volume, and conducted business with her publisher. But when he imposed upon Macmillan for an advance to help finance her excursion to Italy in May of 1865, he overstepped his mandate and earned his sister's decorous rebuke. Declining the self-sufficiency contingent on a literary income in favor of "unfailing family bounty," she apologized to Gabriel for, as she said, the "annoyance brought on you by your brotherliness" and relieved him of further action on her behalf (Packer, ed., 51). Yet in drawing attention to her dependency as a woman, Rossetti also asserted her independence from fraternal control. The same method of polite circumvention had sustained her throughout the production of *The Prince's Progress and Other Poems*.

As early as 1863, Rossetti had considered the possibility of bringing out a successor to *Goblin Market and Other Poems*; unwilling to relinquish her "system of not writing against the grain," however, she twice abandoned the idea of a second volume because she lacked "materials, equal both in quantity and quality," to her previous work (Packer, ed., 19). Ironically, when she later allowed Gabriel to take an active role in shaping the focus of "The Prince's Progress," the centerpiece of the new volume, she committed herself to a system of writing that she found inimical to her genius. But while "The Prince's Progress" represents, in

William's view, "almost the only instance in which she wrote anything so as to meet directly the views of another person" (*PW,* 461), Rossetti writes against rather than submits to the masculine poetic paradigm that Gabriel urged on her. Broadening her resistance to his controlling influence in other works composed for the volume, she experiments with a variety of dramatic and lyric forms to examine the literary and cultural assumptions that shape women's experience of life, love, and art. In such poems as "Under the Rose," "Songs in a Cornfield," and "Autumn," she unsettles the masculine priority assumed in traditional narratives of desire by privileging the feminine voice of thought and feeling. But although Gabriel's brotherliness, however annoying and presumptuous, challenged Rossetti to stretch and grow as a poet, she resented his attempts to appropriate her creativity to his inspiration and never again invited such close cooperation from her familiar critic.

The Poetics of Compromise in "The Prince's Progress"

For "The Prince's Progress," Rossetti grafted a long quest narrative onto the short choral dirge, "The Fairy Prince Who Arrived Too Late," which had appeared in *Macmillan's Magazine* in 1863. At Gabriel's suggestion, she marginalized the female characters central to the original lyric, a redaction of *Sleeping Beauty,* and incorporated a masculine plot featuring the prince and his alter ego, the alchemist. While Rossetti adopted her brother's advice and kept him closely apprised of her progress on the poem, she devised various tactics to fight his efforts to usurp her prerogative as a creative artist. Thus, her first report, made two days before Christmas of 1864, documents the reluctance with which she adopted the method of writing against the grain: "True, O Brother, my Alchemist still shivers in the blank of mere possibility; but I have so far overcome my feelings and disregarded my nerves as to unloose the Prince, so that wrapping-paper may no longer bar his 'progress'" (W. Rossetti, ed., 1903, 69). Announcing the prince's arrival in mid-January, she then sent the manuscript to Gabriel and turned her attention to the alchemist. She refused, however, to rush. Restive under her brother's superintendence, she observed, "The Alchemist makes himself scarce, and I must bide his time" (W. Rossetti, ed., 1903, 73). Nevertheless, when Gabriel returned "the annotated *Prince*" toward the end of the month (W. Rossetti, ed., 1903, 74), she had finished with the alchemist. Forwarding the outstanding episode to Gabriel, she attempted to forestall his criticism by insisting imperatively, if also apologetically, on the unpremeditated nature of her craft. "He's not precisely the Alchemist I prefigured," she adroitly confessed, "but thus he came and thus he must stay: you know my system of work" (W. Rossetti, ed., 1903, 75). Indeed, if the alchemist was not exactly the one Rossetti had prefigured, the poem as a whole was certainly not the one her brother had envisioned.

After reading a completed draft of the poem, Gabriel raised two points for reconsideration. First, he objected to the poem's metrical irregularity. Although Rossetti conceded that her choice of rhythm was less than felicitous, she nonetheless maintained that "it would [not] have done to write the Alchemist without the metric jolt" (W. Rossetti, ed., 1903, 77). More to the point, it would not have done to write the prince without the metric jolt, for the poem's spasmodic rhythm, evident especially in the shortened final line of each stanza, complements the fitfulness of his progress. Second, Gabriel advised the addition of a tournament, undoubtedly to enliven the prince's "tedious trial" (l. 250), but his sister declined the commission on the grounds of boredom:

> How shall I express my sentiments about the terrible tournament? Not a phrase to be relied on, not a correct knowledge on the subject, not the faintest impulse of inspiration, incites me to the tilt: and looming before me in horrible bugbeardom stand TWO tournaments in Tennyson's *Idylls*. Moreover, the Alchemist, according to original convention, took the place of the lists: remember this in my favour, please. You see, were you next to propose my writing a classic epic in quantitative hexameters or in the hendecasyllables which might almost trip-up Tennyson, what could I do? Only what I feel inclined to do in the present instance—plead goodwill but inability. (W. Rossetti, ed., 1903, 77)

Rossetti's disinclination to the tilt derives, as her phrasing suggests, from a reluctance to enter into open competition with Tennyson. Although "The Prince's Progress" offers a case study in "anxiety of influence," Rossetti's effort to deal with the burden of tradition does not lead, as in the Oedipal model Harold Bloom proposes, to a battle between poet and precursor.[1] Rejecting Tennyson's work as a model for her own, she uses a smile and a yawn to repudiate the tradition of which he is the exemplar.

Even as the subjects and forms favored by male poets inspired her with ennui, Rossetti turned her boredom to critical advantage by deliberately reworking elements drawn from a variety of sources, including fairy tale (*Sleeping Beauty*), epic romance (*Idylls of the King*), and religious allegory (*Pilgrim's Progress*). Through this strategy of parodic appropriation, she simultaneously "preserves literary tradition" and "presents a critique of the ideology underlying that tradition."[2] Thus, making the bugbear of boredom the prince's greatest adversary, she ironizes the concept of masculine heroism, undercuts the narrative paradigm adapted from her literary predecessors, and so creates an antiromance rather than a romance. If, as Dolores Rosenblum suggests, the poem suffers as a result (1986, 47), its very failure as art is a necessary rather than an ancillary effect, for by tripping up the prince, Rossetti managed to trip up her brother.

Rossetti's claims to lack of inspiration and knowledge permitted her not only to depart from the conventions of the quest narrative but to preserve integrity of purpose in a poem written under close fraternal supervision. Defiant of her brother's authority even as she appeared compliant, she drew strength from her supposed limitations as a woman of slight experience and as a writer of spontaneous impulse. While she wrote flatteringly of Gabriel's habits of composition, she had only to plead feminine weakness to dismiss their utility for herself:

> I do seriously question whether I possess the working-power with which you credit me; and whether all the painstaking at my command would result in work better than—in fact half so good as—what I have actually done on the other system. It is vain comparing my powers (!) with yours.
> . . . However, if the latent epic should "by huge upthrust" come to the surface some day, or if by laborious delving I can unearth it, or if by unflagging prodment you can cultivate the sensitive plant in question, all the better for me: only please remember that "things which are impossible rarely happen"—and don't be too severe on me if in my case the "impossible" does not come to pass. (W. Rossetti, ed., 1903, 88–89)

At a later date, she wrote, "Here is a great discovery, 'Women are not Men,' and you must not expect me to possess a tithe of your capacities, though I humbly—or proudly—lay claim to family-likeness" (FL, 31). What she called the "genuine 'lyric cry'" she would always "back against all skilled labour" (FL, 65). At the same time, however, The Prince's Progress and Other Poems shows greater evidence of skilled labor than Goblin Market and Other Poems. Composing most of the material for the volume between 1862 and 1865, Rossetti also made substantial revisions to such poems as "A Royal Princess," "The Poor Ghost," "The Bourne," "Summer," "The Ghost's Petition," "After This the Judgment," "Songs in a Cornfield," and "The Prince's Progress." But although Gabriel's editorial assistance clearly made a difference to her work, Rossetti's acquiescence was neither absolute nor indiscriminate. Even when she made the changes that he recommended, she reserved the right to disregard them upon later reflection because, as she explained, "'I am I' is so strong within me" (Troxell, ed., 142).

While Rossetti's claims to spontaneous composition allowed her to repel threats to her esthetic autonomy, the technical reasons that she advanced in defense of "The Prince's Progress" reveal the deliberation with which she approached her work. Thus, as a final argument against the inclusion of a tournament, she wrote, "My actual *Prince* seems to me invested with a certain artistic congruity of construction not lightly to be despised" (W. Rossetti, ed., 1903, 77). Symmetrically structured, the poem alternates between the attractions of society and the trials of solitude or "barren boredom" (W. Rossetti, ed., 1903, 78). Each of the several episodes that constitute the narrative serves as a test of the prince's character. But although, as Joan Rees observes, the poem involves "two kinds of spiritual testing," Rossetti is less concerned to examine the princess's trial of patience than the prince's failure of effort.[3] Indeed, the princess functions as little more than the marginalized object of "The Prince's Progress." But if the princess remains incidental to the prince's adventures, she is crucial to the poet's design. Her radical effacement puts into focus the way traditional narratives of desire have, as Luce Irigaray contends, "defined [the feminine] as lack, deficiency, or as imitation and negative image of the subject."[4] In accordance with Irigaray's view that "a *disruptive excess*" often accompanies women writers' subversive appropriation of masculine discourses (78), the princess's death further exaggerates her absence to clinch the failure of the prince's quest. Likewise, by exaggerating the dilatoriness of the errant prince, Rossetti not only exposes the corrupt values that inform the structure of romance but trivializes the prerogatives of masculine desire.

Patently unheroic, the prince embodies the paradox of physical strength and moral infirmity. "Strong of limb if of purpose weak" (l. 47), he is "Tough to grapple tho' weak to snare" (l. 407). The poem begins, therefore, with the prince lingering even before he embarks upon his journey. "Taking his ease on cushion and mat" (l. 14) within "his world-end palace" (l. 13), he apparently wiled away the time by smoking his pipe, but Gabriel cavilled at the impropriety of such a detail in a medievalized romance. Although the pipe was subsequently "immolated on the altar of sisterly deference" (W. Rossetti, ed., 1903, 81), Rossetti yet possessed other means to indicate her hero's defects. For instance, when urged to start by the voices of his bride's attendants, the prince proclaims, "Now the moon's at full; I tarried for that, / Now I start in truth" (l. 17–18). One of several "refined clues" included for a more sophisticated audience, the full moon was, according to Rossetti, "happily suggestive of the Prince's character" (W. Rossetti, ed., 1903, 81). Just as the moon, a familiar symbol of temporal mutability, waxes and wanes, so too does the prince's sense of purpose. Initially, he is crudely confident that "his bride will be won and worn, / Ere fall of the dark" (ll. 53–54), but he only reaches his destination some "ten years" (l. 491) later just as "Day wears apace" (l. 468). His advent is, of course, "too late" (l. 481), since the darkness that then falls upon his quest is that of death as well as night.

The prince's unpunctual appearance owes, in part, to three encounters that he has in the course of his journey. While he incurs obligations that involve a betrayal of the princess in each instance, the first and third of his encounters also strongly suggest sexual promiscuity to be an affect of moral irresolution. "Starting at length" (l. 48), the prince has "journeyed at least a mile" (l. 59) when he stops to talk to a comely milkmaid loitering with her pail. Ever inclined to caustic understatement, the narrator deliberately confuses the attractions of the milkmaid and her wares to remark that the prince "Grew athirst at the sight" (l. 60). Asking her for "a morning draught" (l. 61), he fails to fix a fee before quenching his thirst and, in so doing, reveals his impetuosity. Requested to set her own price, the maid "laughed, 'You may give the full moon to me; / Or else sit under this apple-tree / Here for one idle day by my side'" (ll. 80–82). Although she is clearly a version of Wanton, whom Faithful successfully resists in John Bunyan's *Pilgrim's Progress,* the prince agrees to her price in order to requite "his own royal pledge" (l. 88):

> So he stretched his length in the apple-tree shade,
> Lay and laughed and talked to the maid,
> Who twisted her hair in a cunning braid
>   And writhed it in shining serpent-coils,
> And held him a day and night fast laid
>   In her subtle coils. (ll. 91–96)

As the Edenic allusions suggest, the prince has fallen to temptation and has, by honoring the maid's demands, dishonored his pledge to the princess. Indeed, idling "a day and night," he has not only "stretched his length in the apple-tree shade" but lengthened the requisite duration of his stay. Similarly, when he later parts from the shorefolk, he stretches time interminably to exchange with his fair companions "last words, and last, last words" (l. 374). Eager in both instances to avail himself of the temptress's charms, he seems wholly unaware of the moral dilemma that his impulsiveness has occasioned, but the achievement of his immediate desires—the milkmaid and the shoremaid—will nonetheless exact another price and frustrate him of his ultimate desire—the bride.

Leaving the maid, Rossetti's hero next traverses a "Tedious land for a social Prince" (l. 152). Just as the conventions of romance inspired disaffection in the poet, the barren wilderness "of chasm and rent" (l. 127) that confronts the prince provokes in him a feeling of "discontent" (l. 168). Yearning for human diversion, he again loses sight of his purpose when he meets the alchemist, "An old, old mortal, cramped and double" (l. 178), whom he asks for lodging. Superseding the defunct tournament and doubling upon the hero's previous experience, this encounter constitutes a central episode in the narrative, for the questions that Rossetti raises about the nature of moral turpitude are, in effect, cramped and double. Thus, while the alchemist, like the milkmaid, exacts a fee, he makes the terms of the bargain clear to the prince at the outset:

> If you're fain to lodge here with me,
> Take that pair of bellows you see—
> Too heavy for my old hands they be—
>   Take the bellows and puff and puff:
> When the stream curls rosy and free
> The broth's boiled enough.

> Then take your choice of all I have;
> I will give you life if you crave.
> Already I'm mildewed for the grave,
>   So first myself I must drink my fill:
> But all the rest may be yours, to save
>   Whomever you will. (ll. 205–16)

Although the alchemist's statement of terms shifts the grounds of the bargain from a night's lodging to the "draught of Life" (l. 257), the prince's assent clearly follows upon an act of conscious and voluntary will rather than, as in the previous episode, unconscious and involuntary desire. At the same time, his intentions and subsequent actions appear good and honorable: first, he determines to share the elixir with his bride and so to save her; second, he indentures himself to the alchemist and, in so doing, commits himself to labor, not leisure. As Walter E. Houghton observes, the Victorians considered work "an end in itself, a virtue in its own right," and "a life of work was identical in outward action . . . with a life of moral earnestness."[5] The prince's labor provides no Carlylean self-knowledge, however. Impervious to the suspicious resemblance between the alchemist's and the milkmaid's draughts, he also fails to consider the import of the old man's long and futile vigil. Indeed, even when the alchemist perfects his potion by dipping one "dead finger" (l. 242) into the pot, the only thing he proves is his mortality: "The last ingredient was supplied / (Unless the dead man mistook or lied)" (ll. 247–48). At best, the alchemist's success is, as the parenthetical aside suggests, highly qualified.

While Rossetti leaves open the question of whether the old man was a "fool or knave, / Or honest seeker who had not found" (ll. 261–62), the credulous prince, whose path is likewise "Self-chosen" (l. 260), seems to be all three at once. Disregarding the potion's inefficacy for the alchemist, he secures a phial as his wage and, lingering for "One night's rest" (l. 253), resolves to "speed with the rising sun" (l. 254). He remains "apt to swerve" (l. 301), however:

> By willow courses he took his path,
> Spied what a nest the kingfisher hath,
> Marked the fields green to aftermath,
>   Marked where the red-brown field-mouse ran,
> Loitered awhile for a deep-stream bath,
>   Yawned for a fellow-man. (ll. 289–94)

Rossetti treats the prince, here as elsewhere, with droll indulgence, but she also reifies his spiritual vagrancy in the wayward movements of eye and foot. In addition, the word *aftermath,* retained against Gabriel's advice, foreshadows the consequences of distraction, for "it gives a subtle hint (by symbol) that any more delays may swamp the Prince's last chance" (W. Rossetti, ed., 1903, 81).

Ironically, the prince's last chance is almost literally swamped when, encountering "a curve" (l. 303), he decides to traverse the torrent, now Bunyan's River of Death. Nearly drowned "in whirling strife" (l. 310) and clearly disoriented by "the dizzying whirl" (l. 314), he finds the thought of death in his mind for the first time. "Life is sweet," he realizes, "and the grave is grim" (l. 317). But despite this awareness, he refuses to relinquish his hold of the phial and, able to use only one hand, "catches—misses—catches a rope" (l. 322) thrown to him by those on the shore. Again relying on parenthetical intrusion, Rossetti effectively interprets the prince's actions as comic or, at least, embarrassingly unheroic even as she hints at the tragic repercussions for the princess: "(If many laugh, one well may rue: / Sleep on, thou Bride)" (ll. 335–36). Furthermore, she reveals the whole episode to be perilously unnecessary as well as unnecessarily perilous when the prince apparently doubles back and once more crosses the stream, albeit more prudently, "where a ford was plain" (l. 393). Moving in circles, he makes little progress.

Unfortunately, the prince's brush with death does not arouse in him a sense of obligation toward his bride. Before crossing the stream, he had yearned in his solitude "for a second maiden, at least, / To bear the flagon, and taste it too" (ll. 298–99). He finds the desired companionship in the woman whose face he beholds upon awakening among the shorefolk:

> Oh a moon face in a shadowy place,
> And a light touch and a winsome grace,
> And a thrilling tender voice which says:
>   "Safe from waters that seek the sea—
> Cold waters by rugged ways—
>   Safe with me." (ll. 343–48)

The woman's "moon face" recalls not only the full moon of the prince's initial departure and of the milkmaid's fanciful request but also the potion that the alchemist watched "wane or wax" (l. 202) until "the hundredth year was full" (l. 235). As such, it belongs to a network of refined clues indicative of the prince's inconstancy. Whether he shares with this second maiden a taste of the elixir, he has once more been unfaithful to his waiting bride, for just as his feet, upon touching the safety of shore, "slip on the slipping sand" (l. 323), the sands of time "Slip past, slip fast" (l. 361). Lulled into false assurance by the shorewomen's promises of safety, he gives no thought to the consequences of delay until, freed of their enchantment, he comes within sight of his goal and views "a valley spread / Where fatness laughed" (ll. 421–22). The prince's mood is not one of laughter, however, for upon seeing the princess's palace, he begins to doubt and, consequently, "lags the more" (l. 435). Approaching the palace gate with "slackening steps" (l. 457), he stops only to meet the cortege that bears "his promised Bride" (l. 464), now beyond the help of any elixir, to her grave. "The long promise," as the voices have foretold, "has not been kept" (l. 382).

At the end of a similar quest, Robert Browning's Childe Roland sees his lost peers become "a living frame / For one more picture" (ll. 200–201) and announces his arrival: "'*Childe Roland to the Dark Tower came*'" (l. 204). Rossetti's prince, on the other hand, cedes the last word to the bridal attendants who act as a living frame for the dead princess. Their closing "bride-chant" (l. 478)—the salvaged remnant of the original lyric, "The Fairy Prince Who Arrived Too Late"—not only serves as a rebuke to the tardy hero but takes up and consolidates those voices heard intermittently throughout the narrative. United at one point with the "clear réveillée" (l. 110) of "the watchman lark" (l. 109), the chorus reifies the voice of awakened conscience and brings an external point of view—one both moral and feminine—to bear on the fickleness of masculine desire.

Making the prince the subject of the chorus's criticism as well as encouragement, Rossetti wittily redirects her brother's efforts at "unflagging prodment" (W. Rossetti, ed., 1903, 89). Nevertheless, the urgency that informs the "hundred sad voices" (l. 37) and "hundred glad voices" (l. 38) may well derive from the poet's own sense that time might rob her of the opportunity to see a second volume through to press. "One motive for haste with me," she confided to Gabriel, "is a fear lest by indefinite delay I should miss the pleasure of thus giving pleasure to our Mother" (W. Rossetti, ed., 1903, 74). But while the prospect of her own death prompted the ailing Rossetti to persevere, her strong prince delays indefinitely. At the beginning of the poem, the "true voice of . . . doom" (l. 19) urges him to begin his journey. Later, "sad glad voices" (l. 115) twice summon him to resume his journey and upbraid him when he shows that he is only "prompt to crave / Sleep on the ground" (ll. 263–64): "He can sleep," they angrily observe, "who holdeth her cheap" (l. 267). He remains unresponsive, however, until he hears "bodiless cries from far away— / Chiding wailing voices" (ll. 375–76). Arriving at the princess's palace, he then becomes the audience for the bride chant that is also a funeral dirge.

Initially fragmented in its censure of the prince, the female chorus gives its united attention to the princess, who is, like her intended groom, slow of movement: "There was no hurry in her hands, / No hurry in her feet" (ll. 527–28). But because the princess's refusal to act or indeed "speak in haste" (l. 521) demonstrates her patience, she wins the commendation of the singers who, as women, identify closely with her. On her behalf, therefore, they repudiate the flowers that betoken the prince's love as well as the tears that betoken his grief:

> You should have wept her yesterday,
>> Wasting upon her bed:
> But wherefore should you weep today
>> That she is dead?
> Lo, we who love weep not today,
>> But crown her royal head.
> Let be these poppies that we strew,
>> Your roses are too red:
> Let be these poppies, not for you
>> Cut down and spread. (ll. 531–40)

Death, as in so many Rossetti lyrics, administers a balm to long-suffering womanhood. By contrast, when the groom of "A Bird's-Eye View" marries another woman in place of his dead bride, the poet denies such sorrow as the prince feels the value of endurance. The choral bride chant that closes "The Prince's Progress" thus provides neither the last nor the most bitter commentary on masculine inconstancy in the 1866 volume. But although the women's final chorus effectively supersedes the narrative of princely adventure, it also displaces the princess's "patient song" (l. 462).

While the princess remains an ever elusive figure on the periphery of "The Prince's Progress," she occupies a privileged position in the illustrations that Gabriel provided for the 1866 volume. Indeed, she is the sole subject of the design for the title page—"The long hours go and come and go" (l. 3)—that "emphasizes anticipation and cyclicity" (Goldberg, 156). By retrieving the waiting bride from the margins of the text, Gabriel preemptively recovers and prominently resituates her as the erotic object of the quest narrative. Her arms resting upon the window ledge, her shoulders inclined forward, her gaze directed outward, the princess incarnates languor and longing. "Watching athwart the golden grate" (l. 461), she has doffed her crown, beneath which "her white

The long hours go and come and go

D. G. ROSSETTI'S TITLE-PAGE ILLUSTRATION FOR *THE PRINCE'S PROGRESS AND OTHER POEMS* (LONDON: MACMILLAN, 1866).

brows often ached" (l. 517), and placed it below the window sill. "Spell-bound" (l. 23), she is the prisoner of time and desire. While the narrowness of the open window heightens the sense of claustrophobic enclosure, the circular pattern inscribed upon the closed windows of the princess's chamber—and repeated in the scene that serves as the object of her gaze—conveys her entrapment within the sterile round of her existence. On the other hand, the formal gardens beyond her window, framed as a distant perspective, suggest desire's fulfillment as well as its frustration: the maze recalls the prince's "labyrinthine" (l. 154) progress while the gushing fountain at its center promises, however illusively, the princess's release.

The design for the frontispiece, like that for the title page, includes significant deviations from the text. At the top of the design, seven lamps, one for each of the attendants shown below the princess's body, burn in readiness for the bridegroom's arrival and so constitute a pictorial allusion to the parable of the wise virgins (Matt. 25:1–13). In the foreground, one of the princess's attendants faces the prince and, in a gesture ambiguously suggestive of both comfort and restraint, presses her hands to his chest. His head bowed with grief, the prince stands inside the princess's chamber door rather than, as in the poem, outside the palace gate. But while Rossetti did not object to this particular change, she was far from satisfied with the preliminary sketch and asked her brother whether "two small points . . . might advisably be conformed to the text" (W. Rossetti, ed., 1903, 83). The "two small points" that she wished changed—"to wit, the Prince's 'curly black beard' and the Bride's 'veiled' face" (W. Rossetti, ed., 1903, 83–84)—were, in fact, two big points. On the one hand, the prince's "curly black beard like silk" (l. 64) provides a symbolic clue to his mature masculinity. On the other hand, the bride's veil, a conventional emblem of feminine modesty, is ultimately suggestive of death's shroud. "Veiled figures" (l. 475) bear the princess's body away and explain that the dead woman, who should have been a "veiled bride in her maiden bloom" (l. 20), "Must wear a veil to shroud her face / And the want graven there" (ll. 507–508). But although Rossetti used veiling to symbolize the inaccessibility of feminine interiority and to suggest the princess's identity with her attendants, none of the women in initial sketch was so veiled.

Reluctant to publish the 1866 volume without the illustrations, Rossetti told Gabriel, "your protecting woodcuts help me to face my small public" (W. Rossetti, ed., 1903, 97). The woodcuts, acting as a veil or screen through which she encountered her readers, allowed her to bring her poetic ambitions into line with a need for womanly modesty. However, she was also reluctant to publish with the unrevised frontispiece and attempted to cajole her brother into making the necessary changes. "Surely," she remarked, "the severe female who arrests the Prince somewhat resembles my phiz" (W. Rossetti, ed., 1903, 84). Indeed, by daring to criticize her brother's work, she had assumed the role of the arresting female while he, on the other hand, took that of the dilatory prince in making revisions. Seeking to expedite publication, she again had recourse to sisterly deference. "Your woodcuts," she told Gabriel, "are so essential to my contentment that I will wait a year for them if need is—though (in a whisper) six months would better please

You should have wept her yesterday

D. G. ROSSETTI'S FRONTISPIECE FOR *THE PRINCE'S PROGRESS AND OTHER POEMS* (LONDON: MACMILLAN, 1866).

me" (W. Rossetti, ed., 1903, 95). Her words were prophetic. Because of the delays occasioned by the illustrations, *The Prince's Progress and Other Poems* appeared more than a year later, even though Rossetti had, as early as March of 1865, softened her demands: "Never mind the Prince's beard, if you please, though I won't record his waste of time in shaving: only please don't mulct me of the Bride's essential veil" (Troxell, ed., 142). Although the changes that Gabriel eventually made to the illustration brought it into alignment with the text, they did so without yielding entirely to his sister's request for the prince's beard and the princess's veil. In the final design, the prince's hand covers his face and deep shadow renders the draped figure of the princess indistinct. Thus the policy of compromise, the most salient feature of all Rossetti's negotiations with her brother during the preparation of *The Prince's Progress and Other Poems,* again prevailed.

The Dramatic Moment of "Under the Rose"

Rossetti's aversion to compromise emerges most clearly in "Under the Rose," later "The Iniquity of the Fathers upon the Children." Revealingly placed at the furthest remove from "The Prince's Progress" in the secular section of the 1866 volume, the poem attests to a deliberate effort to cultivate a poetic space outside her brother's purlieu. Gabriel, receiving the monologue in the spring of 1865, however, advised its exclusion along with two other long poems—"A Royal Princess" and "The Lowest Room"—which, as he explained in 1875, possessed "a real taint . . . of modern vicious style" or "falsetto muscularity" reminiscent of Barrett Browning's verse (D. G. Rossetti 1967, 3:1380). But Rossetti, considering "such a diminution of bulk . . . abhorrent" (Troxell, ed., 142–43), lobbied strenuously for the inclusion of all three poems. In the end, her arguments carried enough weight to facilitate the appearance of "Under the Rose" and "A Royal Princess."

Eschewing medievalized romance for modern realism in "Under the Rose," Rossetti chooses for her subject a girl who, on the verge of womanhood, comes to terms with her illegitimacy. In dramatizing Margaret's situation, however, she was compelled to defend the legitimacy of her attempt, as a woman poet, to treat subjects deemed vulgar by polite society. As usual, she answered Gabriel's objections with respect:

> Whilst I endorse your opinion of the unavoidable and indeed much-to-be-desired unreality of women's work on many social matters, I yet

incline to include within female range such an attempt as this: where the certainly possible circumstances are merely indicated as it were in skeleton, where the subordinate characters perform (and no more) their accessory parts, where the field is occupied by a single female figure whose internal portrait is set forth in her own words. Moreover the sketch only gives the girl's own deductions, feelings, semiresolutions; granted such premises as hers, and right or wrong it seems to me she might easily arrive at such conclusions: and whilst it may truly be urged that unless white could be black and Heaven Hell my experience (thank God) precludes me from hers, I yet don't see why "the Poet Mind" should be less able to construct her from its own inner consciousness than a hundred other unknown quantities. (Troxell, ed., 143)

When Barrett Browning, affronted by W. M. Thackeray's refusal to publish "Sir Walter's Wife" in *Cornhill Magazine,* was likewise moved to defend her work against a charge of coarseness, she wrote, "It is exactly because pure and prosperous women choose to *ignore* vice, that miserable women suffer wrong by it everywhere."[6] Unlike Barrett Browning, however, Rossetti elects to focus on her method rather than her motive in writing. Thus, while the delicacy with which she approaches her subject—only hinting at circumstances and characters that might offend superfine sensibilities—allows her to conduct a searching interrogation of legitimacy in all of its rational, social, and legal forms, she implies that her interest lies in the treatment of feminine subjectivity rather than in the redress of social evils. But by stressing that Margaret's "internal portrait" provides "her own words" and her "own deductions, feelings, semiresolutions," she also insists on the authenticity and, hence, the legitimacy of the experience related.

Rossetti, by maintaining that her heroine is a fictive construct of the disinterested "Poet Mind," exercises her right as a creative artist to imagine an experience not her own. Indeed, her exclusion from Margaret's experience, far from being a barrier to expression, provides her with the moral imperative necessary to address the issue of sexual license and its consequences. But while Rossetti's work among "fallen women" certainly suggested to her the topic of illegitimacy, she was also concerned with the affairs of pure and prosperous middle-class women.[7] As a result, the heroine's experiences are, if literally exclusive, figuratively inclusive of the poet's own, for "Under the Rose," like "A Royal Princess" and "The Lowest Room," examines questions relating to the position of single women within nineteenth-century society. Even though Rossetti, after "several paroxysms of stamping, foaming, hair-uprooting," stifled at least one "screech" to win her brother's reluctant endorsement of the poem (W. Rossetti, ed., 1903, 93), Margaret remains her most muscular exponent of women's rights and most astute critic of patriarchal wrongs.

In some respects, Margaret resembles Barbara Bodichon, whose illegitimacy, insofar as it exempted her from traditional codes of behavior and belief, galvanized her feminism. However, Bodichon, the daughter of a milliner's apprentice and a Radical M.P., received from her father, Benjamin Leigh Smith, two things Margaret lacks—a name (which she lost upon her marriage in 1857) and an annuity of £300. Moreover, unlike Rossetti's heroine, Bodichon worked doggedly on behalf of women's political emancipation. Yet, inasmuch as Margaret's exclusion from the privileges of lawful birth doubles upon women's exclusion from the privileges of legal citizenry, her illegitimacy functions as a symbol for women's disenfranchisement under Victorian patriarchy. While the point of view of the illegitimate daughter freed Rossetti to scrutinize the entitlements of class and sex, "Under the Rose" also acknowledges women's collusion, both willing and unwilling, in the very structures that work to disempower and, thus, to silence them. Even Margaret is silent: her speech, its dramatic directness notwithstanding, assumes the form of an interior monologue. Ironically, this strategy of covert revelation sanctions Rossetti to an unprecedented candor.

Margaret's growth into adult awareness involves the realization that her existence has, from birth, been predicated upon secrets that are tantamount to lies. The thematics of secrecy, allied to the thematics of power, Rossetti brings to the fore in the opening lines of the poem: "Oh the rose of keenest thorn! / One hidden summer morn / Under the rose I was born" (ll. 1–3). Playing with the Latin phrase *sub rosa,* Rossetti not only suggests the hidden circumstances of Margaret's birth but uses floral symbolism to ally these circumstances with passion and pain. The secret of Margaret's birth, her illegitimacy, becomes the grounds for an alienation that Rossetti then figures in spatial as well as relational terms. Margaret, separated from her mother at birth and consigned to the care of a trusted nurse, "was sent away / That none might spy the truth" (ll. 28–29). Dispatched to an undefined location "somewhere by the sea" (l. 84) where "Men spoke a foreign tongue" (l. 85), she returns to England as "a little maid" (l. 82) and, with her nurse, settles in a remote village, situated "A long mile from the town" (l. 44). Physically displaced twice, she becomes, in her illegitimacy, twice foreign. In other words, her early childhood, spent "On that fair foreign shore" (l. 96), as well as her looks and behavior distinguish her from the village children who, like the ladies and gentlemen later entertained at the Hall, either snub her or "hang about . . . / In sheepish mooning wise" (ll. 41–42).

Margaret's difference, the mark of her present estrangement and future independence, inspires her with curiosity about her origins. Remembering her youth, she says, "I often sat to wonder / Who might my parents be, / For I knew of something under / My simple-seeming state" (ll. 111–14). Her nurse, of course, knows the complex circumstances beneath this "simple-seeming state." A maternal surrogate, Margaret's nurse represents the past and, thus, holds the key to the girl's self-knowledge. When she dies, however, she leaves the secret of her charge's parentage "unsaid" (l. 130). Consequently, even as the child in Margaret also dies, the emergent adult remains estranged from herself. At this juncture, the Lady of the Hall arrives and, renown for her openhanded goodness, virtually adopts the orphaned girl. Margaret, however, remains perplexed. "What was my Lady to me," she wonders, "The grand lady from the Hall?" (ll. 187–88). This simple-seeming question, concerned as it is with the nature of relationship, finds an answer when Margaret realizes that "my Lady" is really her mother. But although my Lady is Margaret's true mother, she is also a false mother, for she refrains from open recognition of her child. As a result, the possessive pronoun *my* used in connection with the Lady of the Hall functions as an ironic marker of the irrelation that characterizes her association with her daughter.

Margaret's knowledge of her mother depends on her ability to draw reasonable and legitimate conclusions from the kind of "refined clues" that Rossetti had, in writing "The Prince's Progress," reserved for what she called "such minds as mine" (W. Rossetti, ed., 1903, 81). Effectively giving birth to herself, Margaret bases her narrative upon oblique impressions, fragmentary intuitions, indefinite surmises, and other highly enigmatic proofs. As a result, her story formally reproduces the anxiety that arises from the uncertainty of her social position.[8] At first, she responds to my Lady because she hears "something in her voice" (l. 220):

Something not of the past,
Yet stirring memory;
A something new, and yet
Not new, too sweet to last,
Which I never can forget. (ll. 223–27)

This vague, instinctive "something," recalling the something that also lies under Margaret's simple-seeming state, causes her to look at my Lady and to see that "Her hair like mine was fair" (l. 230). While this physical resemblance provides but uncertain evidence of their relation, Margaret possesses another clue in the ring given to her by her dying nurse. Seeing this ring "Of gold wrought curiously" (l. 134), my Lady conjectures a meaning that, as Margaret later says, "Sounds not improbable" (l. 370):

> She said she should infer
> The ring had been my father's first,
> Then my mother's, given for me
> To the nurse who nursed
> My mother in her misery,
> That so quite certainly
> Some one might know me, who . . .
> Then she was silent, and I too. (ll. 325–32)

Like the nurse's deathbed speech, the most important part of my Lady's tale remains unsaid. Even though Rossetti's use of aposiopesis cuts off further speculation concerning the ring's purpose as a sign to someone of Margaret's identity, my Lady's words have already provided her daughter with the means to know her: Margaret's nurse was, as the sexton's wife has previously revealed, "my Lady's nurse" (l. 154). Indeed, my Lady openly claims Margaret's nurse as her own "dear nurse" (l. 249), but instead of acknowledging the girl as her daughter, she invites her to assume a threefold identity—"Friend, servant, almost child" (l. 421)—that further complicates the ambiguities of their relation.

Margaret's reunion with her mother, albeit under false pretenses, initially inspires her with joy, but she soon realizes that this rose also has its thorn. Tormented by an awareness that everyone—servants, villagers, visitors—knows my Lady's carefully guarded secret, Margaret wishes herself dead and her "Mother safe at last / Disburdened of her child" (ll. 498–99). Her situation reaches its most intolerable when visiting gentlefolk bring the codes and conventions of respectable society to bear on their relationship. Recoiling at the hypocrisy of those women who "mean to be so civil" (l. 335) and who "praise my Lady's kindness" (l. 338), Margaret admires "the proud ones best / Who sit as struck with blindness" (ll. 340–41). As for the men, she resents them because her mother, "fear[ing] / Some downright dreadful evil" (ll. 346–47), confines her to her room. By depriving Margaret of her liberty, my Lady gives physical embodiment to the moral restrictiveness of the "decent world" (l. 407), which, if she were to avow her motherhood, "would thrust / Its finger out at her" (ll. 407–408) and "sink / Its voice to speak of her" (ll. 411–12). Yet what is unsaid, though clearly not unknown, goes unchallenged and uncensured. The voice of public decency is, Rossetti insinuates, the voice of social hypocrisy.

Seeking shelter in privacy, Margaret rebels against the strictures of decency as incarnate in her mother:

> In spite of all her care,
> Sometimes to keep alive
> I sometimes do contrive
> To get out in the grounds
> For a whiff of wholesome air,
> Under the rose you know:
> It's charming to break bounds,
> Stolen waters are sweet,
> And what's the good of feet
> If for days they mustn't go?
> Give me longer tether,
> Or I may break from it. (ll. 352–63)

Just as Margaret breaks from conventional proprieties, Rossetti breaks from conventional prosody. Thus, whereas the formal tercets and closed rhymes of "A Royal Princess" mirror the heroine's rigidly constrained existence, the irregular rhymes and rhythms of "Under the Rose" suggest Margaret's desire to escape the limited range of feminine expression as well as experience. Moreover, as if to dramatize the baleful consequences of excessive restraint, Rossetti sets her heroine's stolen moments in the garden and under the rose, establishing thereby an implicit parallel between Margaret's physical freedom, her mother's sexual indiscretion, and Eve's originating sin.

However much Margaret appreciates the charms of transgression, she does not seek the freedom of the garden to meet a lover but to escape from the unwelcome advances of gentlemen whose valets mount "watch

/ To speak a word with me" (ll. 491–92). Her vulnerability to such insults not only gives her a unique understanding of the indignities suffered by single women as well as illegitimate children, but it encourages her to challenge other truths anointed by decency:

"All equal before God"—
Our Rector has it so,
And sundry sleepers nod:
It may be so; I know
All are not equal here,
And when the sleepers wake
They make a difference.
"All equal in the grave"—
That shows an obvious sense. (ll. 501–509)

Margaret, a precursor to the woman who "knows the parsons' tags" in Charlotte Mew's "Madeleine in Church," empirically qualifies the immediate truth of religious platitude, but she also reposes faith in the ultimate truth of God's justice. Likewise, Rossetti, though convinced that "the instinct of inequality" regulated the affairs of "this world," took encouragement from the prospect of "celestial equality."[9] Trusting to God's magistracy, she believed that each soul would be held accountable to itself: "The soul that sinneth, it shall die. The son shall not bear the iniquity of the father, neither shall the father bear the iniquity of the son" (Ezek. 18:20; quoted in *FD,* 77). In this light, the later title for "Under the Rose"—"The Iniquity of the Fathers Upon the Children"—is doubly ironic, for the poem treats the social stigma that attaches to daughters as a consequence of their mothers' sexual misconduct.

While Margaret, discriminated against on the basis of her illegitimacy, bears her mother's shame, my Lady struggles "with something worse, / A lifelong lie for truth" (ll. 528–29). Yearning for her mother to "drop for once the lie" (l. 429), Margaret nonetheless realizes that a woman's reputation depends entirely upon a show of decency. Therefore, unlike the heroine of "A Royal Princess" who vows "to speak before the world" (l. 106) and so to expose patriarchal iniquity, she resolves, "Never to speak, or show / Bare sign of what I know" (ll. 415–16). Ironically, this resolution, though right and necessary from Margaret's point of view, makes her an accomplice to patriarchal iniquity, for by protecting my

Lady, she also protects the man whom she "could almost curse" (l. 519). Although Margaret refrains from openly and wholly anathematizing her father, she clearly holds him responsible for her (mother's) shame. As she says, he "Flawed honour like a glass" (l. 379) and "set his snare / To catch at unaware / My Mother's foolish youth" (ll. 524–26). Indeed, the mysterious ring—passed from father to mother to daughter—suggests in what manner he baited his snare. Nevertheless, insofar as my Lady is also the victim of her own foolhardiness, Rossetti does not, like Barrett Browning, absolve the unwed mother of complicity in her disgrace. But while my Lady is not, like the speaker of "The Runaway Slave at Pilgrim's Point" or Marian Erle in *Aurora Leigh* (1857), enslaved and raped, she does resemble the woman whose marriage—and consequently whose child—is "Void in Law," for her lover, having given her a token of marital commitment, has a moral, if not a legal, obligation to fulfill his promise.

In reneging on his commitment to marriage, Margaret's father deprives his daughter of legal legitimacy and her mother of social legitimacy. As Rossetti's treatment of names in "Under the Rose" suggests, however, a valid identity is impossible for women under patriarchy. This problem is precisely the one Margaret faces when she contemplates how to "make / The name I bear my own" (ll. 513–14). Similarly, although my Lady's "is the oldest name / In all the neighbourhood" (ll. 61–62), it is not hers, but her father's. Women, Rossetti suggests, are essentially anonymous: they do not own names; names own them. Accordingly, the name of the father and of the husband, the sign of patriarchal legitimacy, becomes also the sign of spurious integrity in "Under the Rose." Thus, when my Lady, promising her daughter a dowry of £200, attempts to purchase her respectability, Margaret refuses her well-meaning effort: "I'll not be wooed for pelf; / I'll not blot out my shame / With any man's good name" (ll. 535–37). At the same time, however, she fully acknowledges the attractions of a good name in marriage:

> A home such as I see
> My blessed neighbours live in
> With father and with mother,
> All proud of one another,
> Named by one common name
> From baby in the bud
> To full-blown workman father;
> It's little short of Heaven. (ll. 459–66)

Here Rossetti broadens her investigation of various forms of social legitimacy to include issues of class as well as sex. The "common name" that
the heroine desires is both a family cognomen and a name common to
the working classes. As such, this wished-for name differs from the aris-
tocratic one by which my Lady is known, but Margaret, defining nobility in personal rather than social terms, would rather be an honest
cottager than a nominal lady. Thus, she asserts, "I'd give my gentle
blood / To wash my special shame" (ll. 467–68). Possessing truly "noble
blood" (l. 387), she will not publish her mother's "fame" (l. 384) and so,
as she says, "shame / Our honourable name" (ll. 385–86). Rossetti
deprives the honorable name of any inherent virtue, however, by uniting
it with the concept of fame that is, in fact, shame.

Rossetti's exhaustion of the possibilities for honor in any man's good
name makes her choice of her heroine's Christian name all the more significant. Writing of St. Margaret in *Time Flies,* Rossetti advised her readers to "picture her in accordance with her name . . . as a modest daisy,
growing where for the present we cannot come: or as a pearl not yet
brought up from hidden depths to the sunlighted surface" (*TF,* 139).
The circumstances of her birth notwithstanding, Margaret fully embodies the modesty, purity, and beauty that her name suggests. Moreover,
unlike her namesake in "Maggie a Lady" or, for that matter, in "Maiden-
Song," she fulfills the promise of her name by eschewing what seems
"little short of Heaven"—marriage—for heaven itself. But even though
she thereby takes her "stand" (l. 538) and arraigns the whole idea of
patriarchal legitimacy, she does not attempt "to change the system."[10]
Instead, Margaret, like the heroines of "A Royal Princess" and "The
Lowest Room," commits herself to personal change, announces her
intention to remain "nameless" (ll. 538, 540), and awaits such time as a
perfect accord exists between the two propositions, "All equal in the
grave" (l. 542) and "All equal before God" (l. 544).[11]

A believer in celestial equality, Rossetti translates the political issues
raised in her monologues into spiritual concerns, thus bypassing the
possibility for systemic change as a remedy to sexual discrimination
under patriarchy. Her egalitarianism runs in quite a different channel
from that of Bodichon whose name headed the petition that the
Women's Suffrage Committee presented to J. S. Mill in June of 1866.
Unlike Bodichon, Rossetti felt that the problem of women's freedom
and equality was subordinate to the attainment of an identity in Christ.
Therefore, as a signal of her intentions in "Under the Rose," she placed
the poem immediately before the section in *The Prince's Progress and
Other Poems* allotted to devotional lyrics. "Under the Rose" is neverthe-

less exemplary of the way Rossetti's uncompromising Christianity allows her to assume "an ideological position which is," as Jerome McGann asserts, "far more radical than the middle-class feminist positions current in her epoch" (1980, 254).

The Poetics of Song and the Possibilities for Women's Lyric Utterance

Eager to stifle "perverse suggestions of monotonous tedium in the final beatitude," Rossetti discovered in music, promised as one of the rewards of heaven, "a reassuring figure of variety" (*FD*, 352). As she observes in *Time Flies*, "Change, succession, are of the essence of music" (*TF*, 29). Imagining the "ceaseless music" of heaven, she foresees a realm "of endless progression, of inexhaustible variety," for as "one sound leads unavoidably to a different sound, one harmony paves the way to a diverse harmony" (*TF*, 29). The principles of music also govern the design of lyrics, both individually and collectively, in *The Prince's Progress and Other Poems*. Indeed, several poems, including "Maiden-Song," "Songs in a Cornfield," "Autumn," and "Martyrs' Song," function as polyphonic variations on the choral bride chant that closes "The Prince's Progress." Moreover, because these pieces show a marked preoccupation with "vocal music" that, wedding sound to intellectual sense, was for Rossetti "the highest form of so high an art" (*TF*, 29), their self-reflexivity serves valuably to elucidate her esthetic concerns. Working against the masculine ethos of romantic individualism, Rossetti constructs in the female singer, often singing in concert with others, a type for the woman poet that is, in turn, a type for the Christian saint.

Rossetti first focuses on the formal constituents of song in the poem that succeeds "The Prince's Progress." Indeed, "Maiden-Song," which "was deservedly something of a favourite with its authoress" (*PW*, 462), received praise from the *Athenaeum* for demonstrating "the melody and beauty with which melody itself can be described."[12] But although this deceptively innocuous fairy tale takes musical form for its theme, Rossetti also explores the power of women's song to fascinate men and subdue them to "silent awe" (l. 80). Much of this power proceeds from the poet's revision of folkloric and romantic materials in accordance with the articles of Christian belief.[13] For Rossetti, emulating in her verse the "celestial ever fresh delight" of music invests her singers with authority by drawing on the "special appositeness [of song] in an illustration of heaven" (*TF*, 29). At the same time, though, the poem's concerns are decidedly secular, since they relate to the achievement of marriage, which is, as Margaret of "Under the Rose" observes, somewhat short of heaven. Like *Cinderella,* "Maiden-Song" features three sisters: "tall Meggan" (l. 5), "dainty May" (l. 6), and "fair Margaret" (l. 7). Rossetti's reinscription of familiar motifs, however, works against the moral certitudes of the traditional fairy tale. Thus, while the dark shadow of feminine competition that lends such dynamic force to a poem like "Noble Sisters" lies beneath the simple whimsy of "Maiden-Song," none of these maidens is vicious. Moreover, as with Lizzie and Laura of "Goblin Market," the resemblance between the three girls' names confuses any distinction among them. Informed that Margaret and Meggan were virtually "the same name," Rossetti answered, "This does not disturb me. . . . May, Meggan, Margaret sound pretty and pleasant" (W. Rossetti, ed., 1903, 98). Nevertheless, when the alliterative trio breaks up, Meggan and May seem a little less than pleasant. Proposing to gather "strawberry leaves" (l. 25), they leave Margaret and pursue "the winding way" (l. 30) until they find "the choicest spot, / Clothed with thyme-alternate grass" (ll. 55–56). But while their route suggests guile, both girls are endued with "innocent will" (l. 33). And though their goal seems frivolous, Rossetti's floral imagery suggests its hidden importance: strawberries represent foresight; thyme, activity and courage; grass, submission or utility.[14] Singing to themselves husbands, the sisters reveal their possession of these attributes.

Insofar as Meggan and May seek to marry rather than destroy the men whom they charm, Rossetti departs from conventional associations of feminine sexuality with evil. Moreover, by translating sensual experience into pure musical form, she authorizes the expression of the sisters' sexual power. "Honey-smooth the double flow" (l. 71), their songs strike a circuitous note and follow, like their walk, the winding way. While Meggan pipes "A fitful wayward lay" (l. 68), May sings "With maiden coy caprice / In a labyrinth of throbs, / Pauses, cadences" (ll. 119–21). Ranging through notes clear and wild, soft and loving, their songs render their male listeners "breathless" (l. 131) and "speechless" (l. 132), unable to "speak or think or wish / Till silence broke the spell" (ll. 133–34).

Only in fantasy do women have the power to prevail over men. Thus, when the speaker of "A Farm Walk"—Rossetti's version of Wordsworth's northern tourist in "The Solitary Reaper"—stops to hear a rustic maiden's "country ditty" (l. 12), he does not, like the swains of "Maiden-

Song," propose marriage. Furthermore, though he has borne her music in his heart for seven years, he realizes that the expedient of the early train will not deliver him again to her magic. "Alas," he thinks from his London home, "one point in all my plan / My serious thoughts demur to: / Seven years have passed for maid and man" (ll. 59–61). But while this lass, the realistic counter to the milkmaid of "The Prince's Progress," cannot countervail the disenchantment wrought by time and the city, Meggan and May are largely immune to such forces.

Denizens of fairy tale, the two sisters are clearly aware, however, of the danger posed by the one who is fairest in all the land. Therefore, having wooed a herdsman with her song, Meggan thinks, "Better be first with him, / Than dwell where fairer Margaret sits, / Who shines my brightness dim" (ll. 97–99). Likewise, May, though perplexed for "a dubious while" (l. 143), smiles to imagine herself wedded to a lowly shepherd and outside the orbit of her sister's influence. Inasmuch as Margaret's power of fascination is, as her sisters well know, much greater than their own, she jeopardizes their chances at fairy-tale fulfillment. In this light, Rossetti makes their decision, otherwise unexplained, to abandon Margaret a matter of crude pragmatism. But even the fairest sister, left at home "to sing and sew" (l. 44) while the others "play and rest" (l. 58), must move beyond the domestic enclosure before she can exert her power. Finally suspending her labor, Margaret walks toward the garden gate where, leaning upon the rail, she awaits her sisters' return. This return she accomplishes through her own marriage. Raising her voice in response to "a distant nightingale / Complaining of its mate" (ll. 163–64), Margaret sings to herself "The king of all that country" (l. 188). No longer a threat to Meggan and May, she also sings them "home / In their marriage mirth" (ll. 210–11).

By ending with feminine accord as well as marriage, "Maiden-Song" seems to exceed the fulfillments of traditional fairy tale, but Rossetti undercuts the maidens' achievement in the final lines of the poem. "So," she concludes, "three maids were wooed and won / In a brief May-tide, / Long ago and long ago" (ll. 227–29). Although these final lines, recalling the reiterated "long ago" in the introduction to the poem, give to "Maiden-Song" a satisfying sense of closure, Rossetti's use of the passive voice gives a check to complacence. As the objects of performed action, the three maidens are no longer the agents of their own destiny. A celebration of the power of the feminine voice, the poem ends paradoxically by assigning victory not to the maids but to their mates.

Abjuring epithalamion for elegy, Rossetti further qualifies the triumph of "Maiden-Song" in "Songs in a Cornfield." This piece, another of the poet's "own favourites" (W. Rossetti, ed., 1903, 88), epitomizes her ideal of music as an embodiment "not of monotony, but of variety" (*TF,* 29). Like "The Bourne" which Alice Macdonald (later Kipling) "set to music very prettily" (W. Rossetti, ed., 1903, 99), "Songs in a Cornfield" was in fact one of several Rossetti lyrics to find a composer (*PW,* 478). According to William Rossetti, however, the poem, though beautifully arranged for performance by Sir G. A. Macfarren, "did not take much with the public, perhaps because of its extremely melancholy tone at the close" (*PW,* 485). As a remedy, William suggested reversing the position of the last two songs, but this solution betrays a cavalier disregard for the care his sister lavished on the poem's construction. A veritable paragon of caprice, "Songs in a Cornfield" alternates between subjective and objective points of view, between lyric and narrative modes of expression, in order to explore the theme of unrequited love from plural perspectives. Consequently, the poem offers "no security, only discontinuity, dislocation, disorientation, displacement, and anomie" (Harrison 1988, 44). This radical insecurity owes much to the figure of the fugitive lover whom Marian, unlike Margaret of "Maiden-Song," cannot sing home. Indeed, because of his absence, she initially cannot sing at all.

Awaiting a lover who does not come, Marian is a rusticated version of Tennyson's Mariana, beloved icon of Pre-Raphaelite art. Whereas paintings such as J. E. Millais's *Mariana* (1851) eroticize the idle monotony of the abandoned woman's existence, Rossetti chooses instead to make the lover's absence a focus for keen, if oblique, inquiry. Accordingly, the narrator's question—"Where is he gone to / And why does he stay?" (ll. 9–10)—supplies the intention for the three songs that follow. In the first song, Marian's three companions—Lettice, Rachel, and May—caution their listeners to reap wheat rather than "a false false love" (l. 38), for when winter comes and the "summer friend has fled, / Only summer wheat remaineth, / White cakes and bread" (ll. 50–52). Tacitly identifying Marian's sweetheart as a doubly false love, the women's chorus also proposes work as an antidote to love. Moreover, Rossetti's language suggests that reaping, an activity metonymically associated with singing at the beginning of the poem, can have but two objects: eternal life or ephemeral love. Singing and reaping together, Lettice, Rachel, and May energetically espouse life rather than love. The certainties of their chorus collapse, however, when Rachel sings a second song to fill the interval as the reapers pause from work. In so doing, she further complicates the question of the lover's absence.

Originally, Rachel's aria began with the line, "We met hand to hand," but this lyric, later achieving "an independent existence" as "Twilight Night" in *Goblin Market, The Prince's Progress and Other Poems,* constituted "a blemish" because it possessed a "less simple character" than the other interpolated songs in a cornfield (W. Rossetti, ed., 1903, 94). Although Gabriel proposed as an alternative the poem later known as "Spring Quiet," Rossetti rejected this solution because the opening words, "Gone were but the Winter," made nonsense of the lyric's surrounding context. Finally, she settled on "There goes the swallow," which one reviewer, irritated by its "too audacious" simplicity, deemed an "unsuccessful piece of affected jingle."[15] Its simplicity notwithstanding, Rachel's song acquires, like the other lyrics in "Songs in a Cornfield" (as well as *The Prince's Progress and Other Poems*), a complex meaning from its immediate situation within the text and from its relation to other works, such as the swallow song in Tennyson's *The Princess,* outside the text. Looking forward in the volume to the poignant reflections on the migratory swallow found in "Autumn" and "A Bird Song," added in 1875, Rachel's song implicitly rejects the explanation of the lover's truancy provided by the preceding cantata. For although the "sunny swallow" (l. 80) is clearly another summer friend, Rachel describes it as "good" (l. 85) and "wise" (l. 80). Moreover, although the song begins with a wish to follow the bird and so to consummate desire, it ends with a gracious, though resigned, expression of farewell.

More sympathetic to the absent lover than the first song, Rachel's pensive melody elicits a response from the taciturn Marian. Adhering to a model of expression that is feminine and communal rather than masculine and individual, both Rachel's and Marian's solos use first-person plural pronouns to articulate a shared experience of loss. Thus, Marian sings about "Our delight" (l. 97), which lies buried "Deeper than the hail can smite, / Deeper than the frost can bite, / Deep asleep thro' day and night" (ll. 94–96). The inaccessibility of delight—literally buried at the end of Marian's first stanza—resembles that of the dead who, in "The Bourne," rest "Underneath the growing grass, / Underneath the living flowers, / Deeper than the sound of showers" (ll. 1–3). Indeed, for Marian, singing "Like one who hopes and grieves" (l. 93), death provides the only satisfactory explanation of her lover's absence. If he has not, as the first song implies, been false, he must be dead. Marian's song is, however, more than an elegy for a dead lover or even for past pleasure. Dwelling on the coldness of the underworld, she demonstrates her estrangement from the other reapers, resting in the "full noontide heat" (l. 57), and virtually consigns herself to the grave.

Rossetti undermines the necessity of Marian's conclusions respecting her lover, if not herself, by reverting to the perspective of narrative in the final lines of "Songs in a Cornfield." The narrator, by way of complement to the pluralizing perspectives afforded by the three foregoing songs, provides the reader with three alternative endings, each beginning with the conditional phrase, "If he comes" (ll. 110, 112, 114). To achieve the openness of this ending, Rossetti cut 12 lines from the original manuscript version of the poem and, in so doing, removed overt evidence of Marian's death and her lover's perfidy. Nevertheless, the truncated poem suggests, albeit more advisedly, the same unhappy outcome, since all three of its alternatives are contingent on the lover's return. This contingency, of course, leaves the question of the lover's absence unanswered and returns the reader to the possibilities advanced in the first two songs in a cornfield.

Coy and self-reflexive, "Songs in a Cornfield" offers a paradigm for understanding Rossetti's arrangement of lyrics in *The Prince's Progress and Other Poems*. By balancing three sad songs sung in a cornfield against the three merry songs sung by Margaret and her sisters, the poet recapitulates the notes of the sad-glad voices that punctuate "The Prince's Progress" and, in this way, establishes the volume's double flow or contrapuntal melody. Then, in "Autumn," she deconstructs the poetics of song by taking monotony rather than variety for her keynote. Rossetti's speaker opens, as she also closes, on a repetitive, uninflected cadence that aptly conveys the utter tonelessness of her existence: "I dwell alone—I dwell alone, alone" (l. 1). This woman, the sister to the bride in "The Prince's Progress," listens as "Slim, gleaming maidens swell their mellow notes, / Love-promising, entreating— / Ah! sweet, but fleeting" (ll. 9–11). But just as the flagging wind becalms the maidens aboard their boats, the speaker twice iterates the imperative "Hush" (ll. 13, 14) in an effort to silence their songs. Quickening the dormant misery that lies within herself, these songs have, however, already awakened, as she says, "singing echoes in my land" (l. 16). An antisong, "Autumn" proliferates with singing echoes derived from works as diverse as Shelley's "Ode to the West Wind" and Mary Howitt's "The Spider and the Fly," but Rossetti alludes most frequently to "The Lady of Shalott," in which the eponymous heroine sings "a song that echoes cheerly / From the river winding clearly, / Down to tower'd Camelot" (ll. 30–32). The insistence of these literary echoes works, like the verbal echoes in the poem's first line, to point the exhaustion of conventional poeticisms.

Designing in "Autumn" to trip up Tennyson, Rossetti replaces the mellow ripeness of Camelot with a landscape of dearth that mirrors the speaker's emptiness, with a climate of impending storm that mirrors her repressed anger. Even the speaker's "fertile trees" (l. 31), as distinct from those "rent by thunder strokes" (l. 29), "are not in flower" (l. 60). But while Rossetti's speaker is more radically withdrawn than the Tennysonian lady, she is not so obviously an artist nor is the web that separates her from the world so explicitly one of her own creation. Nevertheless, Rossetti's revisions of Tennyson's work enable her "to construct and criticize an increasingly self-enclosed version of poetic subjectivity."[16] Reflecting on the spider's web that resembles "a rainbow strung with dew" (l. 36), the speaker says, "few creatures guess it is a trap: / I will not mar the web, / Tho' sad I am to see the small lives ebb" (ll. 38–40). Although the speaker's refusal to mar the web marks out her difference from the Lady of Shalott, her inaction yet argues that she has fallen prey to the spider's cunning. According to Rossetti, the web provides "an apt figure of the world" because "it exhibits beauty, ingenuity, intricacy," especially when "jewelled with dewdrops," but "its beauties of brilliancy and colour [are] no real part of it" (TF, 81–82). In other words, art is illusion. Even as the web's beauty fascinates the speaker of "Autumn," however, she is largely immune to its necrotic properties, for Rossetti, having dealt expeditiously with the PRB in "Goblin Market," here uses a similar strategy to diminish Tennyson— the spider's analogue—and so contain the threat that he posed to her as a woman poet.

By making the Lady of Shalott a figure for the artist, Tennyson pre-empts the emergence of a poetic voice authentic to feminine experience. At the end of "Autumn," therefore, Rossetti is not content to leave the spider's art intact. Hitherto in abeyance, the wind begins to shake not only the web but the trees, the tower, and the boats aboard which the Tennysonian maidens sing. But while the wind, rising gradually to a "full-throated gale" (l. 45), suggests an angry inspiration capable of muting the singing echoes heard from afar, the speaker does not turn her inaudible moan to a corresponding wail. Instead, she projects upon the distant singers three possibilities for an art not her own:

> Perhaps they say: "She grieves,
>> Uplifted, like a beacon, on her tower."
>> Perhaps they say: "One hour
> More, and we dance among the golden sheaves."
>> Perhaps they say: "One hour
>> More, and we stand,
>> Face to face, hand in hand;
> Make haste, O slack gale, to the looked-for land!" (ll. 52–59)

Self-consciously constructing herself as the unhappy inspiration for "love-songs, gurgling from a hundred throats" (l. 5), the speaker is another woman betrayed by the esthetic ideal of romantic love. She implicitly refutes this ideal, however, not only by devising two other alternatives to the last song of the Lady of Shalott but by imagining female singers who are no longer subject to Tennysonian languor. Their final songs—euphoric in tone, apocalyptic in image, collective in expression—offer a vision of feminine community and creativity. Of course, the lady, marooned upon her strand, cannot participate in this vision or claim it as her own. But Rossetti, by making her heroine the flowerless, bowerless chatelaine of a drafty old tower, exposes the fraudulence of the esthetic elaborated in "The Lady of Shalott."

Moving from "Maiden-Song" through "Songs in a Cornfield" to "Autumn," Rossetti tests and gradually exhausts the possibilities for women's lyric utterance in *The Prince's Progress and Other Poems*. But as "Martyrs' Song" and "After This the Judgment" suggest, she does not abandon the poetics of song. These two poems, the longest of the nine religious lyrics in the volume, elaborate the vague allusions to the new song of Revelation found at the end of "Autumn." The wearied speaker of "After This the Judgment," for example, envisions heaven as a place where voices, "All blent in one yet each one manifest" (l. 18), sing "Hallelujahs full of rest, / One, tenfold, hundredfold, with heavenly art" (ll. 14–15). For Rossetti, heaven is "the home-land of music" where each voice, the clarified distillation of "the saint's self," shall be "in a harmony, yet as individually listened to, approved, commended" (*FD*, 352). Moreover, "the actual voices of the redeemed" are also "the selfsame which spake and sang on earth, the same which age enfeebled and death silenced" (*TF*, 30). In this respect, the jubilant singers of "Martyrs' Song," nearing "their home of Heaven-content" (l. 14) and "the rest that fulfils desire" (l. 16), are identical with the singing maidens of the secular lyrics, the solitary speakers of the monologues, and the voices of exile and complaint heard in such devotional poems as "Despised and Rejected," "Long Barren," and "Weary in Well-Doing." Consequently, while Rossetti ultimately seeks an apotheosis beyond rather than in poetry, she nonetheless orchestrates her work within *The Prince's Progress and Other Poems* to achieve a diverse harmony that, emulating the celestial and ever-fresh delight of music, aspires to the condition of heavenly art.

Self-Censorship in *Goblin Market, The Prince's Progress, and Other Poems*

Rossetti found the process of preparing *The Prince's Progress and Other Poems* for publication extremely trying. Reaching toleration's end in April of 1865, she remarked tartly, "I hope after this vol. (if this vol. becomes a vol.) people will respect my nerves, and not hint for a long long while at any possibility of vol. 3" (W. Rossetti, ed., 1903, 100). Ten years, a long while indeed, passed before she produced her third volume of adult verse. Published in 1875, *Goblin Market, The Prince's Progress, and Other Poems* features, in addition to older material, 36 previously uncollected poems. Rossetti did not, however, submit the new pieces to Gabriel's scrutiny before publication. He was startled to discover then that she had added "The Lowest Room." Provoked, he told Theodore Watts-Dunton that this work, which he considered "only fit for one room viz. the bog," constituted a blot on her career: "So now the world will know that she *can* write a bad poem" (D. G. Rossetti 1967, 3:1390). While the relaxation of her brother's control seemingly freed Rossetti to publish material that he had formerly suppressed, she also used the opportunity availed of a new edition to withdraw five poems from her canon. These included "Cousin Kate," "A Triad," "Sister Maude," "Light Love," and "A Ring Posy." Because Rossetti, as she grew older, became more attuned to issues of responsibility and influence, the most likely reason for the omission of these lyrics lies, as William Rossetti believed, in their liability to misconstruction "from a moral point of view" (quoted in Bell, 213). *Goblin Market, The Prince's Progress, and Other Poems* is, therefore, an expurgated, albeit expanded, text.

Pressure from Rossetti's contemporary readership seems to have influenced, at least in part, her decision to self-censorship, for the works that she chose to remove from the 1875 volume are also those that her professional critics had chosen for censure.[17] The *Athenaeum,* for example, identified "Sister Maude" as the poem "which we least like" (1862, 558). Much harsher criticism came from the sectarian press, which was less worldly indulgent of Rossetti's work and more unabashedly forthright about its objections. Thus, the reviewer for the *Catholic World*, attacking Rossetti's "morally dangerous tendency" to "misdirected mercifulness" especially on "the rather delicate subject of our erring sisters," took special exception to "Sister Maude" and "Cousin Kate":

> In each the heroine has sinned, and suffered the penalties of discovery, and in each she is given the upper hand, and made a candidate for sympathy, for very bad reasons. There is no word to intimate that there is anything so very dreadful about dishonor; that it may not be some one else's fault, or nobody's fault at all—a mere social accident. A few faint hinting touches there may be of conventional condemnation, but somehow Miss Rossetti's sinners, *as sinners,* invariably have the best of the argument and of the situation, while virtue is put systematically in the wrong, and snubbed generally. (Rudd, 845)

Before 1875 the *Catholic World,* if not the world at large, had already convicted Rossetti of writing bad poems. But by choosing to withdraw the lyrics to satisfy one class of readers, she drew to herself other criticisms. Indeed, when William later resurrected the lyrics for publication, he opined that "overstrained scrupulosity" had motivated his sister to banish them to undeserved obscurity (*PW,* 480). This was also the view of Edmund Gosse, who as early as 1875 had lamented their loss. Understandably annoyed, Rossetti told Gosse, "I do not suppose myself to be the person least tenderly reminiscent of them . . . but it at any rate appears to be the commoner fault amongst verse-writers to write what is not worth writing, than to suppress what would merit hearers."[18]

Contending that "the morality of art consists in the perfect use of an imperfect medium," Oscar Wilde would dismiss the artist's "ethical sympathies" as "an unpardonable mannerism of style."[19] Rossetti's ethical sympathies, however, apparently as objectionable to the esthetically refined as the morally righteous among her audience, lend a toughness to her work that requires no apology even if she felt compelled to effect a retraction. The strength of the proscribed lyrics resides in the way that they, as a group, call into question conventional morality. For Rossetti was, as Virginia Woolf once said, "not a pure saint" but one who "pulled legs" and "tweaked noses" in her "war with all humbug and pretence."[20] Thus in "A Ring Posy" the speaker's smug spite belies her claim to virtue as a woman chosen in marriage. Likewise, in "A Triad" Rossetti complicates the relation between personal integrity and social respectability by contrasting "three central types of Victorian womanhood—the fallen woman, the old maid, and the wife."[21] Closely associating the single woman and the "fallen woman," Rossetti sets them both against the "sluggish wife" (l. 10). This woman, the antithesis to Patmore's angel in the house, "temperately / Grew gross in soulless love" (ll. 9–10) and "droned in sweetness like a fattened bee" (l. 13). The language of para-dox—allying moderation with immoderation, physical fullness with spiritual emptiness, and marital success with moral failure—allows Rossetti to indict the Victorian ideal of feminine fulfillment in marriage. In those poems specifically concerned with "fallen women," she broadens the challenge posed in "A Ring Posy" and "A Triad."

In "Cousin Kate" and "Light Love," Rossetti separates marriage from motherhood in order to examine licit as well as illicit forms of feminine gratification. Consequently, while she approximates "conventional Victorian moralizing" in her use of "conventional images and diction for didactic effect," she manages nonetheless "to subvert conventional atti-tudes" (Rosenblum 1986, 151–52). In "Cousin Kate," the nameless speaker explains how, having become a sexual "plaything" (l. 12), she also became "an unclean thing" (l. 15) and "an outcast thing" (l. 28). Literally transformed into an object of scorn, she tells how her faithless lover married her cousin, thereby transforming her into "Lady Kate" (l. 17). But while Kate's marriage compromises her integrity, her kinswoman's motherhood brings her pride. By so conflating the roles of the shameless woman and the proud mother, Rossetti demonstrates the tolerance that earned her the opprobrium of moralists. Indeed, most missions dedicated to the rescue of "fallen women" forced penitents to renounce their children as well as their sins (Vicinus, 79). Rossetti is not interested in making an object lesson of these women, however, but in uncovering the complex social forces that contribute to their exploita-tion. In "Cousin Kate," as in "Under the Rose" and "Light Love," she moves beyond conventional condemnation to impute the social license that permits men to philander. Moreover, by doubling Kate's betrayal upon that of the ignoble lord, she insinuates that the ladyhood of some women depends on and perhaps even necessitates the degradation of other women. In "Light Love," on the other hand, she reverses conven-tional expectations by making the chosen bride the object of the forsak-en mistress's compassion. This perspective again undermines the distinction between pure and impure women to suggest that both are, as Ronald Morrison argues, "victims of marriage."[22]

Rossetti, of course, addresses the theme of betrayal in much of her other work. In "Cousin Kate" and "Light Love," however, she not only treats her subject in an open and realistic manner but engages readers' sympathies on behalf of the unwed mother rather than, as in "Under the Rose," the illegitimate child. As a result, the two poems were open to reproach on moral grounds, and rather than revise them, she chose to remove them from her oeuvre. Indeed, even the small change made to "Under the Rose" suggests just how arduous she found the attempt to reconcile good art with good, if inoffensive, morality. Initially, "a distinct aim at conciseness" informed her poetic, but when her sister, Maria, told her that she had sacrificed distinctness to concision, she "then endeavoured to avoid obscurity as well as diffuseness" (quoted in Harrison 1988, 10).[23] Rechristening "Under the Rose" as "The Iniquity of the Fathers upon the Children," she forfeited concision in order to clarify the work's moral impetus and thus to forestall adverse criticism. But less than satisfied with the "unwieldiness" of the revised title, she admitted that she should "have chosen something briefer than one and more lucid than the other" (*FL,* 53). Yet, as the poems added to the collected edition suggest, the tendency to obscurity that had elicited her sister's caution enabled Rossetti to treat potentially objectionable material without offending delicate Victorian sensibilities.

"From Sunset to Star Rise" and "Once for All (Margaret)," two sonnets added to the 1875 volume, are exemplary of the way Rossetti deals responsibly, albeit circumspectly, with the same questions found in the suppressed poems. Dated February 1865, "From Sunset to Star Rise" was composed shortly before the completion of "Under the Rose" and probably derived its inspiration from the same source. According to William, his sister penned in the margins of her manuscript, "House of Charity" (*PW,* 485). Extratextual information suggests, therefore, that the speaker of "From Sunset to Star Rise" is a "fallen woman." Rossetti, however, avoids gendering the experience of the sonnet, thus leading the reader "away from an emphasis on sexual sin and fallen women to a more general consideration of sin and fallen nature."[24] Indeed, she goes even further by eradicating any overt suggestion of sin. As the poem's title suggests, the speaker's "benighted" (l. 3) consciousness inhabits a liminal darkness between sunset and star rise. In words reminiscent of "Songs in a Cornfield," the speaker says, "I am no summer friend, but wintry cold" (l. 2). This desolation, figured as coldness and barrenness, becomes an admonition directed to the speaker's audience: "Take counsel, sever from my lot your lot, / Dwell in your pleasant places, hoard your gold; / Lest you with me should shiver on the wold, / Athirst and hungering on a barren spot" (ll. 5–8). Yet the speaker, having renounced the past in favor of present exile, remembers those "buried years and friends" (l. 12) with fond nostalgia rather than revulsion. Giving few details of the past, Rossetti preserves the speaker's emotional authenticity and takes a position even more morally ambiguous than that assumed in "Cousin Kate," "Light Love," or "Sister Maude," all of which make some token acknowledgment of shame. By refusing to particularize the speaker's condition, the poet underlines the existential rather than the sexual dimensions of the experience related and circumvents the need to make any concession to conventional morality.

The diffuseness of "Once for All (Margaret)" permits a similar latitude. Of the name cited in the title, William notes that his sister intended a private allusion to the first wife of James Hannay, a Pre-Raphaelite associate (*PW,* 486). At the same time, the reference to Margaret recalls the heroine of "Maggie a Lady," whose husband calls her "the rose of roses" (l. 25). While the sonnet has superficially nothing whatsoever to do with either sexual betrayal or "fallen women," Rossetti's floral imagery also suggests a connection with "Under the Rose" and "Light Love." In the latter poem, the unwed mother, nursing her child on her knee, pities the rival who incarnates her former self: "Alas for her, poor faded rose, / Alas for her, like me, / Cast down and trampled in the snows" (ll. 61–63). The image of the traduced rose, resembling Blake's sick rose, relates both women as subject to sexual despoilation. "Once for All," on the other hand, begins with the speaker's admiration for the "beautiful fresh rose" (l. 1) and "its lovely curve of languishment" (l. 3). Eager to "watch its leaves unclose, its heart unclose" (l. 4), the speaker raises the expectation of imminent disclosure. In the sestet, however, the rose abruptly and mysteriously disappears:

> So walking in a garden of delight
>   I came upon one sheltered shadowed nook
> Where broad leaf shadows veiled the day with night,
>   And there lay snow unmelted by the sun:—
> I answered: Take who will the path I took,
>   Winter nips once for all; love is but one. (ll. 9–14)

The speaker's physical movement into the "sheltered shadowed nook" effects a temporal regression that yet suggests the future fate of the beautiful fresh rose, which, like the poor faded rose in "Light Love," will eventually be trampled in the snows. While the speaker's ramble in the garden allegorizes the individual's experience of life and death, Rossetti does not make any overt connection between the rose—displaced by the abstract noun "love" in the last line—and feminine sexuality. Instead, the rose functions as a symbol for love in all of its mundane forms. Thus, the speaker's gnomic answer, clearly monitory, remains enigmatic. Rossetti's obscurity opens the sonnet to multiple possibilities for meaning and closes it to moral objection.

In "From Sunset to Star Rise" and "Once for All" Rossetti shows her ability to reach a compromise between her two classes of readers without lowering either her moral or her esthetic standards. This compromise had, however, a price. When Macmillan inquired about new material for the collected edition, she told him that, aside from some "waifs & strays . . . from Magazines," she possessed only a couple "of *never-printed* pieces" suitable "for use" (Packer, ed., 107). In addition to more than 50 poems published and hitherto uncollected, however, she had some 300 never-printed pieces at her disposal. In the end, *Goblin Market, The Prince's Progress, and Other Poems* included eleven entirely new poems and 25 "waifs and strays." The other work remained unpublished for several reasons: some lyrics, like those privately printed in 1847, were undoubtedly too immature; mature poems, like "Il Rosseggiar Dell'Oriente" and "By Way of Remembrance," were evidently too personal; and others, like "Margery," were probably omitted on the same basis that "Cousin Kate," "Light Love," and "Sister Maude" were suppressed.[25] As a result, what *Goblin Market, The Prince's Progress, and Other Poems* omits is perhaps more important than what it contains. Having fought hard for her right of control only 10 years before in *The Prince's Progress and Other Poems*, Rossetti had not merely grown cautious about publicly flouting moral and esthetic proprieties; she had come to rely on self-censorship as a means to retain her poetic autonomy.

Chapter Four

Fresh Fields of Endeavor: Short Stories and Nursery Rhymes

The demand for *Goblin Market, The Prince's Progress, and Other Poems* put the seal on Rossetti's success as a serious poet. She was, however, more than a poet and had, in the years before 1875, expanded her published oeuvre to include prose as well as verse. During these years she also made the unlucky decision to change publishers. Leaving Macmillan in 1870, she approached F. S. Ellis with a manuscript of nursery rhymes illustrated, as she modestly said, with her "own scratches" (Packer, ed., 74) and broached to him the plan for a collection of prose tales. Published later that year, *Commonplace and Other Short Stories* contains most of the fiction she had composed since 1852. While the volume thus realized an ambition heralded in *Maude,* it fared poorly with critics and booksellers. As a result, Rossetti freed Ellis from his obligation to her nursery rhymes and, in so doing, dispensed with the unwelcome necessity of offending Alice Boyd, whose illustrations, taking the place of the original scratches, had proven unsatisfactory.

When George Routledge and Sons agreed in the following year to publish the rhymes, she had decided on Arthur Hughes as her illustrator. Dated 1872, *Sing-Song: A Nursery Rhyme Book* was released in time for Christmas of 1871. Encouraged by the praise her nursery rhymes received, Rossetti then produced a series of interlinked stories, *Speaking Likenesses,* which she offered to Macmillan in 1874. But when Ruskin, for one, read the tales, he was revolted. "How," he wondered, "could she or Arthur Hughes sink so low after their pretty nursery rhymes?" (Ruskin, 37:155). Nevertheless, insofar as *Speaking Likenesses* succeeds to *Sing-Song* as a work for children and to *Commonplace and Other Short Stories* as a work of fiction, the volume brings to a culmination the experiments in form and genre that Rossetti conducted at the height of her career.

Speaking Likenesses in *Commonplace and Other Short Stories*

Rossetti's reputation as a poet worked to the disadvantage of *Commonplace and Other Short Stories*. Touting the title work among his acquaintance as "very good (in the Miss Austen vein rather)," Gabriel told his sister: "It certainly is not dangerously exciting to the nervous system, but it is far from being dull for all that" (D. G. Rossetti 1965, 2:826). "Of course," he added, "I think your proper business is to write poetry, and not *Commonplaces*" (2:827). Contemporary reviewers made similar criticisms of the volume as a whole. Disappointed to discover "that the authoress of such exquisite verses can indeed write commonplaces," the reader for the *Spectator* observed: "Not that evidence of the same fancy is entirely wanting, but it is chiefly exhibited in the grotesque variety of the wares offered for our acceptance, and which are adapted to such opposite classes of customers, and belong to such different periods of life."[1] The eclecticism that the *Spectator* chose to condemn, however, demonstrates one of Rossetti's strengths as a writer of fiction: her versatility.

In addition to such everyday domestic fare as "Commonplace" and the slightly more exotic "Vanna's Twins," *Commonplace and Other Short Stories* includes one brilliantly vivid historical tale ("The Lost Titian"), two fairy stories ("Nick" and "Hero: A Metamorphosis"), and three avowedly polemical pieces ("A Safe Investment," "Pros and Cons," and "The Waves of this Troublesome World"). Arranging her prose for publication in much the same way as her poetry, Rossetti opens the volume with a secular novella, "Commonplace," and ends with a devotional narrative, "The Waves of this Troublesome World." But despite "individual differences," her tales possess, like the three sisters in the title story, a "strong family likeness."[2] Experimenting with a range of realistic, fantastic, and didactic forms, Rossetti returns time and again to the same motifs—birth and death, loss and gain—that distinguish her verse. Moreover, her stories, whether oriented to secular or religious ends, rely on a symbology informed by an Anglo-Catholic appreciation of the spiritual significance of physical phenomena. "All the world over," says Rossetti in the devotional work *Seek and Find*, "visible things typify things invisible."[3] As a result, her fiction emulates the structure of parable, defined as "a spoken emblem," and uncovers in mere commonplace a resource for "hidden meaning" (*CSS*, 309–10).

"Commonplace," written in 1870, returns to the preoccupations of *Maude*. But whereas Rossetti's juvenile novella explores alternative forms of feminine fulfillment, "Commonplace" focuses on marriage as woman's ordinary lot in life. Finding hidden meaning in the platitudinous phrase and the everyday event, Rossetti examines the romantic illusions and economic realities that shape women's decision to marry. The tale opens as Lucy and Catherine, the eldest of the three Charlmont sisters, attend to the "meat-and-drink responsibilities" of breakfast (*CSS*, 5). Ironically, the youngest sister's frivolous perusal of the *Times* supplement speaks no less to the meat-and-drink affairs of Victorian women:

> Jane read aloud: "'Halbert to Jane'; I wish I were Jane. And here, positively, are two more Janes, and not me. 'Catherine'—that's a death. Lucy, I don't see you anywhere. Catherine was eighty-nine, and much respected. 'Mrs. Anstruther of a son and heir.' I wonder if those are the Anstruthers I met in Scotland: she was very ugly, and short. 'Everilda Stella,'—how can anybody be Everilda?" Then, with a sudden accession of interest, "Why, Lucy, Everilda Stella has actually married your Mr. Hartley!" (*CSS*, 6–7)

The notices devoted to births, marriages, and deaths, though ancillary to the reports of men's business in the *Times* proper, constitute the whole of women's business. In this respect the three envied Janes, all recently wed, reveal the youngest Miss Charlmont's dedication to marriage as a career. Catherine's future, on the other hand, is parabolically encoded in fate of the aged and venerable woman whose obituary Jane reads. Not interested in marriage for herself, Catherine looks, at the end of the novella, to a future that lies "further off" (*CSS*, 142). By contrast, Lucy's situation is, as Jane's inability to see her in the *Times* suggests, rather more ambiguous. Having met Alan Hartley at Appletrees House, the home of her father's cousin in London, she has allowed his charm to win her over and, believing herself loved, refused several offers of marriage. Consequently, when Alan marries the "only child and presumptive heiress of George Durham, Esq., of Orpingham Place" (*CSS*, 19), Lucy receives a shock. In effect, her disappointment comes of her childish confidence in the "copy, 'Manners make the Man,'" set her as a girl; Catherine, having also been taught "how in that particular phrase 'Man' includes 'Woman,'" amends the rule to "'Morals make the Man' (including Woman)"; and Jane believes "'Money makes the Man'" (*CSS*, 93). The final maxim, as Jane's circumstances confirm, is not gender inclusive.

Moving the scene from Brompton-on-Sea to London, Rossetti advances the narrative of Jane's career to demonstrate how women's disadvantaged position under patriarchal law undermines the sanctity of marriage. Taking Lucy's place in a second breakfast triptych, Mrs. Tyke observes that Jane has made a conquest of George Durham. Although his daughter Stella's inheritance is thus imperilled, she remains unruffled by her father's courtship of a woman young enough to be her sister. For this reason, however, Jane treats Stella as a rival. The posthumous daughter of William Charlmont, she receives nothing under the terms of her father's will and, hence, is "dependent on her sisters" (*CSS*, 16). Like Margaret's illegitimacy in "Under the Rose," Jane's disinheritance, albeit unintentional, symbolizes the legal exclusion under which the Victorian woman suffers. Unlike Margaret, however, Jane is corrupted by her experience. Courting in George a father to restore her lost patrimony, she transfers her envy of her sisters, as favored daughters, to Stella.[4] Even when Catherine makes Jane her sole heir, she resents the £20,000 that George settles upon his daughter.

Mean-spirited toward Stella, Jane is no more charitable toward her aged suitor, who is merely a means to an end. As she says, "George is Orpingham Place, and Orpingham Place is George" (*CSS*, 95). Although "she would certainly have entered upon Orpingham Place with added zest had it not entailed George" (*CSS*, 104), her love of money outweighs her aversion for the man. "If the pines and the pigs are smitten," she asks, "why shouldn't I marry the pigs and the pines?" (*CSS*, 38). While Jane's objectification of George reveals the crassness of her material ambitions, her jokes at his expense demonstrate her intelligence as well as her scorn. Sending his photograph to Lucy, she facetiously asks, "Don't you see all Orpingham Place in his speaking countenance?" (*CSS*, 60). For her part, Lucy settles on "an arrangement which, in her eyes, showed a symbolic appropriateness" and returns to her sister "Mr. Durham's portrait wrapped in a ten-pound note" (*CSS*, 64). This symbolic gesture suggests, of course, that marriage is but a form of prostitution. Jane, allowing herself to be bought, nonetheless tolerates her husband "as the 'habitation-tax' paid for Orpingham Place" (*CSS*, 141).

The artfulness of Jane's campaign to acquire a wealthy husband, whatever the cost, is epitomized in the event that serves as a prelude to George's proposal: an elaborate three-part charade performed for a party of 200 guests at Appletrees House. While Charlotte Brontë, in a similar episode in *Jane Eyre* (1847), employs the name of a British prison, Bridewell, to associate marriage with captivity, Rossetti's choice of "love-

apple" for the "charade word" (*CSS*, 75) exposes romance as pretense, for
the grandiloquent "love-apple" is only the commonplace tomato. In each
of the charade's three scenes, therefore, Rossetti emphasizes the artifi-
ciality of the construct from which the audience must guess the answer.
In the first scene, representing *love*, "a file of English-Grecian maidens,
singing and carrying garlands, passed across the stage towards a pasteboard temple, presumably their desired goal, although they glanced at
their audience, and seemed very independent of Cupid on his pedestal"
(*CSS*, 78–79). The maidens' self-conscious awareness of their audience
casts doubt on their devotion to love as an ideal. In the second scene,
representing *apple*, the stage props—"woolly toy lambs" and a peacock
"ingeniously mounted on noiseless wheels" (*CSS*, 80)—draw attention
once more to the pasteboard unreality of the action. Having made a real-
life choice between Lucy and her "unconscious rival" (*CSS*, 39), Alan
Hartley plays the part of Paris. Constrained to choose among three "rival
goddesses" (*CSS*, 80), he wavers between Juno and Minerva before passing the prized apple to Venus, played by Jane. Bringing *love* and *apple*
together, the third scene grounds the meaning of the charade word in
the vulgar context of the marketplace and hence defines love as a commodity on which women trade competitively for economic security. In
this act, Stella takes the role of a market girl who, like the little men of
"Goblin Market," cries, "'Grapes, melons, peaches, love-apples,' with the
most natural inflections" (*CSS*, 82). Her down-to-earth performance is
less affecting, however, than Jane's act as a trumped-up goddess. In
another charade enacted behind the scenes, Jane crowns her performance
as Venus when she accepts George's proposal. Eclipsing Stella on stage
and off, she has thereby "attained both her objects" (*CSS*, 84).

    That marriage need not be a charade Rossetti suggests by contrasting
Jane and George Durham with Sarah and Gawkins Drum. The family
likeness between the two couples emerges when Miss Drum, the
Charlmont sisters' former teacher, expounds "the Drum-Durham theory": "Our family name of Drum," she tells Lucy, "though less eupho-
nious than that of Durham, is in fact the same" (*CSS*, 90). Nevertheless,
the Durhams' marriage is a very different affair from the Drums', for
Sarah, having "devoted herself during an ordinary lifetime" to a "bedrid-
den brother" (*CSS*, 69), marries Gawkins when both are in their sixties.
Provoking laughter among their acquaintance, their belated marriage so
outrages his sister's sense of propriety that she indicts the aged bride and
groom as "culprits at the moral bar" (*CSS*, 73). Unconventionality is not
immorality, however. Indeed, while the Drums have remained faithful to

each other through a lifetime of courtship, Jane refuses to commit her-
self to George during their short engagement. An incorrigible flirt, she
tells Catherine, "Mr. Durham isn't Bluebeard; or, if he is, I had better
get a little fun first" (*CSS*, 99). Thus, she attends, upon her return to
Brompton-on-Sea, a picnic at which she initially designs to fascinate Mr.
Ballantyne, a widowed solicitor, and so dash the marital hopes of Edith
Sims. Modifying her plan for amusement, she turns her attention from
Ballantyne to a young viscount. Narrated with zest and humor, Jane's
activities nevertheless betoken her desperation in the face of her forth-
coming marriage.

The picnic is a pivotal event in "Commonplace," for it marks the
resumption of Lucy's career as well as the climax of Jane's romantic
adventures. But Lucy, far from seeking to conduct a flirtation or initiate
a courtship, chooses to take charge of Ballantyne's five-year-old son, who
futilely searches for strawberries out of season. While Catherine fails to
divert Jane from the viscount, Lucy successfully saves little Frank when
he attempts to escape her control and run into danger. In so doing, she
wins the admiration of the child's father, who proposes shortly after her
birthday in November. Pleased "to find herself not obsolete even at thirty" (*CSS*, 128), she refuses to rush headlong into marriage and declines
his offer. Indeed, her rescue of Frank provides a spoken emblem of
immature passion restrained by mature conscience.

Through Lucy's experience, Rossetti validates marriage as a vocation
based on principle. Having drawn "a false conclusion" from Alan
Hartley's superficial charm (*CSS*, 23), Lucy has learnt to appreciate the
sincerity of his friend Arthur Tresham, whom she had formerly refused.
Accepting an invitation to Appletrees House, she looks forward to
renewing his acquaintance. Rossetti ironizes Lucy's newfound happiness,
however, by placing her courtship against the mourning of the widowed
Mrs. Tyke, born Lucy Charlmont, and by emphasizing Arthur's dullness.
Diligent on behalf of London's East End poor as well as Lucy's bereaved
kinswoman, Arthur is a moral man and a lackluster lover. Lucy momen-
tarily rues his shortcomings, but "weighing her second love against her
first, tears, at once proud and humble, filled her eyes, and 'one cannot
have everything' was forgotten in 'I can never give him back half
enough'" (*CSS*, 137). Although their courtship and marriage admits "no
stereotyped hypocrisies" (*CSS*, 140), Lucy experiences one "romantic
moment" before she returns to Brompton-on-Sea to prepare for the wedding: "At the noisy, dirty, crowded railway-station, . . . Arthur terrified
Lucy, to her great delight, by standing on the carriage-step, and holding

her hand locked fast in his own, an instant after the train had started"
(*CSS,* 138). This moment doubles upon Jane's departure from London
before her marriage. Having produced a "show of sentiment" for George
(*CSS,* 92), Jane "never in her life had experienced a greater relief than . . .
when the starting train left him behind on the platform," but soon "it
would be too late to leave him behind" (*CSS,* 93). The thought of Paris—
the city rather than the Trojan prince—overcomes Jane's feelings of mis-
giving. Rossetti enhances the significance of these two departures not
merely by interposing the death of Dr. Tyke, but by making "London-
Bridge Station, with its whirl of traffic," an "emblem of London itself:
vast, confused, busy, orderly, more or less dirty" (*CSS,* 33). The site of
departures and arrivals, London-Bridge Station is also an emblem of the
world in all its tawdry confusion. Consequently, because Lucy's wedding
necessitates a return to London, Rossetti ultimately figures marriage as a
decision to live *in* rather than *apart* from the world.

While Lucy's marriage to Arthur refuses to "lend itself to any tribute
of lies, miscalled white" (*CSS,* 140), Rossetti includes as an epigraph to
"The Lost Titian," the second selection in *Commonplace and Other Short
Stories,* the enigmatic phrase, "A lie with a circumstance" (*CSS,* 145).
Although this tale, richly opulent in the telling, seems the reverse of
commonplace, it is a companion piece to the title story. In both, Rossetti
addresses the problem of judging from appearances and of distinguishing manners from morals. But turning from the female world of love to
the male domain of art, she provides in "The Lost Titian" a critique of
post-Raphaelite decadence rather than of amatory ideology. In so doing,
she offers a rejoinder to Gabriel's short story "Hand and Soul," which she
once described as "rich in beauty and power: *that* even my anxious eyes
see and admit" (quoted in Bell, 123). Whereas "Hand and Soul," first
published in the *Germ,* describes the provenance of a thirteenth-century
painting by Chiaro dell' Erma that hangs in Florence's Pitti Gallery,
"The Lost Titian" relates the disappearance of a sixteenth-century work
of Venetian art. And whereas Chiaro dell' Erma's painting incarnates
Pre-Raphaelite sincerity in art, the lost Titian symbolizes the loss of
moral principle in Victorian as well as Renaissance painting.

For Rossetti, esthetic degradation is a reflex of moral degradation.
Drawing perhaps on her understanding the rivalry among her eldest
brother, Hunt, and Millais, she opens her post-Raphaelite story as Titian,
in company with "his two friends—Gianni the successful, and
Giannuccione the universal disappointment" (*CSS,* 146)—completes
"the masterpiece of the period; the masterpiece of his life" (*CSS,* 145).

Yet Gianni, for all his success, suffers from jealousy and so contrives to rob Titian of his achievement during a game of dice. Wagering all in one desperate gamble, he wins the painting and loses his friend. When financial insolvency threatens to deprive him of his sordid triumph, Gianni again compromises his integrity by employing art in the service of guile: "Taking coarse pigments, such as, when he pleased, might easily be removed, he daubed over those figures which seemed to live, and that wonderful background, which not Titian himself could reproduce; then, on the blank surface, he painted a dragon, flaming, clawed, preposterous" (*CSS*, 158). Consequently, when Titian arrives with Gianni's other creditors, he seeks his "one unforgotten beauty . . . in vain; only in the forefront sprawled a dragon, flaming, clawed, preposterous; grinned, twinkled, erected his tail, and flouted him" (*CSS*, 159). The dragon's tail, suggestive of phallic power, delivers an insult that Titian, unable to see through Gianni's latest device, fails to appreciate. But although the painting is a lie, it reveals a truth. Just as Chiaro's depiction of a beautiful lady symbolizes his purity of heart, Gianni's preposterous dragon reveals the monstrous perversity of his soul. Furthermore, the dragon's usurpation of beauty, represented in Titian's masterpiece, signifies coarse art's succession to fine art. Thus, insofar as the renovated painting epitomizes the betrayal of art as well as friendship, Rossetti uses the dragon to show the loss of sincerity following the dissolution of the PRB.

Ironically, Gianni's revenge redounds against him, for a publican claims the sign of the dragon to settle an outstanding account and the painter fails to redeem it before his death. But even as the Titian is thus twice lost, the story ends with the tantalizing possibility of the painting's recovery:

> Reader, should you chance to discern over wayside inn or metropolitan hotel a dragon pendent, or should you find such an effigy amid the lumber of a broker's shop, whether it be red, green, or piebald, demand it importunately, pay for it liberally, and in the privacy of home scrub it. It *may* be that from behind the dragon will emerge a fair one, fairer than Andromeda, and that to you will appertain the honour of yet further exalting Titian's greatness in the eyes of a world. (*CSS*, 162–63)

While the final address to the reader is redolent of allegory, an earlier allusion to "an oral tradition of a somewhere extant lost Titian having survived all historical accuracy" (*CSS*, 162) enhances the story's realism. Indeed, because some credulous readers had taken "The Lost Titian," first published in the *Crayon* (1856), to be literally true, Rossetti prefaced *Commonplace and Other Short Stories* with a reminder that her work was "not . . . founded on fact" (*CSS*, [v]). Yet, in fiction, she discovered a means to make a lie serve the circumstance of truth.

Following her historical tale of moral degeneracy with two allegories of spiritual regeneration, Rossetti abandons realist conventions in "Nick" and "Hero: A Metamorphosis." Written in 1853, the first of these companion tales deals with an old man who suffers from envy and discontent, while the second, published in the *Argosy* in 1866, concerns a young maiden who, mistaking the diffidence of her father and her lover for indifference, desires "to become the supreme object of admiration" (*CSS*, 190). Nick's adventures begin when he wishes destruction to farmer Giles's orchard. An outraged fairy, brandishing "her tiny fist . . . in a menacing attitude," responds immediately: "Now listen, you churl, you! henceforward you shall straightway become everything you wish; only mind, you must remain under one form for at least an hour" (*CSS*, 168–69). The vengeful fairy's final "slap in the face" (*CSS*, 169) anticipates the sadism of Rossetti's *Speaking Likenesses* and foreshadows the violence that follows on each of Nick's wishes. When, for example, he becomes a flock of sparrows and begins to devour Giles's cherries, the farmer arms himself and "soon reduce[s] the enemy to one crestfallen biped with broken leg and wing" (*CSS*, 170). After several punishing transformations, Nick finally decides that "if he merely studied his own advantage without trying to annoy other people, perhaps his persecutor might be propitiated" (*CSS*, 176). Consequently, he wishes himself "the rich old man who lived in a handsome house just beyond the turnpike" (*CSS*, 176). In this incarnation, however, he discovers that his miserly wealth makes him the object of envy and spite. Robbed and murdered, he returns to himself just as his assassins toss the first clods of the grave upon his body. Symbolically reborn, devilish old Nick becomes good saint Nick. After making his former victims secret restitution, he "was never again heard to utter a wish" (*CSS*, 179).

"Hero," the feminine complement to "Nick," is likewise a cautionary fairy tale. But when Hero utters her wish, the fairy court is reluctant to burden her with the "perilous preeminence she demanded" (*CSS*, 192). Instead, the Queen Fairy decrees that the girl's "restless spirit" be returned to Man-side in "a heavy blazing diamond" (*CSS*, 195) while her body remains on Elf-side for one year until she understands the magnitude of the gift that she desires. A commodity sold at "the best market of Outerworld" (*CSS*, 196), Hero comes into the possession of Princess

Lily, who wears the jewel on her wedding day. But even though "Hero eclipsed the bride, dazzled the bridegroom, distracted the queen-mother, and thrilled the whole assembly" (*CSS,* 197), Lily's husband esteems his wife over the diamond. Experiencing "a shock," Hero then moves into "Lily's pure heart [where] she almost found rest" (*CSS,* 198).

Restlessness returns to Hero when, upon the return of the prince and princess to the public world, they attend the final operatic performance of Melice Rapta. Moving from Lily to Melice, Hero finds herself again eclipsed when the singer's uncle, an avid gardener, turns his attention from his niece to a rare seedling. Reborn in the plant, she is, however, scorned by the woman who takes over Uncle Treeh's estate after his death and who covets, above all else, a picturesque garden ruin. As the object of admiration to one of degraded taste, Hero realizes the ruin of her ambition and feels "a passionate longing for the old lost life, the old beloved love" (*CSS,* 207). At that moment, her spirit returns to her body. Reconciled to herself, she awakens from death to life under the care of Forss, her lover, and Peter, her father. The moral of the story, which Hero, like Laura of "Goblin Market," tells her children, is "that though admiration seems sweet at first, only love is sweet first, and last, and always" (*CSS,* 211).

Apart from "Vanna's Twins," the remaining stories in *Commonplace and Other Short Stories* appeared initially in the *Churchman's Shilling Magazine* in 1867. Although all three take Rossetti's tendency to moral exempla to doctrinal ends, "A Safe Investment," a parable of the apocalypse, and "Pros and Cons," a sermon on pew rents and Christian equality, are of less significance than "The Waves of this Troublesome World." Another story of loss and recovery, "The Waves" concerns the return of Sarah Hardiman Lane to her childhood home and eventually to her childhood faith. The parable of the lost sheep (Luke 15:4–7) that Mrs. Grey, the curate's wife, assigns Sarah's niece, Jane, as a lesson gives meaning to the widow Lane's experience. As a young woman, Sarah had met and, against her father's will, married a traveling photographer and itinerant Methodist preacher. For Rossetti, Sarah's action represents a grave error. "A wife's paramount duty," she explains in *Letter and Spirit,* "is indeed to her husband, superseding all other human obligations: yet to assume this duty, free-will first stepped in with its liability to err; in this connexion woman has to reap as she has sown, be the crop what it may: while in the filial relation all is safe and flawless."[5] Thus Sarah, having substituted her father for her husband, also substitutes Anglicanism for Methodism. As a dissenter, she rebels against her heavenly as well as her earthly father. Her punishment, wreaked by a truly jealous God, follows in the deaths of the three male relatives she most loves: her father, Henry Hardiman; her son, Henry Lane; and her husband, John Lane. In other words, heaven's trinity cancels Sarah's earthly trinity. The near death of another Henry Hardiman, the nephew whom Sarah dotes on because he is "so like his grandfather" (*CSS*, 328), precipitates her return to Anglicanism.

Dispatching Jane and her brother Henry on an innocuous errand that ends in disaster, Sarah resembles the mother who unwittingly sends her children to their deaths in "Vanna's Twins," which Swinburne, despite his "physical shock" at Rossetti's heartlessness, considered "the sweetest story of them all."[6] But whereas the twins, after fulfilling Vanna's commission to a poor woman with three sick children, get lost in a sudden snowstorm and perish "huddled together in a chalky hollow close to the edge of the cliff" (*CSS*, 236), the Hardiman children find themselves pinned on "a narrow shelf" beneath the cliff as the tide rises inexorably toward them (*CSS*, 323). During their ordeal, Jane prays for the protection of the Good Shepherd. Indeed, even as Rossetti's allusion to "one Holy Innocents' Day" (*CSS*, 228) serves to put the death of Vanna's twins within the context of divine mystery, the miraculous salvation of Sarah's niece and nephew corresponds to the parable of the lost sheep and reveals "its lesson of mercy or warning" (*CSS*, 327). To this lesson, Sarah pays heed and, moved by Jane's plea, accompanies the Hardimans to church to give thanks for the children's restoration. Still torn in her allegiance to her dead father and dead husband, she finds comfort in Mrs. Grey's assurance that John Lane provided her "husband a living lesson of boldness, self-denial, and trampling false shame under foot" (*CSS*, 326). This assurance allows her to respond to the voice of conscience and return to the fold. While Rossetti's emphasis on the Anglican Church as the one true fold is obviously dogmatic, she also suggests that the Church has much to learn from those, like Sarah's husband, who have, as the name "Lane" suggests, chosen other avenues of worship.

Insofar as Sarah's return to the Church follows on her return to celibacy, *Commonplace and Other Short Stories* implicitly rejects marriage as woman's best destiny. Moving from courtship in "Commonplace" to widowhood in "The Waves," Rossetti broadens her treatment of feminine experience to reevaluate the situation of the single woman. Making England's cliff-lined shore the scene for liminal subjectivity, she not only sets her opening and closing tales in coastal towns but chooses for the motto of *Commonplace and Other Short Stories* "From sea to sea" (*CSS*, [iii]).

Although the waves of this troublesome world threaten to engulf the unwary, the sea also symbolizes the other world and the afterlife. At the end of "Commonplace" Catherine looks toward the sea that has claimed her earthly father's life and, awaiting his return, trusts her future to her heavenly father. Similarly, at the end of "The Waves" Sarah awaits Christ's second coming. "Thankful that her idol was removed for a season" (*CSS,* 329), she returns to the flawless safety of the filial relation that Catherine, never marrying, has never left. Choosing to remain a widow, she keeps faith not so much with her dead husband as her beloved father(s). In "The Waves," therefore, Rossetti reorients the imperatives of feminine existence from the secular ideal of marriage to the spiritual ideal of self-devotion and brings *Commonplace and Other Short Stories* full circle.

Sing-Song and Full-Grown Femininity

Sing-Song: A Nursery Rhyme Book occupies a position at the center of Rossetti's poetic career. Describing the volume as "alternating between the merest babyism and a sort of Blakish wisdom and tenderness," Gabriel swore that "no one could have written anything so absolutely right for babies but herself" (D. G. Rossetti 1965, 2:797). *Sing-Song* belongs, however, to a tradition that also includes such undisputed classics as Jane Taylor's "The Star" ("Twinkle, twinkle, little star") and Sarah Josepha Hale's "Mary's Lamb" ("Mary had a little lamb"). In these and other works, Rossetti's female precursors annexed juvenile verse to the prerogatives of feminine lyricism and so pioneered an esthetic of literary maternalism that granted them, as women poets, unparalleled authority.[7] Indeed, as if to acknowledge the expressive freedom she discovered in nursery rhyme, Rossetti opens *Sing-Song*—the only volume of verse not dedicated to her mother—with the delightfully provocative announcement: "RHYMES DEDICATED WITHOUT PERMISSION TO THE BABY WHO SUGGESTED THEM" (*CP,* 2:19). Although the unnamed muse was, in all likelihood, Charles Cayley's nephew, the cryptic impersonality of the dedication widens the frame of reference from a child to all children. At the same time, the inspirational baby functions as an ideological cipher that not only yields before feminine power in the nursery but reproduces feminine powerlessness outside the nursery. In other words, the construct of the child ironically reconstructs the experience of Victorian wives and mothers who, reading *Sing-Song* to their children, comprised the poet's other audience. Speaking for as well as to nineteenth-century femininity in *Sing-Song,* Rossetti accommodates the childlike simplicity of nursery rhyme to the adult voice of duty and desire, power and passion, doubt and dependence.

Although Rossetti considered herself "deficient in the nice motherly ways which win and ought to win a child's heart" (*FL,* 75), she respected the power that motherhood conferred on women. Polarizing rather than conflating juvenility and femininity, her first four lyrics exploit the dramatic directness of maternal speech to convey women's relationship with children as one of intimacy as well as authority. Furthermore, while the opening quartet includes some of the most babyish of Rossetti's singsongs, it also inscribes an antithetical turn from life to death and, in so doing, encapsulates the total movement of the volume. The first two poems—"Angels at the foot" and "Love me,—I love you"—depict the mutual joys of mother and child. The second two—"My baby has a father and a mother" and "Our little baby fell asleep"—reveal their mutual sorrows.[8] Indeed, the initiatory lyric alone hints at Rossetti's breadth of scope in *Sing-Song:* "Angels at the foot, / And Angels at the head, / And like a curly little lamb / My pretty babe in bed" (ll. 1–4). Supernature, represented by the angels, hovers at the outer limits of the child's domain. Nature, suggested by the lamb, constitutes its center.

Reinvoking the resemblance between the child and the lamb several times in the course of *Sing-Song,* Rossetti playfully captures the innocence of youth. In "Minnie and Mattie" a "Woolly white lambkin / Frisks all about" (ll. 11–12); in "Dancing on the hill-tops" a young girl, Alice, cavorts "with lambkins / In the flowering valleys" (ll. 5–6); in "A frisky lamb" the lamb frolics with an equally "frisky child" (l. 2). In "On the grassy banks," moreover, Rossetti widens the analogy inaugurated in "Angels at the foot" and makes the flock a metaphor for the family. "Woolly sisters, woolly brothers" (l. 3) gambol under the watchful eyes of "their woolly mothers" (l. 5). Missing from "On the grassy banks," however, is the "patriarchal ram" that, at the end of "An Old-World Thicket," calls and leads the flock "with tinkling bell" (l. 171). Indeed, in *Sing-Song,* the new world of childhood is, as "On the grassy banks" suggests, matriarchal.

Making an explicit comparison between babies and lambs in "Angels at the foot," the speaker reveals the vulnerability as well as the innocence of childhood. The poet, on the other hand, ascribes to womanhood a protective power by creating an implicit resemblance between angels and mothers. Rossetti does not, however, subscribe unqualifiedly to the angelic ideal of Victorian femininity. When, for example, the maternal angels that act for the speaker in the opening lyric reappear in "Three little children," their presence marks the mother's radical absence. The mother's death, in other words, brings seraphic woman-hood to its logical dénouement. In the interests of balance, therefore, Rossetti broadens her treatment of maternity to include lyrics like "On the grassy banks" and "A white hen sitting." In these poems she not only puts motherhood into a natural context but elaborates the ideal of heroic femininity that prompted her to lay aside, if only for the sake of argument, her objections to the women's rights movement. Proposing the enfranchisement of married women, she asked Augusta Webster, "Who [are] so apt as Mothers . . . to protect the interests of themselves and of their offspring? I do think if anything ever does sweep away the barrier of sex, and make the female not a giantess or a heroine but at once and full grown a hero and a giant, it is that mighty maternal love which makes little birds and little beasts as well as little women match-es for very big adversaries" (quoted in Bell, 112). Defined in terms of love and might, motherhood possesses a power that transcends generic as well as sexual difference.

Assimilating little women to little birds and little beasts, Rossetti aligns maternity to nature. The likeness between human and animal mothers Arthur Hughes cleverly depicts in his design for "A white hen sitting": the hen whose chicks huddle beneath her wing faces a young woman whose daughter stands within her embrace. Implicit in the illus-tration is the idea of protective or, more properly, heroic motherhood. Giving more explicit form to maternal might in the poem, Rossetti describes the threat posed by three winged adversaries—an owl, a hawk, and a bat—to the hen's newly hatched brood. But just as the orphans of "Three little children" are "Safe as safe can be / With guardian Angels" (ll. 9–10), the "chicks beneath their mother's wing / Squat safe as safe can be" (ll. 7–8). By reiterating the phraseology of "Three little children" in "A white hen sitting," however, Rossetti ironizes the relationship among angels, women, and animals. Indeed, the resemblance between winged beasts, both protective and predatory, and winged beings strong-ly suggests the poet's ambivalence toward the conventional ideal of ethe-real femininity.

Love as well as might is integral to Rossetti's construction of mother-hood in *Sing-Song*. Thus in the second of her lyrics she turns from protec-tive to passionate maternity. Superseding the intercessory angels of the previous poem, her speaker assumes a tone of address that is, at once, more immediate, more intimate, and more intense:

Love me,—I love you,
    Love me, my baby;
Sing it high, sing it low,
    Sing it as may be.

Mother's arms under you,
    Her eyes above you;
Sing it high, sing it low,
    Love me,—I love you. (ll. 1–8)

The mother holds the child with her arms, her eyes, and her words. The
internal symmetry of the poem's framing lines suggests, moreover, a reciprocity between mother and child. But insofar as the baby's "very limited subjectivity" raises a "justified doubt" about its ability to sing and to
feel the desired response, the poem articulates an unrealized ideal.[9] The
child's limitations as a reciprocating subject, however, actually maximize
the speaker's capacity for pleasure. Dependent, the baby needs its mother's care. Unself-conscious, it cannot reject her love. Thus the mother's
relationship with her child, far from being "egalitarian," provides satisfaction because it ratifies her power.[10]

James R. Kincaid's argument that literary and cultural constructions
of childhood as "pure nothingness" readily accommodate such strong
emotions as adult erotic desire provides further insight into the way
Rossetti figures babyhood in *Sing-Song*.[11] Because the baby represents an
emptiness more profound than the child, it is infinitely more seductive.
In "Your brother has a falcon," then, the baby's nothingness invites the
mother's fulfillment:

Your brother has a falcon,
    Your sister has a flower;
But what is left for mannikin,
    Born within an hour?

I'll nurse you on my knee, my knee,
    My own little son;
I'll rock you, rock you, in my arms,
    My least little one. (ll. 1–8)

In the first stanza, the contrast between the baby and its siblings establishes the infant's absolute lack. But when the mother poses herself as the object of the child's fulfillment, she reveals her own insufficiency, for her elder son and daughter are, as the falcon and the flower suggest, no longer completely dependent on her. Turning to the infant, she finds the most emotional satisfaction in the least of her children precisely because his total need exceeds her partial want.

As a legitimate object of maternal attention, the baby authorizes the expression of feminine desire. But whereas distance defines sexual desire in the conventional amatory sonnet, nearness characterizes the articulation of maternal desire in Rossetti's nursery rhymes. Indeed, her eroticization of babyhood becomes overtly fleshly in those lyrics which, functioning as infantine blazons, catalog the child's physical charms. In "My baby has a mottled fist" the fatness that mottles and creases the child's body makes him "the very thing for kisses" (l. 4). In "I know a baby, such a baby," on the other hand, the knowing mother not only rejoices in the baby's "Round blue eyes and cheeks of pink" (l. 2) but dwells with sensuous languor on "an elbow furrowed with dimples" (l. 3) and "a wrist where creases sink" (l. 4). Having rapturously itemized the baby's attractions in the first stanza, the speaker begins the second by attributing a meaning to the child's crowing: "'Cuddle and love me, cuddle and love me'" (l. 5). The child's imagined response, a projection of the mother's desire, resembles the chiastic refrain of "Love me,—I love you" and echoes the ending of "The dog lies in his kennel": "And cuddle and kiss my baby, / And baby kiss me" (ll. 7–8). At the same time, the thrice-repeated "oh" of the lyric's final lines brings the mother's wonder and admiration to a new pitch: "Oh the bald head, and oh the sweet lips, / And oh the sleepy eyes that wink!" (ll. 7–8). The baby's sleepy eyes form a fitting prelude to the volume's two final lullabies, which, with their rocking rhythms and repetitive phrasings, recall the opening cradle songs. But even as these poems return the reader to the beginning of *Sing-Song*, the concluding lines of the last lyric, "Lie a-bed," possess an air of finality: "Never wake:— / Baby, sleep" (ll. 5–6).

While the faint intimation of mortality in "Lie a-bed" has alarmed some twentieth-century critics, it provides an instance of "the ulterior, intenser quality" that nineteenth-century readers such as Sidney Colvin esteemed in *Sing-Song*.[12] Indeed, Colvin describes the volume as "having always a music suited to baby ears, though sometimes a depth of pathos or suggestion far enough transcending baby apprehension" (23). Likewise, another of Rossetti's contemporaries observes that "her devo-

tion to the children" does not deter her "from opening now and then the
sluices of pathos and wider meanings, to flood the merry rill of *Sing-Song*
for babes."[13] Introducing this note of pathos in the third lyric of the
sequence, Rossetti reveals that maternal love, however mighty, cannot
safeguard the child from all life's hazards. Thus "My baby has a father
and a mother," which one reviewer praised as "not too wise or grave for
three years old," develops a contrast between the "Rich little baby" (l. 2)
and a "Poor little baby" (l. 5) who, having neither mother nor father, is
"Forlorn as may be" (l. 4).[14] Possessing an economic as well as an emotional resonance, the opposition between wealth and poverty distances
the threat of parental abandonment to the middle-class child.
Nevertheless, the affluent are not immune to the tragedies of life and
death in *Sing-Song*.

Whereas poems like "Love me,—I love you" figure the relationship
between mother and child as private and self-enclosed, Rossetti makes
sorrow an emotion to be shared by both parents. In the fourth lyric,
therefore, the speaker uses the possessive plural pronoun ("our" rather
than "my") to communalize her expression of grief: "Our little baby fell
asleep, / And may not wake again / For days and days, and weeks and
weeks" (ll. 1–3). As days lengthen into weeks, the mother's ambiguous
phrasing ("may not wake") becomes less an expression of uncertainty
than a statement of interdicted possibility. But taking comfort from a
belief in eternal life, she asserts that her child will "wake again, / And
come with his own pretty look, / And kiss Mamma again" (ll. 4–6).
Recalling the end of "The Convent Threshold," the anticipated kiss not
only provides an assurance of reunion in the hereafter but partakes of the
here-and-now intimacy of lyrics like "Love me,—I love you" and "My
baby has a mottled fist."

The consolatory function performed by Rossetti's singsong dirges
acknowledges death as a familiar aspect of life in the Victorian nursery.
The high rate of mortality affecting infants and toddlers meant that, in
all probability, at least one of the six children born to the average mid-
Victorian family would not survive beyond its fifth birthday.[15] In addition
to fearing and grieving the loss of a child, a mother had cause for anxiety
on her own behalf, for the maternal mortality rate remained steady at 5
per 1,000 live births until the turn of the century. Furthermore, women's
chances of hemorrhaging to death or contracting puerperal septicemia,
as high after a stillbirth as a live birth, were even higher after a miscar-
riage.[16] Yet while the number of nineteenth-century poems featuring
dead infants and mothers is thus understandable, Rossetti's precursors

offered little in the way of comfort for the aggrieved. For example, Jane and Ann Taylor's "The Poor Little Baby," published in *Rhymes for the Nursery* (1806), opens with a macabre description of an infant's interment—"Down, down, in the pit-hole poor baby is gone"—and ends with the child speaker's grim self-admonition: "And let me remember, that I too shall die, / And then in the pit-hole I also must lie."[17] In "The Little Child," on the other hand, a toddler casually remarks, "If my dear mamma were gone, / I should perish soon, and die" (3:38). "The Baby," included in *Original Poems for Infant Minds* (1804–1805), makes a similar point about the child's helplessness: "Without a mother's tender care / The little thing must die" (2:70). While the Taylors' lyrics use the prospect of a mother's demise to frighten children into obedience and gratitude, later poems such as Henry Sharpe Horsley's "The Death of a Mother," which appeared in *The Affectionate Parent's Gift, and the Good Child's Reward* (1828), rely on sentiment to achieve a similar end. By contrast, Rossetti's nursery rhymes possess remarkable restraint. Spare and subtle, they are neither "mawkish" nor "sentimental."[18]

Avoiding the moral tendentiousness of much Victorian verse, Rossetti's singsong elegies provide emotional comfort by presenting death "as one point in a larger pattern, and as a natural event."[19] Furthermore, they provide spiritual comfort by representing nature in accordance with the Tractarian principles of analogy and reserve.[20] The ulterior or sacramental significance of "Brown and furry," for example, resides in the poet's use of nature to impart the mystery of the resurrection: the lowly caterpillar may "Spin and die, / To live again a butterfly" (ll. 9–10). In "Why did baby die," on the other hand, nature supplies a tacit answer to the anguished question of infant mortality:

> Why did baby die,
> Making Father sigh,
> Mother cry?
>
> Flowers, that bloom to die,
> Make no reply
> Of "why?"
> But bow and die. (ll. 1–7)

"Spring blossoms and youth" are, as Rossetti says in "What are heavy? sea-sand and sorrow," both "frail" (l. 3). Related metonymically rather than sylleptically to youth in "Why did baby die," the unresponsive flowers reveal the natural inevitability of death. The lyric's position immediately before "If all were rain and never sun" suggests, moreover, that joy and sorrow, like rain and sun, are both necessary to life.

By the same token, the consecutive arrangement of "Hear what the mournful linnets say" and "A baby's cradle with no baby in it" puts the experience of bereavement into a broader consolatory context. In "Hear what the mournful linnets say," Rossetti takes the point of view of the parent birds to condemn the destruction of their eggs by marauding boys. More than an indictment of childish cruelties, the linnets' lament offers a means to understand the paradox of "A baby's cradle with no baby in it." The ruined nest, in other words, functions as an analogue for the empty crib. But while the first lyric addresses, albeit obliquely, a mother's sense of impotent rage and despair following the delivery of a stillborn child or the death of an infant, the second redeems the hope that has miscarried: "The sweet soul gathered home to Paradise, / The body waiting here" (ll. 3–4). Similarly, the snowdrop that the speaker of "Baby lies so fast asleep" places within the hands of the dead child, now beyond any pain that might "grieve her" (l. 6), represents hope. This hope, inspired by a belief in the resurrection, helps to assuage the mother's pain.

Rossetti's use of nature to express grief and offer religious solace lends her lyrics a succinctness that distinguishes them from contemporary works, such as Jean Ingelow's popular adult sequence, "Poems Written on the Deaths of Three Lovely Children Who Were Taken from Their Parents within a Month of One Another." Rossetti does not, however, make all comfort contingent on the prospect of paradisal reunion. The shortest lyric in *Sing-Song,* for example, delivers the orphaned child to a new mother: "Motherless baby and babyless mother, / Bring them together to love one another" (ll. 1–2). Although Hughes's illustration depicts a woman accepting her foster-child over a tiny grave, Rossetti does not specify, as Alice Meynell does in "Maternity," that the paradox of the babyless mother follows on her child's death. Indeed, in *The Face of the Deep* she argues that single women need not be excluded from the rewards of maternity, for "the childless who make themselves nursing mothers of Christ's little ones are true mothers in Israel" (*FD,* 312). In "Minnie and Mattie," therefore, "the nursing hen" (l. 13) is as true a mother to her brood of ducklings as "the mother hen" (l. 17) to her chicks. Amplifying her depiction of true motherhood in "A motherless

soft lambkin," Rossetti returns to the parable of the lost sheep used in
"The Waves of this Troublesome World" to create a spoken emblem for
juvenile as well as feminine heroism. Thus the child's rescue of the
orphaned beast doubles on Christ's redemption of the lost soul and symbolizes the woman's adoption of an orphaned baby. By mothering the
lost lamb, the speaker—child and woman—becomes a full-grown hero.

Refusing to confine her treatment of femininity to maternity, Rossetti
seeks to embrace all aspects of the lives of girls and women in *Sing-Song*.
Consequently, while pastoral lyrics like "Minnie and Mattie" and
"Dancing on the hill-tops" nostalgically celebrate the freedom of youth,
others, such as "A pocket handkerchief to hem," put work before play
and so anticipate the emphasis on duty in *Speaking Likenesses*. Using work
to distinguish children from adults, Rossetti thus depicts the women in
"Rosy maiden Winifred" and "Margaret has a milking-pail" as dairy-
maids. The allusions to the harvest in these lyrics help, moreover, to
emphasize the maturity of the maids. Arising early in the morning,
Winifred walks through a late summer landscape of ripening grain,
while Margaret meets Thomas, who "has a threshing-flail" (l. 3). The
produce of the harvest, marital as well as agricultural, Rossetti relates in
"Minnie bakes oaten cakes," for Minnie not only makes cakes and ale
but awaits her husband, Johnny, as he returns "Home from sea" (l. 4).
But although Minnie "glows like a rose" (l. 5) in anticipation of Johnny's
arrival, *Sing-Song* generally portrays wifehood as less rewarding to
women than is motherhood.

Rossetti's marital singsongs provide a critique of Victorian domestic
ideology. Restricted to home, her little wives lack full-grown experience.
Thus in "Wee wee husband" the wife demands money of her husband to
purchase comfits and honey—that is, the sweet desserts of marriage.
Because her husband has "no money" (l. 6), however, they must learn to
live without even such plain fare as milk, meat, and bread. While this
wee parable of marital economics illuminates the frustrations consequent
on the wife's financial dependence, "I have a little husband" makes the
woman's dissatisfaction a function of her emotional dependence:

I have a little husband
    And he is gone to sea,
The wind that whistle round his ship
    Fly home to me.

The winds that sigh about me
        Return again to him;
So I would fly, if only I
        Were light of limb. (ll. 1–8)

The wind aptly suggests the difference between husband and wife as
they pursue their separate existences: he whistles briskly while she sighs
sadly. Their physical distance becomes, therefore, a measure of their
emotional distance.

While the speaker's desire for flight in "I have a little husband" may
appear childish, it yet reveals a concomitant desire for the freedom and
independence of adulthood. Returning to the motif of flight in "I caught
a little ladybird," Rossetti suggests, moreover, that feminine independence would provide greater satisfaction to both husbands and wives.
Described as a "little lady wife" (l. 3), the ladybird travels, like the men in
"I have a little husband" and "Minnie bakes oaten cakes," "far away" (l.
2). Lively and elusive, she is more desirable as a playmate than the lifeless
"dolly wife" (l. 7): "She's such a senseless wooden thing / She stares the
livelong day; / Her wig of gold is stiff and cold / And cannot change to
grey" (ll. 9–12). The dolly wife, forever young and blond, and the lady
wife represent two opposing constructs of womanhood. Playing a masculine role, the girlish speaker positions herself as the ladybird's husband,
validates her own desire for freedom and experience, and rejects the ideal
of childlike femininity as embodied in the unnatural dolly wife.

Divorcing motherhood from wifehood in *Sing-Song,* Rossetti explores
the contradictions implicit in Victorian inscriptions of womanhood to
relate the totality of adult feminine experience. In so doing, she finds in
nursery rhyme a form uniquely adapted to her purposes as a woman
poet. Indeed, so thoroughly had she conquered the constraints of simplicity that she judged the volume to include, as she said, "some of my
best songs" (*FL,* 94). Willing to explore further the expressive possibilities inherent in children's verse, she moved from nursery rhyme into dramatic spectacle with "The Months: A Pageant," which, occupying a
privileged position in her adult canon, appears as the title work in *A
Pageant and Other Poems.* Hopeful as to the poem's "success as a drawing-
room acting piece" (*FL,* 96), she did not confine her ambitions in the
field of juvenile literature to verse. Setting her pen to fiction in *Speaking
Likenesses,* she returns once more to the terrain of feminine experience
examined in *Sing-Song.*

Speaking Likenesses: Tales of Feminine Forbearance

A devoted daughter, Rossetti dedicates *Speaking Likenesses* "To my dearest mother, in grateful remembrance of the stories with which she used to entertain her children."[21] Although she acknowledged her mother in near- ly all of her published works, the dedication to *Speaking Likenesses* serves as an odd introduction to a volume that features, as a narrator, an unamiable maiden aunt rather than a loving mother. Indeed, Aunt refuses to enter- tain her little listeners in either a hospitable or pleasurable manner. Ridiculing their childishness, she instead relates to them a series of stories in which her "small heroines perpetually encounter 'speaking (literally *speaking*) likenesses' or embodiments or caricatures of themselves" (Packer, ed., 101). But while Aunt, presumably a speaking likeness for her mar- ried sister, gives expression to maternal intolerance, she is also the chil- dren's secret ally against the parent whose indulgence masks tyranny, for she embodies the grown-up daughter's animus toward a beloved mother. Idealizing mothers in her stories, Aunt marginalizes and silences them. Coveting their power and prestige, she usurps their authority to ratify her own independence as a single woman. Still, while Rossetti thus reveals her ambivalence toward motherhood, she nevertheless makes maternity a potent symbol for feminine creativity.

The tensions that characterize Rossetti's treatment of mothers and daughters in *Speaking Likenesses* derive, in part, from her reliance on a rather unlikely mixture of elements drawn from the fantastic and didac- tic traditions in juvenile literature.[22] As a moral fiction, *Speaking Likenesses* resembles the tales with which Frances Rossetti had tried—and failed— to amuse her children. But even as the volume follows the pattern of instruction found in Thomas Day's *The History of Sandford and Merton* (1783–89), Maria Edgeworth's *Moral Tales* (1801), and Mary Sherwood's *The Fairchild Family* (1818–47), Rossetti conceived of her work as "a Christmas trifle, would-be in the *Alice* style with an eye to the market" (*FL*, 44). Such blatant imitation worked, however, to the book's disad- vantage with reviewers, who noted that it "would have been more origi- nal if Alice had never been to 'Wonderland.'"[23] Yet Rossetti could not have been unaware of the criticism she would court in *Speaking Likenesses,* for Colvin had followed his favorable estimate of *Sing-Song* with a com- plaint about Lewis Carroll's unoriginality in *Through the Looking-Glass* (1871). As the sequel to *Alice's Adventures in Wonderland* (1865), *Through the Looking-Glass* "has," he said, "the misfortune of all sequels—that it is not a commencement" (Colvin, 24).

If the doubly belated *Speaking Likenesses* is not a commencement, it certainly brings Carroll's work to a resounding denouement. Appropriating Carrollian adventure to moral purpose, Rossetti serves up a confection—a Christmas trifle—that derisively mocks the assumptions of didactic and fantastic fiction alike. Opposed to Carroll's "avuncular" ideal of perpetual girlhood, Rossetti creates in Aunt a narrator who, as U. C. Knoepflmacher argues, tells her listeners "stories which relentlessly discourage their potential indulgence in Alice-like fantasies."[24] Unlike Scheherazade in Rossetti's beloved *Arabian Nights,* Aunt declines to "promise first-rate wonders on . . . extremely short notice" (*SL,* 71) and insists on her prerogative "to utilize . . . a brilliant idea twice" (*SL,* 81). Provokingly uninspired as a story-teller, she attempts to impress upon her would-be Alices the moral that concludes the first and longest of her three tales: "how to bear a few trifling disappointments, or how to be obliging and good-humoured under slight annoyances" (*SL,* 49).

Of the stories told in *Speaking Likenesses,* the first is most obviously a mock-*Alice* adventure. The tale opens with Flora, who, exactly six months older than Carroll's heroine in *Through the Looking-Glass,* awakens to her mother's kiss on the morning of her eighth birthday. Describing the little girl's failure to appreciate this sign of maternal favor, Aunt makes the daughter's negligence the object of her first lesson. Speaking "from the sad knowledge of . . . older experience," she somberly tells her auditors, "To every one of you a day will most likely come when sunshine, hope, presents and pleasure will be worth nothing to you in comparison with the unattainable gift of your mother's kiss" (*SL,* 4). After this gloomy prognostication, Aunt returns to her story and recounts Flora's delight upon opening her presents. From her father, she gets a Carrollian "story-book full of pictures" (*SL,* 4). From her mother and her nurse, on the other hand, she receives a writing case and a pin cushion that, housing pen and paper, pin and needle, are emblematic of dual feminine creativity. Unwittingly slighting her mother a second time, the girl is most impressed by the gifts given by her brother and sister: a box of sugar-plums and an expensive doll that, dubbed Flora by Flora, says, "Mamma" (*SL,* 8). In addition to her other gifts, Flora's mother also gives her a party. Crowning her daughter the "queen of the feast," she asks only that the girl and her guests "be very good and happy together" (*SL,* 5). The children are, however, far from either good or happy, for they wrangle over the sugar-plums, find fault with the tea, and fall to fighting at their games. Paradoxically, Flora's punishment for having three times disesteemed her mother's generosity involves reliving experience through the looking glass. In this way the mother's birthday greeting—"I wish you many and many happy returns of the day" (*SL,* 3)—becomes the ungrateful daughter's curse.

Flora's adventures start in earnest when she leaves her tiresome companions, walks from "the sunshine into the shadow" of "the yew alley," and finds "at its furthest end . . . a door with bell and knocker, and 'Ring also' printed in black letters on a brass plate" (*SL,* 16). This marvelous beginning constitutes, as the symbol of the yew tree suggests, a prelude to sorrow. Nevertheless, Flora, having entered a realm in which looking glasses abound, initially finds the experience "quite delightful," for she is able to gratify her vanity by taking "a long look at her little self full length" (*SL,* 21). This intense narcissism leads to bitter self-knowledge when the little girl meets her alter ego. The angry birthday Queen, whose features are "reflected over and over again in five hundred mirrors," magnifies the choler that distorts "Flora's fifty million-fold face" (*SL,* 26). Reflecting the Red Queen and Queen Alice in *Through the Looking-Glass,* Rossetti's queens likewise double upon Carroll's incarnation of fury, the Queen of Hearts, in *Alice's Adventures.* This movement back through Carroll's several queens allows Rossetti, moreover, to recall the rival card players, one of whom is named Flora, in her own "Queen of Hearts," a poem written and published in 1863 before Alice first went to Wonderland. In the 50 million–fold mirrors of *Speaking Likenesses,* Rossetti makes herself not Carroll's imitator but his originator.

Using the looking-glass motif to heighten discordancy, Rossetti reflects other aspects of the world that her heroine has fled. Like Flora's mother, the yew tree chairs and tables "study everybody's convenience" (*SL,* 21), but the Queen's subjects possess an assortment of "exceptional features [that] could not but prove inconvenient":

> One boy bristled with prickly quills like a porcupine, and raised or depressed them at pleasure; but he usually kept them pointed outwards. Another instead of being rounded like most people was facetted at very sharp angles. A third caught in everything he came near, for he was hung round with hooks like fishhooks. One girl exuded a sticky fluid and came off on the fingers; another, rather smaller, was slimy and slipped through the hands. (*SL,* 28)

These inconvenient children personify all that is vicious and unpleasant: malice, anger, pain, disorder, lubricity. Crudely gendered, the boys are hurtful, and the girls are unctuous. Moreover, the sticky and slimy fluids that the girls exude on hand and finger are, like the boys' phallic quills, angles, and hooks, quite lewdly suggestive. Refusing to romanticize the innocence of the prepubescent eight-year-old, Rossetti establishes a sexual foundation for the three games played subsequently in Flora's dream. Like Carroll, Rossetti uses games to give form to her heroine's experience. But as if to prove herself more original than Carroll, she rejects cards, croquet, and chess as inadequate to her purpose. Asked to propose the first game, Flora timidly suggests *Les Grâces,* which, roundly abused as "a girl's game" (*SL,* 31), receives little support from the ungracious children. Finally, when she fails to think of something "new," the Queen interposes: "Let her alone;—who's she? It's *my* birthday, and we'll play at Hunt the Pincushion" (*SL,* 32). Since her listeners are unfamiliar with this game, Aunt condescends to outline the rules: "Select the smallest and weakest player (if possible let her be fat: a hump is best of all), chase her round and round the room, overtaking her at short intervals, and sticking pins into her here or there as it happens: repeat, till you choose to catch and swing her; which concludes the game" (*SL,* 33). The children, not surprisingly, make Flora the pin cushion. Whereas Mary Ann Kilner subjectivizes a pin cushion's experience in her moral tale *The Adventures of a Pincushion* (1780), Rossetti's heroine, playing the role of *it* in a children's game, undergoes extreme objectification. Consequently, as Aunt's shocked listeners observe, Hunt the Pincushion is "a horrid game" (*SL,* 33). In response to her nieces' protests, Aunt argues that she has "seen before now very rough cruel play, if it can be termed play" (*SL,* 33). Insisting that "Nowhere" and "Somewhere" are "not altogether unlike" (*SL,* 36), she collapses rather than maintains the distance between fantasy and reality. Thus, Hunt the Pincushion truly reflects Flora's earlier experience of Blindman's Buff and Hide and Seek.

Rossetti does not limit herself to a caricature of childish faults in *Speaking Likenesses.* Naming the children's second game after Samuel Smiles's *Self-Help* (1859), she extends her parody to the whole of Victorian society:

The boys were players, the girls were played (if I may be allowed such a phrase): all except the Queen who, being the Queen, looked on, and merely administered a slap or box on the ear now and then to some one coming handy. Hooks, as a Heavy Porter, shone in this sport; and dragged about with him a load of attached captives, all vainly struggling to unhook themselves. Angles, as an Ironer, goffered or fluted several children by sustained pressure. Quills, an Engraver, could do little more

than prick and scratch with some permanence of result. Flora falling to
the share of Angles had her torn frock pressed and plaited after quite a
novel fashion: but this was at any rate preferable to her experience as
Pincushion, and she bore it like a philosopher. (*SL*, 36–37)

In this savage satire of nineteenth-century entrepreneurship, Rossetti
creates an "analogy between sexual and social victimization of the
female" (Gilbert, 18).[25] The burlesque Queen's monstrous subjects are
not simply projections of the id and super ego but reflections of men
and women in Victoria's England as well as the boys and girls at Flora's
party. By presiding over a game from which she, like Flora's mad double, is ceremonially exempt, Victoria colludes in the subjugation of
women. When Rossetti tells her readers to "look at home" (*SL*, 36), she
implies, moreover, that the Victorian wife and mother—the queen of
domesticity—permits similar chaos to reign. As a result, home is not, as
Ruskin posits in "Of Queens' Gardens" (1865), "the place of Peace; the
shelter, not only from all injury, but from all terror, doubt, and division"
(18: 122).

Further ironizing Flora's eventual return to the safe familiarity of
"home precincts" after her experience in the "hall of misery" (*SL*, 47),
Rossetti parodies the activity of Victorian homemaking in the children's
final game. For this sport, the children leave the maternal confines of
the looking-glass parlor. Entering "a spacious playground" (*SL*, 39),
they find themselves in the world as so often described in Rossetti's religious lyrics. Indeed, the epigraph to "A Castle-Builder's World"—"The
line of confusion, and the stones of emptiness" (Isa. 34:11)—aptly mod-
ifies the structures that the children erect. Made from bricks of colored
glass, their castles resemble nothing so much as Joseph Paxton's monument to Victorian consumerism, the Crystal Palace, which held the
Great Exhibition of 1851. Despite the opulence of her surroundings,
Flora is horrified to find herself "being built in with the Queen" (*SL*,
42), who, in defiance of proverbial wisdom, begins to hurl bricks as well
as abuse at her subjects. The girl escapes, however, when the Queen
throws a huge brick at Hooks and shatters the mirrored walls of her
castle. Faced with the murderous implications of her own latent rage,
Flora severs her attachment to self and thus undergoes an experience
akin to that of the soul pierced by the "sharp two-edged sword" of
God's word (Rev. 1:16). As Rossetti says, "Life it is, not death, that thus
cleaves its way into my heart of hearts" (*FD*, 37). If, she continues, "we
[are] afraid of a dividing asunder of our very selves," we should "let fear

nerve us to endure it; for more dreadful will be the cutting asunder of the reprobate servant" (*FD*, 37).

Having survived the apocalypse of self, the regenerate Flora returns home, quietly assumes her place among her guests, and whispers an apology to her cousin Anne for having been bad-tempered. Literally as well as figuratively muted, she has learnt how to be an obliging daughter. On the other hand, her older sister, Susan, assumes the role of the absent mother. During the disastrous game of Hide and Seek, she emerges from "her hiding-place" and tries "her best to please everybody" (*SL,* 13). She picks a basket of mulberries, takes Flora and Anne for a walk, and begins to tell a story about a frog who, unwilling to admit his inability to boil a kettle, says, "I can't bear hot water" (*SL,* 15–16). After her "troubled dream" (*SL,* 48), Flora might better appreciate her sister's meaning, but Aunt's listeners do not understand the joke. In Susan's fragmented narrative, they instead hear another possibility for their own diversion.

Asked to relate the frog's adventures, Aunt unobligingly replies, "I was not there to hear Susan tell the story" (*SL,* 49). Finally agreeing "to try" (*SL,* 49), she provides a truly trying narrative, for she tells the story of Edith, who tries but fails to light the kettle for the gypsy tea that her "loving mother had planned [for] a treat" (*SL,* 52). Although Aunt draws exhaustively on folk convention to include a superabundance of talking animals, she minimizes the frog's part in the story. Moreover, unlike the animal helpers of fairy tale, the several beasts that either accompany Edith to the wood or meet her there are unable to assist her in her desire to light the kettle. Making a brief stage appearance in Edith's story, the fabled fox provides a clue to Aunt's intentions. Unable to avail himself of the luscious grapes hanging above the site that Edith's mother has chosen for the family picnic, "he shook his head, turned up his nose, shrugged his shoulders, muttered, 'They must be sour'" (*SL,* 68). Although the fruit also tempts Edith, she is too "wise" to "stand long agape after unattainable grapes" (*SL,* 57). Nevertheless, her effort to light the kettle and prove herself "as wise as her elder brother, sister, and nurse," if not also "her parents" (*SL,* 51), betokens a comparable presumption.

Ironically, while Edith's unhelpful animal helpers—speaking likenesses for Aunt's many bothersome nieces—reify childish incompetence, they also reflect the absent-minded preoccupation of the mother who is deaf to her daughter's demands. Contained within the outer margins of the central story, the conflict between Edith and her doting, albeit inattentive, mother finds form in the little girl's relationship with two other adult female figures—cook and nurse—who perform their mistress's will. At the beginning of Aunt's story, Edith goes into the kitchen and attempts "to talk, whilst cook, with a good-natured red face, made her an occasional random answer, right or wrong as it happened" (*SL,* 53). Indeed, cook's responses answer as little to Edith's questions as the advice she later receives from a pair of pigeons. When the birds, speaking "like two gurgling bottles," tell her to flee the scene of her failure, she says, "I wish you'd advise something sensible, instead of telling me to fly without wings" (*SL,* 63). At the same time, the pigeons' gurgling speech recalls the sound of Edith's voice when she quietly volunteers to light the fire. Distracted, "cook heard nothing beyond the child's voice saying something or other of no consequence" (*SL,* 55).

Cook's negligence notwithstanding, Edith is a pint-sized Prometheus. Surreptitiously taking a box of matches, she covets the maternal knowledge and power that fire represents. Although Rossetti thus uses a standard trope of the cautionary tale, her heroine does not, as in Ann Taylor's "Playing with Fire," suffer horrid disfigurement. Nor is she reduced in one spectacular blaze to a pile of ashes like the disobedient daughter of Heinrich Hoffman's "The Dreadful Story about Harriet and the Matches," included in *The English Struwwelpeter* (1848). Instead, the fire that the girl lights with her last match goes out. At this point, nurse appears, heralding the imminent arrival of Edith's "relations, friends, and other natural enemies" (*SL,* 60). A manifestation of the adversarial mother, nurse tacitly rebukes the ill-prepared girl, for she comes bearing "a box of lucifers in one hand, two fire-wheels in the other, and half-a-dozen newspapers under her arm" (*SL,* 69). Moreover, nurse crowns Edith's disgrace by telling her of the disruption her absence has caused the household. Sent indoors to her mother, the girl finds herself in metaphoric hot water at the end of Aunt's story.

Although Aunt is, like Edith's nurse, an enemy to childhood, she also sympathizes, as a daughter, with her nieces' desire for independence. Thus her next story, which begins on Christmas Eve in a shop tended by the heroine's grandmother, provides a fulfilling pendant to Edith's frustrating adventure. Indeed, Aunt's description of Dame Margaret's shop as the point of origin for the games, gifts, and dolls hitherto mentioned in *Speaking Likenesses* forges an oblique connection between her successive stories. Her heroine, a child of working-class diligence rather than middle-class indulgence, has no leisure to play in this childish vanity fair, however, for unlike Edith and Flora, she does not have a mother. But even though Aunt, at the beginning of her first story, characterizes a mother's death as a daughter's profoundest misfortune, Maggie's orphanhood helps her to succeed insofar as it allows her to overcome her impotence as a daughter and to advance to her mother's place. A miniature version of Dame Margaret, Maggie is, furthermore, a regenerate Red Riding Hood, who, offering to deliver the parcels that the doctor's heedless daughters have left behind in the shop, travels both away from and back toward her grandmother. Setting forth into the darkening day, she abides by her promise "to make great haste" (*SL*, 74) and so succeeds where the folk-tale heroine fails.

Recapitulating the tripartite movement of the volume as a whole, Rossetti triples the wolfish temptations that her heroine must face before she reaches the doctor's house. After an overly hasty beginning that ends with a punitive fall on the ice, Maggie encounters her first temptation to loiter in a group of children, surrounded by barking dogs, who appeal to her desire for play. Recollecting her promise, she hurries away from the sportive children—Flora's erstwhile companions—and next meets a boy with a "wide mouth . . . full of teeth and tusks" (*SL*, 85). This boy, shadowed by "a fat tabby cat, carrying in her mouth a tabby kitten" (*SL*, 84), reifies the hunger that so nearly tempts her to eat the chocolate meant for the doctor's daughters. Indeed, just as the mother cat seems ambivalently poised between devouring and nurturing her offspring, Maggie vacillates between gratifying her hunger and adhering to the purpose of her journey. Conquering her unreasoning appetite, she moves on to find a "tempting group" (*SL*, 88) of sleepers near a fire that attracts a number of birds. Despite her weariness, the girl proceeds with her journey.

Here Aunt interrupts herself to remark that Maggie, if she had stopped to sleep, would have brought the story to "an abrupt end" (*SL*, 87). More than a chilling reminder of the dangers of winter weather, Aunt's comment returns her listeners to the abrupt and unceremonious conclusion of the previous story. In effect, Maggie's tale symbolically redeems and completes Edith's abortive action. Persevering to arrive at the doctor's house "wide awake and on tiptoe with enchanting expectation," Maggie is neither fed nor warmed nor entertained nor given "a glimpse of the Christmas tree" (*SL*, 91). She accomplishes all her desires on the homeward journey, however. Revisiting the sites of her temptation, she meets a half-frozen wood pigeon, a famished kitten, and an abandoned puppy. While these infantile and commonplace editions of Edith's cockatoo, Persian cat, and Newfoundland dog represent remnants of the girl's desire for warmth, food, and companionship, they have themselves valid claims on the child's attention. Adopting these animals, Maggie becomes, like the speaker of "A motherless soft lambkin," a full-grown hero. Reaching home as the northern lights transform the landscape into a spectacle more brilliant than any illuminated Christmas tree, Maggie receives the necessary creature comforts from her grandmother and, in turn, gives them to her new and needy foster children. In Aunt's final story, therefore, the fruit of feminine forbearance is not, as in so many fairy tales, marriage but motherhood.

Concluding her three stories with the narrative of the daughter's triumph, Aunt responds not merely to her listeners' request for a winter tale but to their growth over the course of three days. Named after the would-be poet of Rossetti's juvenile novella, Maude best exemplifies the progress made by the children under Aunt's tutelage. Compelling her nieces to learn doubly the lesson of feminine forbearance, Rossetti's tasking narrator makes her tales contingent on labor. On the first day, Maude's sulky expression registers her resistance to Aunt's system and provokes a chiding rebuke: "Put away your pout and pull out your needle" (*SL,* 1). Once satisfied that the child has obeyed, Aunt announces, "Now I start my knitting and my story together" (*SL,* 2). By the second day, however, Maude has completed her darning. Ordered to sew for others rather than herself, she expostulates: "But we got through our work yesterday" (*SL,* 50). By way of response, Aunt reproves the girl for her selfishness: "Very well, Maude, as you like: only no help no story. I have too many poor friends ever to get through *my* work. However, as I see thimbles coming out, I conclude you choose story and labour" (*SL,* 50). Since "whoso clothes the poor, weaves for himself (still more obviously weaves for *herself*) a white garment" (*FD,* 138), Aunt's demands on the children serve their spiritual needs. However coercive, her arguments are effective, for Maude complies and, on the third day, makes an effort to be obliging. Although she receives a reprimand for whispering to Jane and for taking a defensive tone in revealing the purport of their murmured conference, she addresses her elder with affection, articulates the children's desire for another story, and utters no complaint when Aunt issues the inevitable order to work.

In *Speaking Likenesses* the relationship between sewing and storytelling serves an esthetic as well as a moral function. Associating industrious and imaginative creativity, manual and oral productivity, textile and textual materiality, Aunt not only insists on feminine cooperation but makes needlework a metonym for narrative. In other words, her stories are yarns. Indeed, just as she and the children sew the breadths of cloth "together, three and three" (*SL,* 50), Rossetti runs her three tales together within a three-part metafictional framework. When the irrepressible Maude asks why Edith hangs her kettle upon a tripod, Aunt's answer illuminates further the rationale for the volume's tripartite design: "Three sticks, Maude, are the fewest that can stand up firmly by themselves; two would tumble down, and four are not wanted" (*SL,* 57). While each tale within Rossetti's "narrative tripod" helps "to prop up the whole" (Knoepflmacher, 323), the frame story features a woman and five girls who work together, three and three, to augment the productivity of the whole. Even as the children's questions and comments form part of the fabric of Aunt's stories, their contributions to her charity basket enlarge the scope of the whole and create a seamless link between domestic and social service.

Engaged in the relief of the poor and the destitute, Rossetti's spinster maidens, old and young, conform to the model of maternity advanced in the last of Aunt's tales. Reversing the order of Catherine's experience in "Commonplace," they succeed to a "motherly position" by emulating "the motherly instinct of self-postponement" (*CSS,* 18). But whereas "postponement means deferment in time" or "personal deference or subordination," Rossetti's ideal of maternal self-postponement paradoxically allows women, single as well as married, to obtain gratification in the here and now as well as the hereafter.[26] Raising maternal self-postponement to an art in storytelling and sewing, *Speaking Likenesses* valorizes feminine creativity over female procreativity and, in this way, establishes the unwed daughter's claim to self-worth.

Chapter Five

"What Doth Remain": The Impetus to Devotion in the Sonnets

Having served her apprenticeship to rhyme in the sonnet, Rossetti returns to explore the formal and conceptual possibilities of this most rigorous and concentrated of lyric genres in her final volumes of verse. Published in 1881, *A Pageant and Other Poems* features, in addition to other work, a total of 56 sonnets. Of these, all but 14 appear in two major sequences, "Monna Innominata: A Sonnet of Sonnets" and "Later Life: A Double Sonnet of Sonnets." Twelve years later Rossetti released *Verses*, which, with more than 60 sonnets, contained the largest number of any previous volume. In these works she uses the religious sonnet to express the soul's devotion to self.

Whereas Rossetti's first experiments in the genre reveal the problems of accommodating the sonnet to the demands of feminine subjectivity, her mature poems assimilate fixed form to the flux and reflux of fluid consciousness. Frequently arranging her sonnets in sequences, she fiercely defended the structural integrity of the interlocking lyrics to those who sought permission to reprint them. "I do not mind what piece you select," she told one anthologist, "subject only to your taking any piece in question *in its entirety*; and my wish includes your *not* choosing an independent poem which forms part of a series or group. . . . Such compound work has a connection (very often) which is of interest to the author and which an editor gains nothing by discarding" (Packer, ed., 154–55n3). Within such sequences as "Monna Innominata" and "Later Life," each sonnet not only dramatizes a discrete moment of cognitive or emotive awareness but also contributes to the dynamic of the whole. Shaping the sonnet sequence to the structure of inwardness, Rossetti creates what Gabriel Rossetti, describing Dante's *La Vita Nuova,* called an "autopsychology."[1] Indeed, each successive sequence presents a study of the soul more comprehensive than the last. Striving toward a universalized conception of self, Rossetti finds in the compound lyric a way to connect the voice of individual experience to a vision of communal identity, for just as each independent poem forms part of a series or group, each independent person shares in the life of the spirit.

Early Sonnets: Preparing the Soul's Canvas

Quickly mastering the technical challenges posed by the sonnet, Rossetti included several of her *bouts-rimés* in *Maude*. By 1850, moreover, she had begun using the sonnet as a means to articulate the soul's yearning for Christ. In this respect, "What is it Jesus saith unto the soul?" acts as an indicator of change and continuity in Rossetti's career, for she resurrected and revised the poem, originally placed at the end of *Maude,* for inclusion in *Time Flies* and *Verses.* But while "What is it Jesus saith unto the soul?" reveals the relative ease with which the poet harnessed the exigencies of form and content to the exercise of devotion, other early poems demonstrate the difficulties that she encountered in her attempt to adapt the sonnet's generic protocols to the prerogatives of feminine self-expression. Nevertheless, as experiments in voice and point of view, such lyrics as "Remember," "Dead before Death," and "In an Artist's Studio" brilliantly communicate the sonnet's estranging impact on feminine consciousness and attest to the need for a superior authority to preserve a female speaker against literary and cultural injunctions "to suffer, and be still."[2]

"Remember" and "After Death," both written in 1849, feature female speakers whose efforts at self-memorialization are fraught by contradiction. But insofar as the two sonnets, published side by side in *Goblin Market and Other Poems,* constitute a rudimentary sequence chronicling two consecutive moments of awareness, they anticipate the compound works of later years. Tacitly affirming the continuance of consciousness beyond the grave, "After Death" quite logically follows the prophetic glimpse of the afterlife of subjectivity found in "Remember":

> Remember me when I am gone away,
>> Gone far away into the silent land;
>> When you can no more hold me by the hand,
> Nor I half turn to go yet turning stay.
> Remember me when no more day by day
>> You tell me of our future that you planned:
>> Only remember me; you understand

It will be late to counsel then or pray.
Yet if you should forget me for a while
    And afterwards remember, do not grieve:
    For if the darkness and corruption leave
    A vestige of the thoughts that once I had,
Better by far you should forget and smile
    Than that you should remember and be sad. (ll. 1–14)

Poised between going and staying, between life and death, the speaker inhabits a subject position that is rife with indeterminacy. The prospect of separation that serves conventionally to inspire the Petrarchan poet to love's immortalization causes anxiety in the female speaker who, imagining her death, proleptically translates her presence into absence. Framing herself as the object of memory rather than desire, she envisions a "future" quite different from the one her lover has "planned" and posits remembrance as a way to "hold" onto love and defy death. In the sestet, however, the ambiguity that vexes the sonnet becomes more pronounced, for the speaker qualifies and relinquishes her request for remembrance. Although the question of whether death will "leave" some kind of vestigial or trace awareness to the speaker remains unresolved, she gives her suitor leave to find happiness with another. In so doing, she takes absolute and final leave of life.

Death, whether imagined or realized, admits the possibility of feminine self-expression in "Remember" and "After Death." In "Dead before Death" and "In an Artist's Studio," on the other hand, Rossetti explores the circumstances leading to the cancellation of vital awareness in women. In "Dead before Death," for example, she takes a point of view external to the subject who has "Grown hard and stubborn in the ancient mould, / Grown rigid in the sham of lifelong lies" (ll. 5–6). Rossetti's diction hints at a key contradiction, for the woman's growth implies death rather than life. Indeed, her "stiffened smiling lips and cold calm eyes" (l. 2) suggest rigor mortis. Concerned to examine the reasons for such a "changed" (ll. 1, 3) state of being, the poet relies on the first-person plural point of view to maintain a subject position amenable to an understanding of buried consciousness. In the process she also invites readers to participate directly in the vision that shapes the sonnet. "We" assume the role of sympathetic observers who once "hoped for better things" (l. 7). Reiterating the word *lost* six times in the sestet of the sonnet, the composite speaker notes, however, that the woman, like "the blossom that no fruitage bore," has "fallen" (l. 9). A hardened sinner and a lost soul, she has so far forgotten self as to contribute to her own objectification. In other words, her outward obduracy manifests an inward paralysis.

In "In an Artist's Studio" and "A Study (A Soul)," which, like "Dead before Death," were written in 1854, Rossetti once more treats feminine interiority from a perspective outside the self. Although the poet chose not to publish either during her lifetime, both are beautifully conceived and executed experiments in point of view. A third-person lyric, "A Study" personifies the soul as a woman who "stands as pale as Parian statues" (l. 1). As the end of the sonnet makes clear, the woman's statuesque pallor reifies her strength of spirit: "She stands there patient, nerved with inner might, / Indomitable in her feebleness, / Her face and will athirst against the light" (ll. 12–14). But while "A Study" positively reinscribes the stillness of the "fallen woman" in "Dead before Death," Rossetti's use of sculptural metaphors to objectify inward states yet denies the soul the likelihood of vital change or progress. Indeed, as "In an Artist's Studio" devastatingly reveals, art effectively eradicates feminine subjectivity.

During the 1850s Elizabeth Siddall's face came to epitomize the ideal of Pre-Raphaelite beauty. Drawing on Gabriel's obsession with his favorite model for "In an Artist's Studio," Rossetti constructs a critique of a consuming masculine subjectivity that projects its own desires upon an idealized other. Again relying on the sympathetic detachment of the first-person plural, she shows, moreover, that the woman's beatific translation into art has pathetic consequences for both model and painter:

> One face looks out from all his canvasses,
>   One selfsame figure sits or walks or leans;
>   We found her hidden just behind those screens,
> That mirror gave back all her loveliness.
> A queen in opal or in ruby dress,
>   A nameless girl in freshest summer greens,
>   A saint, an angel;—every canvass means
> The same one meaning, neither more nor less.
> He feeds upon her face by day and night,
>   And she with true kind eyes looks back on him
> Fair as the moon and joyful as the light:

Not wan with waiting, not with sorrow dim;
Not as she is, but was when hope shone bright;
Not as she is, but as she fills his dream. (ll. 1–14)

Ending the sonnet on the jangling note of imperfect rhyme, Rossetti signals the discord between the artist's luminous "dream" and the woman's
"dim" reality. Art, contradicting the effects of time and change, freezes
the woman into an ideal presence that, as in Robert Browning's "My
Last Duchess," necessitates her real absence. Consequently, the studio is,
despite the proliferation of canvases, eerily empty. Indeed, while the
demonstrative phrasings—"those screens" and "that mirror"—point
emphatically at objects that both conceal and reveal the model's image,
the speaker cannot point to the woman herself. Painting after painting
depicts the "selfsame figure," but none reproduces the real or hidden
self—the woman "as she is." Because her portrait, however lifelike, falsi-
fies the truth, the painter, enamored of an image "with true kind eyes,"
fails of the reciprocity for which he hungers. Self-deceived, he, too, is a
victim of art.

In her early sonnets Rossetti explores feminine inwardness from a variety of peripheral vantage points. Free from egocentrism, her sonnets possess an oddly dispassionate tone. Nevertheless, the voice of the objective
observer allows Rossetti to circumvent, in part, generic conventions that
polarize male and female into fixed positions as subject and object. Often,
however, as in "In an Artist's Studio," she is less concerned with feminine
selfhood than with its erasure. Indeed, the faint imprints of residual
awareness and the lingering traces of former existence that pervade her
lyrics suggest the very elusiveness of the female subject. Thus, while she
deftly manipulates point of view to communicate women's experience of
estrangement, she rarely appropriates the lyric "I" to the purposes of feminine self-expression. With "Monna Innominata," however, Rossetti not
merely empowers the woman as speaker but envisions her as a poet. In
the process, she creates her first full-scale autopsychology.

The Amatory Sequence: Renaissance Iconology and Biblical Typology

"Monna Innominata: A Sonnet of Sonnets," a compound work of both
prose and verse, functions as the centerpiece of *A Pageant and Other
Poems.* Using the structure of the sonnet to govern the sequence's

arrangement, Rossetti engages in "a radical questioning" of the formal and conceptual conventions specific to the genre.[3] This interrogation, evident in the variety of rhyme schemes appropriated for use in her 14 sonnets, involves an effort to redeem fixed form to the nuances of feminine voice and feeling. Rossetti seeks not only a female voice to authenticate women's experience of love, however, but also an indisputable authority to legitimize feminine subjectivity. She therefore relies on scriptural authority to counter the masculine literary tradition militating against the innominate poet's putative existence. But while the concept of Christian selfhood validates feminine selfhood, it also makes the material fact of sexual difference irrelevant and so renders the premises for the sequence obsolete. Consequently, although "Monna Innominata" establishes Rossetti's resistance to masculine hegemony in the amatory sonnet, the sequence signals a major shift in the poet's oeuvre as she moves from secular to devotional subjects, from death as an answer to the problem of carnal love to life as a necessary prelude to the consummation of spiritual love, and from the concept of the self bound in time to one of the self oriented to eternity.

Like the Italian epigraphs that head each of Rossetti's 14 sonnets, the note that prefaces the sequence functions as a reminder of the traditions interrogated in the course of the speaker's self-exposition. Yet William Rossetti, calling "the introductory prose-note a blind interposed to draw off attention from the writer in her proper person" (*PW,* 462), tacitly ignored the challenge posed to Renaissance inscriptions of femininity and virtually authorized the sequence's later reception as part of "the Cayley cycle."[4] Whether Rossetti took her inspiration for the sequence from her love for a middle-aged Dante scholar is, however, somewhat beside the point, for the preface, which she described as a "semi-historical argument . . . full of poetic suggestiveness" (*FL,* 98), clearly situates the series in the context of literary (rather than personal) history. Establishing the need for as well as the plausibility of a female sonneteer, the preface anticipates the dramatization of feminine subjectivity in the sequence itself.

Comprised of three paragraphs, the preface concentrates on three moments in the development of the love lyric. First, Rossetti isolates Beatrice and Laura as the archetypal objects of amatory quest. Then, moving backward to the beginning of the thirteenth century, she speculates that the muses who inspired the early Italian lyricists to verse were themselves capable poets. Finally, moving forward to nineteenth-century England, she cites her own immediate predecessor, Elizabeth Barrett

Browning, as the female sonneteer par excellence. Interested in the conventions affecting the representation of women in the sonnet, Rossetti
uses the preface to identify a spatial and temporal position from which to
admit a revision of traditional iconology:

> Beatrice, immortalized by "altissimo poeta . . . cotanto amante"; Laura,
> celebrated by a great tho' an inferior bard,—have alike paid the excep-
> tional penalty of exceptional honour, and have come down to us resplen-
> dent with charms, but (at least, to my apprehension) scant of
> attractiveness.
>
> These heroines of world-wide fame were preceded by a bevy of
> unnamed ladies "donne innominate" sung by a school of less conspicuous
> poets; and in that land and that period which gave simultaneous birth to
> Catholics, to Albigenses, and to Troubadours, one can imagine many a
> lady as sharing her lover's poetic aptitude, while the barrier between
> them might be one held sacred by both, yet not such as to render mutual
> love incompatible with mutual honour.
>
> Had such a lady spoken for herself, the portrait left us might have
> appeared more tender, if less dignified, than any drawn even by a devoted
> friend. Or had the Great Poetess of our own day and nation only been
> unhappy instead of happy, her circumstances would have invited her to
> bequeath to us, in lieu of the "Portuguese Sonnets," an inimitable "donna
> innominata" drawn not from fancy but from feeling, and worthy to occu-
> py a niche beside Beatrice and Laura. (*CP,* 2:86)

The modestly parenthetical but no less intrusive "apprehension" of the
nineteenth-century woman poet begins to organize the sequence's guiding principles by discriminating "charms" from "attractiveness." In so
doing, Rossetti forces a distinction between women as written and
women as read. In fact, she implies that Beatrice and Laura's desirability
as constituted by male writers—Dante and Petrarch—is the measure of
their undesirability for female readers. Subordinating charms to attractiveness, she repudiates these "exceptional" figures in favor of their
anonymous precursors.

Insofar as the preface's entrenchment in metaphors of portraiture and
sculpture reveals the power of Renaissance iconology to enthrall the
Victorian woman poet, "tradition writes her perhaps as much as she
rewrites tradition."[5] To argue, though, as Margaret Homans has, that
the preface "ends by turning th[e] speaking woman back into the stone
from which Rossetti would wish to redeem her" (1985, 575) is to reach
a premature conclusion. As a beginning rather than an ending, the pref-

ace serves to disturb sonnet conventions by using a female reader's point of view to test the psychological validity of Renaissance iconology. Perceiving a disparity between traditional modes of representation and representative feminine experience, Rossetti, as reader, asserts her critical subjectivity. Because her semi-historical argument draws attention to the fanciful conditions of the poem's production, however, it also reveals the instability of its premises and therefore heightens the problems of a traditional poetics of desire for the woman poet. Forwarded tentatively, formulated elliptically, and phrased conditionally, the preface's postulates constantly jeopardize the very project on which the poet wishes to embark.

By framing "Monna Innominata" as the utterance of a pre-Petrarchan lady, Rossetti uses myth to empower her revisionism. Situating her sequence in a moment of literary prehistory, she takes advantage of the novelty of emergent conventions to furnish the tenderness that Beatrice and Laura, for all their dignity, lack. But while the preface thus occludes later difficulties posed by sixteenth-century encrustations of the visual trope, the fictive lady's early Italian contemporaries had already established charm as a causal basis for love. Anthologized in D. G. Rossetti's *Dante and His Circle* (1874), originally *The Early Italian Poets* (1861), Mazzeo di Ricco's "He solicits his Lady's Pity" demonstrates how feminine beauty visually elicits and sustains masculine desire:

> Lady, though I do love past utterance,
>> Let it not seem amiss,
>> Neither rebuke thou the enamoured eyes.
> Look thou thyself on thine own countenance,
>> From that charm unto this,
>> All thy perfections of sufficiencies. (D. G. Rossetti 1911, 446)

The lady, as pitiless as she is beautiful, rejects the poet's appeal, for her heart is like ice, which, "when it is frozen hard, / May have no further hope / That it should ever become snow again" (D. G. Rossetti 1911, 446). But while the poet is unable to consummate his desire, he finds a compensatory satisfaction in the composition of verse and the creation of art. Thus, Jacopo da Lentino, another pre-Petrarchan poet included in *Dante and His Circle,* writes two canzonette, "Of his Lady, and of her Portrait" and "Of his Lady, and of his making her Likeness," which enshrine the woman's image in art. The lady's intractability, however, even as it provides an additional impetus for both desire and poetry, licenses the poet's contempt. Writing more than three centuries later, Edmund Spenser recognizes in *Amoretti,* for example, "that fairest images / Of hardest marble are of purpose made, / For that they should endure through many ages" (51.1–3). Nevertheless, he abuses his beloved as "no woman, but a senseless stone" (54.14). Objectified, reviled, and maligned, the charming woman pays dearly for inspiring the poet's admiration.

Whereas the Renaissance sonneteer lavishes "exceptional honour" upon his inamorata only to exact an "exceptional penalty," Rossetti holds that the barrier between the lover and his lady need not "render mutual love incompatible with mutual honour." Thus her speaker seeks "to persuade" her beloved "not . . . toward seduction but toward understanding."[6] Indeed, insofar as Rossetti opposes the exaltation of a passion that is both unilateral and adulterous, "Monna Innominata" resembles Barrett Browning's *Sonnets from the Portuguese* (1850), which, preceding such works as George Meredith's *Modern Love* (1862) and D. G. Rossetti's *The House of Life* (1870–81), inaugurated the nineteenth-century revival of the amatory sequence. Alluding to Barrett Browning in the preface, Rossetti also imitates her late contemporary by giving to her sequence a title that suggests a translation.[7] In other words, both poets acknowledge the unconventionality of the female sonneteer by constructing the expression of feminine desire as essentially foreign. But while Barrett Browning, like Rossetti, stipulates equality in love and art as the ideal for amatory lyricism, her sequence, unlike "Monna Innominata," ends with the requital of desire.

Although Rossetti's work functions as an alternative rather than a corrective to *Sonnets from the Portuguese,* critics have sometimes construed her prefatory remarks as a derogation of Barrett Browning's achievement.[8] For instance, Thomas Hall Caine, in his 1881 review of *A Pageant and Other Poems,* took issue with the preface to defend *Sonnets from the Portuguese* on the grounds that "the brighter side of life has its appeal for the imagination and its profound response in the affections."[9] Frustrated at being misunderstood, Rossetti told Gabriel, "Surely not only what I meant to say but what I do say is, not that the Lady of those sonnets is surpassable, but that a 'Donna innominata' by the same hand might well have been unsurpassable. The Lady in question, as she actually stands, I was not regarding as an 'innominata' at all,—because the latter type, according to the traditional figures I had in view, is surrounded by unlike circumstances" (*FL,* 98). Inasmuch as Rossetti conflates the poet and the persona of *Sonnets from the Portuguese* in her references to the "Lady," she makes Barrett Browning's courtship and marriage the basis for disqualifying her speaker as an *innominata*. Because *Sonnets from the Portuguese*—the product of experiential "feeling" rather than imaginative "fancy"—reaches a "happy" consummation, it represents an extreme departure from Renaissance models. In "Monna Innominata," on the other hand, Rossetti uses poetic "fancy" to valorize feminine "feeling," predicates her speaker's "unhappy" situation on circumstances conventional to the sonnet, and enacts a failure to ratify desire in marriage.

In *The Face of the Deep* Rossetti observes that "many women attain their heart's desire: many attain it not. Yet," she continues, "are these latter no losers if they exchange desire for aspiration" (*FD*, 312). Exchanging charm for attractiveness, desire for aspiration, she ultimately looks to the Bible rather than the Renaissance sonnet to authorize feminine self-consciousness in "Monna Innominata." Widening the amatory context to include sacred as well as secular texts, "Rossetti is concerned not so much to render a hitherto untold love story as to demonstrate that the same old story is transcended by its incorporation into the 'new' story of Christian scripture" (Rosenblum 1986, 204). More precisely, she transcends an amatory ideology inimical to feminine self-expression by activating a corrective typology. Invoking Eve, Lot's wife, and Esther in the second sonnet quatrain and developing each allusion at greater length, Rossetti relies on the Bible not only to "intensify the struggle" of a "soul in conflict" but to plot three stages in the female persona's progress toward self-realization.[10] Modeling her *innominata* on Old Testament types rather than Beatrice and Laura, she draws on precedents for women's desire and aspiration that are absent from the Renaissance sonnet. Thus, Eve and Lot's wife, contrary to the conventions of amatory lyricism, conform to the type of the desiring woman. According to Rossetti, they also "suggest Curiosity as a feminine weak point inviting temptation, and doubly likely to facilitate a fall when to indulge it woman affects independence" (*FD*, 520). Esther, on the other hand, epitomizes the desirable woman. Ironically, since she also demonstrates how desire can be transcended, she becomes a prototype for the woman who renounces desire. This type is perfected in the *innominata*, who, unlike her biblical antecedents, remains unmarried. The last six sonnets depart from these types once established, for the *innominata* must herself come to terms with her newly integrated persona.

The first four poems, which function as the opening quatrain in Rossetti's "Sonnet of Sonnets," contain only one explicit reference to the

Bible. The allusion to Ecclesiastes 1:9 that concludes sonnet 3—"there be nothing new beneath the sun" (3.14)—is important for two reasons: it ironizes the poet's attempt to renovate the amatory sonnet for a female speaker and anticipates the *innominata*'s effort to model her relationship with the beloved on Eve's relationship with Adam. Ironically, while Milton was an author whom Rossetti could "not warm towards, even let alone all theological questions," the dynamic of sonnet 5 recalls his ideal of paradisal order between the sexes: "He for God only, she for God in him" (*Paradise Lost,* 4.299).[11] Thus, the *innominata,* having commended her beloved to God's loyal service, pledges fealty to man:

> So much for you; but what for me, dear friend?
>   To love you without stint and all I can
> Today, tomorrow, world without an end;
>   To love you much and yet to love you more,
>   As Jordan at his flood sweeps either shore;
> Since woman is the helpmeet made for man. (5.9–14)

Alluding to the same text (Gen. 2:18) that informs "A Helpmeet for Him," first published in *New and Old* (1888), the *innominata* claims a prelapsarian authority for her devotion. As the inhabitant of a postlapsarian universe, however, the speaker resembles less Eve before than after the fall.

For Rossetti, desire and curiosity are two sides of the same coin. Having indulged curiosity, Eve "received as part of her sentence 'desire': the assigned object of her desire being such that satisfaction must depend not on herself but on one stronger than she, who might grant or might deny" (*FD,* 312). Laboring under the full weight of the penalty levied on "the first and typical woman" (*LS,* 17), the *innominata* devotes herself unstintingly to the beloved, whom she calls "More than myself myself" (5.2). Rossetti affirms that "all reciprocal human love worthy of the name . . . is so far selfless as to be only one harmonious part of a better whole" and "is faithful, fitting into nothing except its own other self"; but "unless it sets Christ before us at least as in a glass darkly, it were good for it not to have been born" (*TF,* 132). While reciprocated human love enables the subsistence of self in a better whole, it also invites a confusion of priorities. In this light, the *innominata*'s dedication to the beloved, though based on biblical precedent, threatens to interfere with her personal obligation to God.

Rossetti's conservatism notwithstanding, she does not ratify woman's exclusive commitment to God in man. At the beginning of the next sonnet, therefore, she recalls the *innominata* to divine priorities. Responding to a traditional lover's complaint, the speaker acknowledges the hazards of reckless desire in her reference to Lot's wife (Gen. 19:26):

> Trust me, I have not earned your dear rebuke,
>> I love, as you would have me, God the most;
>> Would lose not Him, but you, must one be lost,
> Nor with Lot's wife cast back a faithless look
> Unready to forego what I forsook. (6.1–5)

Unable to reconcile action to conviction, Lot's wife is the model of failed renunciation and the exemplar of infirm faith. Moreover, through the serendipity of anagram, Lot's wife becomes the paradigmatic lost soul, wooed by the temptations of the world. Betrayed by curiosity, she forfeits God and self. Given Rossetti's distrust of worldliness, the *innominata*'s earlier compliment to the beloved as her "world of all the men / This wide world holds" (1.7–8) suggests that her desire approximates that of Lot's wife. But while sonnet 6 foreshadows the relinquishment of desire in the six sonnets that conclude the series, the speaker does not yet surrender her love. Nevertheless, her acknowledgment of love's risk moves her one step closer to regenerate self-consciousness.

While the conventional sonneteer devises elaborate poetic conceits to overcome the obstacle to union, the *innominata* quotes scripture (Song of Sol. 8:6) to express her faith in love: "I find comfort in his Book, who saith, / Tho' jealousy be as cruel as the grave, / And death be strong, yet love is strong as death" (7.12–14). Approaching the *volta* or turn of the sequence, she returns to the Bible to find comfort in the narrative of Esther's triumph (Esth. 4:16–5:2):

> "I, if I perish, perish"—Esther spake:
>> And bride of life or death she made her fair
>> In all the lustre of her perfumed hair
> And smiles that kindle longing but to slake.
> She put on pomp of loveliness, to take
>> Her husband thro' his eyes at unaware;
>> She spread abroad her beauty for a snare,

Harmless as doves and subtle as a snake.
   She trapped him with one mesh of silken hair,
      She vanquished him by wisdom of her wit,
         And built her people's house that it should stand:—
         If I might take my life so in my hand,
   And for my love to Love put up my prayer,
   And for love's sake by Love be granted it! (8.1–14)

This sonnet, according to Antony Harrison, "is perhaps the most per-plexing" of the series because it witnesses Esther's transformation into "a morally equivocal figure" who, instead of functioning as "a prototype of Christ," reifies the "false values" of amatory ideology (1988, 180–81). Several of Rossetti's poems, however, including "A Royal Princess" and "Advent Sunday," present Esther as a salutary model for feminine action. In *The Face of the Deep,* moreover, she argues that Esther, "by a conde-scension of grace," illustrates how "'the weakness of God' stands forth as 'stronger than men'" (*FD,* 409). In addition, Esther's succession of Vashti shows how love's "perpetual reality" succeeds "the hollow semblance or the temporary endowment . . . believed in and preferred" on earth (*FD,* 40) and how "the Church looks onward, upward, to the moment of sit-ting down with her Divine King and Spouse in His Throne" (*FD,* 434). Likewise, in sonnet 8, the narrative of Esther's triumph, while it clearly reveals the *innominata*'s longing for sexual power and fulfillment, pos-sesses an ulterior spiritual significance.

In a movement unprecedented in the sequence and seemingly pro-scribed by the preface, sonnet 8 focuses on Esther's charms. Relying on images that appeal vividly to the senses of smell (Esther's "perfumed hair"), touch (her "silken hair"), and sight (the "lustre" of her hair), Rossetti uses a standard trope of amatory verse. Her highly eroticized rendering of Esther's hair recalls, for instance, the opening of Fazio Degli Uberti's canzone, "His portrait of his Lady, Angiola of Verona": "I look at the crisp golden-threaded hair / Whereof, to thrall my heart, Love twists a net" (D. G. Rossetti 1911, 488). A staple of English as well as Italian verse, the trope also informs such works as Spenser's *Amoretti* (sonnet 37), Daniel's *Delia* (sonnet 14), and Barnabe Barnes's *Parthenophil and Parthenophe* (sonnet 68). At the same time, the winsome Esther has analogues in those of Rossetti's religious sonnets that rein-scribe amatory convention to reveal the apocalyptic consequences of sin-ful desire. "The World," published in *Goblin Market and Other Poems,* is exemplary. Personified as a woman, the world appears "soft, exceeding fair" (l. 1) but is actually "Loathsome and foul with hideous leprosy / And subtle serpents gliding in her hair" (ll. 3–4). Similarly, in "Babylon the Great," included in *Verses,* Rossetti feminizes the world and issues a warning "Lest she should mesh thee in her wanton hair" (l. 3). "Gaze not upon her," cautions the poet, "lest thou be as she / When, at the far end of her long desire, / Her scarlet vest and gold and gem and pearl / And she amid her pomp are set on fire" (ll. 11–14). When Rossetti reactivates specular tropes in such devotional sonnets as "O Lord, on Whom we gaze and dare not gaze," also in *Verses,* she asks that vision be regenerated and transformed so "that gazing we may see, / And seeing love, and loving worship Thee" (ll. 2–3). By contrast, her sonnets on worldly desire deal with faithless gazing rather than faithful seeing, with lust rather than love, and with vanity rather than worship.

Subjecting charm's imperilling potency to new purpose in "Monna Innominata," Rossetti transcends convention, for Esther, though a temptress, acts primarily as an active agent of the divine will and only secondarily as the object of masculine desire. "In the Bible," writes Rossetti, "the word *tempt* (or its derivatives) is used in a good or in an evil sense, according to the agent or to the object aimed at" (*FD,* 358). Moreover, temptation, though projected upon the desirable object, proceeds from within the desirous subject. "At the root of every possible temptation," says Rossetti, "I have to overcome myself" (*FD,* 519). Likewise, Esther, vanquishing her fear of death, overcomes temptation to achieve a "self-conquest" (*FD,* 519). Just as aspiration triumphs over desire, she also triumphs over her husband. Consequently, whereas the world in "Babylon the Great" transfixes and destroys those who "dream her fair" (l. 2), Esther "put[s] on pomp of loveliness" to subdue a king and save a people. In this connection, her charm ("loveliness") elicits man's pleasure ("love") to serve God's purpose ("Love"). As a result, while Rossetti does not revise the constituents of charm, Esther's thesis—"I, if I perish, perish"—hints at an inner motivation that yet reconciles charm to attractiveness.

Assimilating Esther's words to her own utterance, the woman poet identifies with the biblical heroine and her conquest of self. Whereas the admonitory example of Lot's wife posits self-annihilation as the consequence of failed renunciation, the kind of self-conquest espoused in "Monna Innominata" tends toward a "form of self-making" that concentrates "on the inner life of a representative Christian absorbed in the heavenly future and not the earthly present."[12] Indeed, the movement from "self-abnegation" to "self-exaltation" in Rossetti's mature work proceeds from an awareness that God has created each soul in his self-image and thus involves a "full acknowledgement of the dignity of personality" (Packer, 324). "Concerning Himself God Almighty proclaimed of old," writes Rossetti, "'I AM THAT I AM,' and man's inherent feeling of personality seems in some sort to attest and correspond to this revelation: I who am myself cannot but be myself. . . . Who I was I am, who I am I am, who I am I must be for ever and ever" (*FD,* 47). As a result, "I may loathe myself or be amazed at myself, but I cannot unself myself for ever and ever" (*FD,* 47). Therefore, the *innominata,* having joined her "I" to Esther's in the first line of sonnet 8, reasserts her autonomy in the final lines of the sestet. The nature of the prayer then uttered by the speaker is not clear. But if these lines relate the speaker's wish to eternize her love, the prayer must mediate her recognition that this objective cannot ultimately be accomplished either by writing poetry, though this is certainly one avenue explored (Whitla, 125), or by asking once more for "God's sanction of her earthly love" (Harrison 1988, 154). Seeking the courage to immortalize her passion by exchanging "love" for "Love," she achieves the victory of Self (spiritual aspiration) over self (physical desire).

The last six sonnets, the sestet of the sequence, reveal the speaker's struggle to come to terms with relinquished desire and suggest an important difference between her sacrifice and Esther's. In these sonnets the *innominata* discovers that the renunciation of desire requires the patience and humility of a lifetime as well as the heroism of a moment. Her integrity and individuality inhere in the strength of her will to deny the importunities of a long life rather than brave the threat of sudden death. Consequently, a "hyperconsciousness of time" prevails in "Monna Innominata" (Blake, 10). When the speaker's devotional vigil succeeds to her amatory vigil, this hyperconsciousness of time intensifies. Ever one to "wait and watch" (1.1), the *innominata* resembles the heroines of "The Prince's Progress" and "The Convent Threshold." Considering herself "unworthy of the happier call" (9.4), she employs images reminiscent of the novice's nightmare struggle to contend that "love may toil all night, / But take at morning; wrestle till the break / Of day, but then wield power with God and man" (9.10–12). Rossetti's use of enjambment ("break / Of day") fittingly suggests how love will succeed after the briefest of pauses. "A little while," the *innominata* tells her lover, "and age and sorrow cease; / A little while, and life reborn annuls / Loss and decay and death, and all is love" (10.12–14). Contracting life to the length of one short night, she determines "to claim [love] anew / Beyond this passage of the gate of death" (11.11–12). Yet time takes a toll upon the woman who awaits death's consummation of desire. Refusing love's crown of "fresh roses" (14.4), she asks, "Youth gone and beauty gone, what doth remain?" (14.9). The answer is a silence that speaks eloquently of "The longing of a heart pent up forlorn" (14.10). Indeed, silence is, as Rossetti writes in "The Thread of Life," "music of an unlike fashioning" (2.8).

Privileging interiority over exteriority, Rossetti's autopsychology rehabilitates the sonnet to eroticize the female subject rather than the female object. In other words, the poet's religious and moral conservatism permits the recovery of feminine selfhood as intrinsically attractive. Concerned with the conflict between aspiration and desire, "Monna Innominata" examines a woman's effort to reconcile her sexuality to her spirituality and thus represents a significant departure from amatory convention. But when the *innominata* transcends her desire for the beloved, the motive for expression expires and the series concludes. Within the terms outlined in the preface, Rossetti has exhausted the possibilities of the conventional amatory lyric and the unconventional female speaker. While the *innominata*'s anonymity seems to act as surety for her representativeness, the outward circumstances of gender yet play a role in determining her subjective responses. Insofar as essential sameness obviates the problem of sexual difference, however, Rossetti's later sonnets circumvent questions of gender and genre to address the inward preoccupations of the truly representative self. As she explains in *Seek and Find,* "one final consolation yet remains to careful and troubled hearts: in Christ there is neither male nor female, for we are all one" (*SF,* 32).

The Devotional Sequence: Works of Self-Conversion

Love assumes three forms in *A Pageant and Other Poems*. Setting out the parameters for her treatment of the sonnet, Rossetti identifies her "first Love" in the dedication to the 1881 volume:

> Sonnets are full of love, and this my tome
> > Has many sonnets: so here now shall be
> > One sonnet more, a love sonnet, from me
> To her whose heart is my heart's quiet home,
> > To my first Love, my Mother, on whose knee

I learnt love-lore that is not troublesome;
    Whose service is my special dignity,
And she my loadstar while I go and come.
And so because you love me, and because
    I love you, Mother, I have woven a wreath
        Of rhymes wherewith to crown your honoured name:
        In you not fourscore years can dim the flame
Of love, whose blessed glow transcends the laws
    Of time and change and mortal life and death. (ll. 1–14)

Echoing the singsong refrain of "Love me,—I love you," Rossetti plays the troubadour to her mother, mimics the conventions of amatory lyricism, and anticipates the demand for reciprocity that stands at the heart of "Monna Innominata": "'Love me, for I love you'—and answer me, / 'Love me, for I love you'" (7.1–2). In effect, the dedicatory sonnet establishes the relationship between parent and child as a model for the relationship between man and woman. Yet even as love, the motive force for Rossetti's "wreath / Of rhymes," "transcends the laws / Of time and change," *A Pageant and Other Poems* returns insistently to the question of temporal mutability and poetic inarticulateness. Thus "The Key-Note," which follows the dedicatory sonnet, opens with the elegiac *ubi sunt*: "Where are the songs I used to know, / Where are the notes I used to sing?" (ll. 1–2). Although the poet determines to "break and cheer the unlovely rest / Of Winter's pause" (ll. 14–15), the threat of inarticulateness returns when she begins to sing of her second love. "Ah me," laments the *innominata*, "but where are now the songs I sang / When life was sweet because you called them sweet?" (1.13–14). While the woman who has lost her heart's desire eventually consigns herself to silence, the poet's third love, God, enables her to break the pause and sing anew in such works as "'If Thou Sayest, Behold, We Knew It Not,'" "The Thread of Life," and "Later Life." Discovering in the devotional sonnet a medium capable of endlessly prolonging poetic expression, Rossetti explores the soul's relationship with God—father and lover— and plumbs the depths of self.

    The companion sequences, "'If Thou Sayest, Behold, We Knew It Not'" and "The Thread of Life," differ from "Monna Innominata" inasmuch as Rossetti refrains from openly constituting the speaker as female. Freed from the constraints of gender, the universal speaker still remains subject to spiritual conflict. Thus, in "'If Thou Sayest,'" the individual's sense of responsibility becomes a source of incomparable anguish: "I have done I know not what,—what have I done? / My brother's blood, my brother's soul, doth cry: / And I find no defence, find no reply" (1.1–3). The opening self-reproach, modeled on God's censure of Cain (Gen. 4:10), modifies the titular allusion to Proverbs: "If thou sayest, Behold, we knew it not: doth not he that pondereth the heart consider it? and he that keepeth thy soul, doth he not know it? and shall not he render to every man according to his works?" (Prov. 24:12). For Rossetti, personal action involves a "certain," albeit "incalculable," influence, which is "inseparable from a proportionate burden of responsibility" (*TF*, 157). On the other hand, the "withholding" of "personal influence" is tantamount "not to neutrality but to evil influence" when it results in "the grievous hurt of those whose due it is" (*TF*, 158).

Tortured by the unknown consequences of action and inaction alike, the speaker of "'If Thou Sayest'" petitions Christ to "undo / Our self-undoing" (2.7–8). This appeal to Christ, ushering in a vision of "the last Appeal" (3.2), occasions a revaluation of anguish: "Disfeatured faces, worn-out knees that kneel, / Will more avail than strength or beauty then" (3.7–8). Such outward defacement provides proof of inward commitment. When, for example, the speaker of "Why?" questions the need to endure lifelong agony, Christ explains that suffering perfects the soul in his image: "Bride whom I love, if thou too lovest Me, / Thou needs must choose My Likeness for thy dower" (ll. 9–10). But while the marred face to which the *innominata* draws attention in her final sonnet becomes a signature of her fitness to be Christ's bride, the speaker of "'If Thou Sayest,'" having also accepted pain as love's dower, is overwhelmed by the magnitude of Christ's suffering: "Thy Face was marred / In sight of earth and hell tumultuous" (3.9–10). Offering not so much a pattern for individual emulation as a remedy for communal insufficiency, Christ's passion becomes the basis for the poet's final appeal: "Lord, for Thy sake, not our's, supply our lacks, / For Thine own sake, not our's, Christ, pity us" (3.13–14).

While the three sonnets in "'If Thou Sayest'" address the perils of doing and not doing, the three sonnets in "The Thread of Life" treat the dynamics of being. Together, the two sequences offer a diptych on works and faith. Moreover, insofar as "The Thread of Life" chronicles an "act of conversion," the series provides a fine example of the way Rossetti's religious lyrics translate "the language of solitude into the language of salvation."[13] At the beginning of the first sonnet, land and sea, both "irresponsive" (1.1, 1.2), come to symbolize the individual's isolation:

"Aloof, aloof, we stand aloof, so stand / Thou too aloof bound with the flawless band / Of inner solitude" (1.4–6). Acknowledging the "self-chain" (1.7) that fetters heart and stifles hope, the speaker moves beyond the torments of solipsism to affirm the eternal grounds of being: "I am not what I have nor what I do; / But what I was I am, I am even I" (2.13–14). The repeated references to self as "still mine own" (3.4, 3.8) and "ever mine own" (3.5, 3.7) underline the instrinsic value of the speaker's "sole possession" (3.3). This possession is, as the pun indicates, the soul. So whereas "Monna Innominata" ends with the "Silence of love that cannot sing again" (14.14), the cherished self of "The Thread of Life" resumes the capacity to sing:

> And this myself as king unto my King
>   I give, to Him Who gave Himself for me;
> Who gives Himself to me, and bids me sing
>   A sweet new song of His redeemed set free;
> He bids me sing: O death, where is thy sting?
>   And sing: O grave, where is thy victory? (3.9–14)

Liberated in song, the soul achieves identity in Christ, who, as Rossetti's verbal echoes suggest, counters the irresponsiveness of nature. Furthermore, the speaker not only renders self unto Self "as king unto my King" but returns word unto Word (1 Cor. 15:55) in the final lines of the sonnet.

As the innominate female speaker cedes to the anonymous Christian speaker in *A Pageant and Other Poems,* the concept of selfhood shifts accordingly to consolidate difference in sameness. In this respect, "Later Life: A Double Sonnet of Sonnets" is particularly important. Unfortunately, although Rossetti hoped this sequence would "claim attention" with "Monna Innominata" (*FL,* 94), its lancinating cycles of self-doubt have rarely attracted the notice of critics.[14] Yet "Later Life," at twice the length of "Monna Innominata," is doubly ambitious. Although Rossetti relies on the sonnet's "curtailing form" to combat "final chaos" (Finn, 143), she simultaneously exceeds its structural limits to include 28 poems within the series. In so doing, she formally reproduces the indecision of a speaker who is torn between the alternatives of life and death.

Universalizing the dialectic between aspiration and desire responsible for the construction of subjectivity in "Monna Innominata," "Later Life" examines the "foolishest fond folly of a heart / Divided, neither here nor there at rest!" (24.9–10). Not surprisingly, images of doubleness pervade this "Double Sonnet of Sonnets," for Rossetti treats the world both as a medium of divine revelation and as a snare to human vanity. "This dead and living world," she observes, "befits our case / Who live and die" (23.9–10). In the interests of unified sensibility, the soul must, as she writes in "Resurgam," a sonnet first published in the *Athenaeum* (1882), allow itself to be "Emptied and stripped of all save only Grace, / Will, Love, a threefold panoply of might" (ll. 7–9). In "Later Life," therefore, the speaker petitions the God of Love to endow grace, strengthen the will, and "furnish me / With that same love my heart is craving now" (5.3–4): "O Love accept, according my request; / O Love exhaust, fulfilling my desire" (5.9–10). But although God's love, which both fulfills and exhausts desire, offers a means to overcome self-division, "Later Life" acknowledges the fallibility of human intention.

However comparable to "Monna Innominata" as an autopsychology, "Later Life" moves beyond the amatory sequence to mediate between individual awareness and collective experience. In sonnet 8, for instance, the persona utters the wish for integrated communal consciousness as a means to self-transcendence: "We feel and see with different hearts and eyes:— / Ah Christ, if all our hearts could meet in Thee / How well it were for them and well for me, / Our hearts Thy dear accepted sacrifice" (8.1–4). Christ's "only sacred Self" (8.11) becomes the means to reconcile difference. "Luring us upward from this world of mire" (11.11), his example compels "us to press on and mount above / Ourselves and all we have had experience of" (11.12–13). If this experience be of sin, a consciousness of shame yet "gives back what nothing else can give, / Man to himself,—then sets him up on high" (13.13–14). Thus as aspiration conquers and succeeds desire, self-abasement precedes and enables self-exaltation.

Using "Man" as a term of generic assembly in "Later Life," Rossetti moves in the two sonnets at the center of the sequence to the genesis of sin and self-division. Locating the origins of fragmented awareness in the fall, she makes ontology or being a matter of etiology or beginning. But while sin transformed the world into a "realm of change and death and pain" (14.14), Adam and Eve continued to "love on and cling together still" (14.2), for "Love in a dominant embrace holds fast / His frailer self, and saves without her will" (15.13–14). Insofar as Eve, Adam's frailer self, misjudged "the inquiring snake, / Whose doubts she answered on a great concern" (15.3–4), Rossetti adheres to the Pauline doctrine (1 Tim. 2:11–12) that women should "fear to teach and bear to learn, /

Remembering the first woman's first mistake" (15.1–2). Eve sinned thoughtlessly, however, whereas Adam, who "deemed poison sweet for her sweet sake" (15.7), entered into transgression with full knowledge. Aspects of a single self, the first couple epitomizes the conflict between emotion and intellect. As Rossetti explains in *Letter and Spirit,* "Eve diverted her 'mind' and Adam his 'heart' from God Almighty," but their separate "courses led to one common result, that is, to one common ruin" (*LS,* 18). This pattern of collective fall—predicated on a single "ill / The twain had wrought on such a different wise" (14.3–4)—implies a pattern of collective redemption. Thus, while the *innominata,* like Eve, is "so apt to fall" (9.5), the speaker of "Later Life" says, "Today we fall, but we shall rise again" (14.10). Nevertheless, the trials of today constantly test the speaker's faith in tomorrow.

Terrified by the prospect of eternity, the speaker of Rossetti's Dantean dream vision, "An Old-World Thicket," endeavors to "cling to dying life; for how / Face the perpetual Now?" (ll. 123–24). Similarly, in the second half of "Later Life" the "Befogged and witless" (16.9) consciousness fears to abandon sublunary existence even though the Old World, described as "one mere desert dust / Where Death sits veiled amid creation's rust" (26.12–13), is, like the monument in Shelley's "Ozymandias," an antiquated ruin. Reluctant to exchange new for old, time for eternity, the speaker understands, however, that "This Life we live is dead for all its breath" (26.9). The same life-and-death paradox Rossetti elaborates in the two sonnets that comprise "'Behold a Shaking'": "Here life is the beginning of our death, / And death the starting-point whence life ensues; / Surely our life is death, our death is life" (2.9–11). But although this life is "Death's self . . . set off on pilgrimage, / Travelling with tottering steps the first short stage" (26.10–11), the speaker of "Later Life" remains entranced by earth's charms. The failure to resist temptation leads to those instances of insurrection that Rossetti recounts in *Called to Be Saints*: "In one moment every instinct of our whole self revolts against our lot, and we loathe this day of quietness and sitting still, and writhe under a sudden sense of all we have irrecoverably foregone."[15] Rebelling against the present, the self turns, like Lot's wife, from hope to memory, from future to past, and from life to death.

In *Time Flies* the parable of a "spider, himself dark and defined, his shadow no less dark and scarcely if at all less defined" (*TF,* 122), conveys the futility of revolt. Observing the way the "self-haunted spider" attempts to elude its "black double," Rossetti sees in this phantom pursuit "a figure of each obstinate impenitent sinner, who having outlived

enjoyment remains isolated irretrievably with his own horrible loathsome self " (*TF,* 122). Unable to unself self, the spider resembles the
speaker of "Later Life," who, in one of the darkest moments of the
sequence, succumbs to self-loathing:

> I am sick of where I am and where I am not,
>   I am sick of foresight and of memory,
>   I am sick of all I have and all I see,
>   I am sick of self, and there is nothing new;
> Oh weary impatient patience of my lot!—
>   Thus with myself: how fares it, Friends, with you? (17.9–14)

The conception of self as hateful is one of the most significant obstacles
to personal salvation, for it represents a refusal of God's redeeming grace
and a denial of Christ's efficacy as "God's sole well-pleasing Sacrifice"
(8.10). In sonnet 17 the speaker's diseased self-consciousness, cleverly
conveyed in the anaphoric repetition of "I am sick," turns on "a something which / Is neither of this fog nor of today" (17.1–2). In the course
of the poem this "something" yields to "nothing." Likewise, in the course
of the sequence the seeming certainties of earthly pleasure—"a something" delusively embodied in "certain cliffs" and "one certain beach"
(17.4)—turn into an empty dream as surely as the fondly remembered
winds "turn the topmost edge of waves to spray" (17.5).

Locating transformative awareness in the liminal spaces of cliff and
beach, Rossetti shows that faith is ever poised on the precipice of self-
doubt. In sonnet 17 the final banal address to "Friends" represents an
effort, albeit meager, to escape solipsistic self-loathing and to reclaim
faith through a sympathetic awareness. The speaker begins to emerge
from the prison of self in response not to the human world, however, but
to the natural world. In fact, nature's patterns of rise and fall double
upon the speaker's experience of psychological ascent and descent. The
cycle of the seasons, the "mellow grieving" (20.3) of "one solitary bird"
(20.2), the topography of Switzerland and Italy, these gradually strike
"harmonies from silent chords which burst / Out into song" (22.4–5):
"All harmonies sang to senses wide awake. / All things in tune, myself
not out of tune" (21.8–9). The speaker's epiphany occurs as the summer
evening flushes with the radiance of "a doubled June" (21.14). Recalling
the relationship between Sirius and the Pole Star, which, though not "in
a visible sympathy" (9.10), orbit in silent accord, nature's symphony

anticipates the union of the speaker's "I" in the fellowship of "we" in the sestet of sonnets that closes the sequence.

Having recovered self-assurance, the speaker relinquishes the world whose beauty is observed in sonnets 19 through 22. In her discussion of romantic and Tractarian influences on Rossetti's nature poetry, Catherine Cantalupo astutely remarks that the changeable world provides no image to satisfy the "eternal identity" of "the stable soul."[16] Thus in "Today's Burden," a sonnet first published in Hall Caine's *Sonnets of Three Centuries* (1882), the ceaseless movement of the celestial bodies symbolizes the dis-ease that affects each person: "Unrest the common heritage, the ban / Flung broadcast on all humankind, on all / Who live; for living, all are bound to die" (ll. 9–11). As the initiatory sonnet in "Later Life" suggests, God alone provides rest and stability, for "God was God" (1.2) before the beginning of the world "And God will still be God" (1.3) after it has ended. But although "God's Presence antedates what else hath been" (24.7), the divided heart, caught "within the screen / Of this familiar world" (24.3–4), "hankers after Heaven, but clings to earth" (24.11). As a result, even though "Later Life" generalizes the dilemma posed, for example, by the *innominata*'s sexual and spiritual goals, it intensifies the effects of self-conflict. In fact, the doubleness to which the persona is subject lends Rossetti's "Double Sonnet of Sonnets" an emotional turbulence more easily compared to G. M. Hopkins's Terrible Sonnets than her own "Monna Innominata." A "wordless tearless dumbness of distress" (3.3) afflicts her speaker, who, though entrammeled "in a wordy maze" (16.9), is quite articulate. This distress persists despite a sense that self-division might be remedied by doubling self on Self, for "If making makes us Thine then Thine we are, / And if redemption we are twice Thine own" (3.9–10).

The final serious challenge to the personal stability craved by the speaker occurs in the penultimate sonnet of "Later Life." Here the "I" reemerges to recount the thoughts elicited by a dream of death. More horrifying than the dream, however, is the prospect of death "in the literal truth" (27.2). Death, accompanied by its "adjuncts ghastly and uncouth" (27.3), holds no romance for Rossetti. Indeed, the account of her awakening to the awful reality of mortal corruption in *Time Flies* may well explain the anxiety that grips her speaker toward the end of "Later Life":

> My first vivid experience of death (if so I may term it) occurred in early childhood in the grounds of a cottage.

> This little cottage was my familiar haunt: its grounds were my
> inexhaustible delight. They then seemed to me spacious, though now I
> know them to have been narrow and commonplace.
>
> So in these grounds, perhaps in the orchard, I lighted upon a dead
> mouse. The dead mouse moved my sympathy: I took him up, buried him
> comfortably in a mossy bed, and bore the spot in mind.
>
> It may have been a day or two afterwards that I returned, removed
> the moss coverlet, and looked . . . a black insect emerged. I fled in horror,
> and for long years ensuing I never mentioned this ghastly adventure to
> anyone. (*TF,* 45)

This experience, tentatively set within an Edenic garden, is "vivid" precisely because death comes grotesquely alive when the black insect
emerges from the grave. At this point the orchard, once the locus of
innocent delight, becomes the scene for horrific knowledge. Indeed,
Rossetti's ellipsis not only retreats from such knowledge but recovers
the sudden abhorrent revulsion that follows on it. As a child, however,
Rossetti took a view of death that was, like the garden, "narrow." A
mature woman in possession of "a wider and wiser view-point," she
"would fain reverse the order of those feelings" of sympathy and horror,
"dwelling less and less on the mere physical disgust, while more and
more on the rest and safety" (*TF,* 45). Yet, as the bouts of hysteria she
suffered in the weeks before her death attest, Rossetti shared with the
persona of "Later Life" an abiding dread of death even as she yearned
for its solace. Thus, seeing self as "A helpless charmless spectacle of
ruth" (27.7) rather than a "saint rejoicing on her bed" (27.13), the
speaker of "Later Life" not surprisingly fears to "miss the goal at last"
(27.14). Although the afterlife—the true end and meaning of "Later
Life"—awaits the soul after the death of the body, self-doubt persists to
the end.

The final sonnet of "Later Life" moves from horror to sympathy, from
physical disgust to rest and safety, and so offers a more consoling vision
of death in which the beloved dead commune with the living:

> The unforgotten dearest dead may be
>   Watching us with unslumbering eyes and heart;
> Brimful of words which cannot yet be said,
>   Brimful of knowledge they may not impart,
> Brimful of love for you and love for me. (28.10–14)

Insofar as the self on the threshold between life and death is attractive to "our absent friend" (28.1), the sequence overcomes its moments of self-loathing and finishes with the lovable self. Nevertheless, Rossetti's conditional phrasings ("may be") and negative formulations ("cannot" and "may not") sustain the tension of uncertainty characteristic of "Later Life" to its conclusion, unsettling somewhat the comfort the speaker seeks to give both self and reader. By contrast with the sense of exhaustion that ends "Monna Innominata," however, "Later Life" seems near supersaturation, possessed of a fullness of possibility, if not of certainty, for death promises to requite life, which Rossetti ironically figures as "full of numbness and of balk, / Of haltingness and baffled short-coming, / Of promise unfulfilled, of everything / That is puffed vanity and empty talk" (26.1–4). By contrast, the final sonnet's emphasis on fullness—a fullness ready to overflow in the thrice-iterated "Brimful"—remedies the speaker's fear of helpless, charmless insufficiency and redeems the "wide vacuity of hope and heart" (25.10) that afflicts all who lead lives "full of toil and pain" (25.2). Consequently, even as the final place in the sequence belongs to the discrete self ("me"), the limits of individual personality begin to dissolve when the speaker, approaching the frontier of the unknown and the unsaid, imagines the union of each and all in "Later Life."

Later Sonnets: Canvassing the Whole

Precisely one year before she herself crossed the frontier between life and death, Rossetti wrote to inform William of the success of her latest work. "Mrs. Garnett," she told him, "called one day and told me that by Christmas there was no meeting the demand for *Verses*: at one considerable shop she tried at she heard that twenty or thirty applications had had to be negatived for the moment" (*FL*, 201). The volume, composed entirely of religious lyrics, continued to sell well and passed into a third edition in the spring of 1894. Although sacred verse had always occupied a privileged place in her oeuvre, Rossetti had never yet presented herself primarily as a devotional poet. As such, however, she has no compeer but Hopkins, who privately acknowledged his debt to her in "A Voice from the World: Fragments of 'An Answer to Miss Rossetti's *Convent Threshold*.'" But whereas Hopkins remained virtually unknown to his contemporaries, Rossetti had gradually acquired, during the course of her career, a loyal following among discriminating readers.

Verses, the crowning achievement of her life's work, won her an even larger audience.

The popularity of *Verses* owes perhaps as much to its lack of pretension as to its confessional sincerity. "Equality," Rossetti argues in *The Face of the Deep,* "tends to annihilate pride: *proud* humility may plant itself in the lowest place; only *humble* humility can revel and rejoice in sitting altogether undistinguished amid peers" (*FD,* 501). The difference between proud and humble humility is integral to an understanding of *Verses,* for the poet, speaking as a peer rather than a prophet, as a Christian rather than a woman, gives voice to an experience that, insofar as it is typical and universal, is undistinguished. Collecting and revising material originally published in *Called to be Saints, Time Flies,* and *The Face of the Deep,* she reassembles her lyrics to create "a unified poetic sequence" that traces a "spiritual pilgrimage" toward "understanding of, and faithful resignation to, God's will."[17] This pilgrimage, divided into eight stages, begins with a series of 17 sonnets. In fact, one-fifth of the 331 poems included in *Verses* are sonnets. Although Rossetti does not restrict herself to the genre, she yet gives priority to the sonnet as the form best suited to contain the soul's inherent feeling of personality and to express its commitment to God.

In the first section of *Verses,* "OUT OF THE DEEP HAVE I CALLED UNTO THEE, O LORD," the Christian soul's longing for its savior mirrors the Petrarchan lover's longing for his lady. But while the series thereby resembles Donne's Holy Sonnets, Rossetti explicitly frames her sonnets as the articulation of collective rather than individual need. Recapitulating the images of temporal change that open "Monna Innominata," the speaker of the inaugural sonnet asks God to "Lift us above this transitory scope / Of earth, these pleasures that begin and cease, / This moon which wanes, these seasons which decrease" (ll. 3–5). Although the soul seeks to transcend its attachment to the transitory world, Rossetti expresses Christian ambition through analogy to sensuous nature: "As on an eastern slope / Wheat feels the dawn beneath night's lingering cope, / Bending and stretching sunward ere it sees" (ll. 6–8). Likewise, in the fourth sonnet, "'As Sparks Fly Upward,'" the sparks' flight symbolizes communal aspiration: "Lord, grant us wills to trust Thee with such aim / Of hope and passionate craving of desire, / That we may mount aspiring, and aspire / Still while we mount" (ll. 1–4). Recurring frequently in *Verses,* the images of light and of ascent reify spiritual objectives and function as unifying motifs lending thematic and structural coherence to the volume as a whole.

In *Verses* the experience of discontinuity both inspires and imperils the quest for reintegrated selfhood. Thus for the title of "'As Sparks Fly Upward,'" Rossetti fractures a biblical text—"Yet man is born unto trouble, as the sparks fly upward" (Job 5:7)—and so makes trouble the unspoken impetus to the soul's devotion. As the opening sequence proceeds, however, trouble threatens to overwhelm the speaker and, indeed, fragments composite utterance. Thus the sixth sonnet, "O Lord, I am ashamed to seek Thy Face," introduces the lyric "I" to the sequence. The voice of solitary anguish emerges quite strongly, for example, in "'Cried Out with Tears'": "Lord, I believe, help Thou mine unbelief: / Lord, I repent, help mine impenitence" (ll. 1–2). But while the poet speaks as an individual, she puts words to "the silence of each soul, / Its cry unutterable of ruth and shame, / Its voicelessness of self-contempt and blame" ("'I Will Come and Heal Him'" [ll. 1–3]). Figuring communal solidarity as the means to personal integrity, the representative speaker later asks, "Lord, make me one with Thine own faithful ones" (l. 1). Christ's atonement, of course, offers to achieve the desired oneness. The sun that draws the wheat and the flame that draws the spark, Christ is, as the final sonnet in "OUT OF THE DEEP" affirms, the "'Light of Light.'"

Although *Verses* begins in the pain of self-doubt, it gradually acquires an elated assurance that "Later Life," for instance, never quite achieves. Thus, while the voice of fear dominates "OUT OF THE DEEP," "CHRIST OUR ALL IN ALL" issues as a call to hope. This hope proceeds from the unitary identity available to all Christians. In "'King of Kings and Lord of Lords,'" for example, the speaker describes the comfort found in Christ's "Blessed Name, / Man's life and resurrection from the grave" (ll. 13–14). Drawing together all "feeble folk" (l. 9) and "many-semblanced ordered Spirits" (l. 6), this Name countervails the anonymity that Rossetti associates with the feminine condition in such works as "Monna Innominata" and "Under the Rose." Indeed, as the sonnet that precedes "'King of Kings and Lord of Lords'" demonstrates, God's "still unchanging Name" ("New creatures; the Creator still the Same" [l. 4]) provides stability as well as identity to the community of the faithful: "We too are still the same: and still our claim, / Our trust, our stay, is Jesus, none but He: / He still the Same regards us, and still we / Mount toward Him in old love's accustomed flame" (ll. 5–8). Annexing linguistic austerity to emotional intensity, Rossetti repeats *same* and *still* to emphasize the soul's ambition to eternal being. In other words, her use of anaphora verbally complements the self's desire for assimilation in Self. Insofar as Christ's sacred Self transfigures and magnifies the soul, love overcomes the terror contingent on the diffusion of individual identity: "Since it is Thou, we dare not be afraid, / Our King of old and still our Self-same King" (ll. 13–14). At the same time, the emotional and expressive restraint evident in Rossetti's religious sonnets tempers the autoeroticism implicit in the aspiration to Self-sameness.

In the third and fourth sections of *Verses*, "SOME FEASTS AND FASTS" and "GIFTS AND GRACES," Rossetti puts the speaker's journey toward reconciliation in Christ in the context of liturgical and sacramental awareness. Not surprisingly, most of the sonnets in "GIFTS AND GRACES" concern love, which, according to Saint Paul, is the greatest of the three theological virtues (1 Cor. 13:13). Indeed, Rossetti contends that "love is more potent to breed faith than faith to breed love," for "'God is Love'; and that which God is must rank higher, and show itself mightier than aught which God is not" (*TF,* 245). Publishing "A Harmony on First Corinthians XIII" in *New and Old* (1879), she quotes the Pauline text in the title of "'The Greatest of These is Charity.'" In this sonnet love, more powerful than "faith and hope, will carry them / Safe to the gate of New Jerusalem" (ll. 12–13). "NEW JERUSALEM AND ITS CITIZENS" is, in fact, the end the pilgrim has in sight beyond the next two sections of *Verses.* The intermediate sections—"THE WORLD: SELF-DESTRUCTION" and "DIVERS WORLDS: TIME AND ETERNITY"—contain between them only two sonnets, which, however, effectively summarize the soul's progress from the Old to the New World. Whereas the Old World, personified as a harlot, woos the unwary to self-destruction in "Babylon the Great," the speaker of the sonnet in "DIVERS WORLDS" commends an earthly lover to abandon the here and now for the hereafter: "Beloved, yield thy time to God, for He / Will make eternity thy recompense" (ll. 1–2). Once Rossetti's speaker reaches the goal of eternity in "THE NEW JERUSALEM AND ITS CITIZENS," her sonnets concern heaven's loveliness and the bliss to be found in reunion with the saints gone before.

Although Rossetti describes eternity as "Finishing sequence in its awful sum" ("Time lengthening, in the lengthening seemeth long" [l. 14]), she chooses to conclude *Verses* with "SONGS FOR STRANGERS AND PILGRIMS" rather than "THE NEW JERUSALEM AND ITS CITIZENS." After all, her audience is one that requires strength and encouragement to persist through time's remainder. Providing the necessary inspiration in "'Heaviness May Endure for a Night, but Joy Cometh in the Morning,'" Rossetti recapitulates the whole movement of the volume in two sonnets. As the poem's title suggests, she models the speaker's conversion experience on the text of Psalm 30:5. At the same time, she derives the images used to convey the heart's heaviness—the "mournful owl" (l. 9) and the "doleful dragon" (l. 10)—from the prophet of woe (Mic. 1:8). "Companion of all monsters of the dark" (l. 11), the speaker yet responds to Christ, who is the Light of Lights. Accordingly, the dawn of day symbolizes the renewal of hope: "When lo! the light cast off its nightly cowl, / And up to heaven flashed a carolling lark, / And all creation sang its hymn anew" (ll. 12–14). While the mournful owl reifies the despair of the unrepentant sinner, the lark, whose scintillating flight propels its song heavenward, becomes an emblem for the Christian poet. Indeed, the speaker, inspired by the lark's anthem, cannot "but sing a stave in tune" (l. 16).

Reminiscent of sonnets 21 and 22 in "Later Life," "'Heaviness May Endure for a Night, but Joy Cometh in the Morning'" functions as a two-part paean to creation. As such, it dramatizes the renewal of poetic as well as religious faith. In this respect Rossetti follows in the steps of her Tractarian predecessors. For example, John Keble, whose work in *The Christian Year* (1827) influenced the direction taken in Victorian devotional verse, felt poetry acted "as a catharsis for the artist, a 'divine medicine' for relieving the 'over-burdened' mind, for 'soothing emotion,' for providing 'release'" (G. B. Tennyson, 58). Likewise, at the end of her double sonnet, Rossetti suggests that art helps to heal the soul:

> Lark's lay—a cockcrow—with a scattered few
>   Soft early chirpings—with a tender croon
>   Of doves—a hundred thousand calls, and soon
> A hundred thousand answers sweet and true.
> These set me singing too at unawares:
>   One note for all delights and charities,
>   One note for hope reviving with the light,
>   One note for every lovely thing that is;
> Till while I sang my heart shook off its cares
>   And revelled in the land of no more night. (ll. 19–28)

Answering and echoing nature's avian chorus, the speaker's antiphon not only redeems the straitened spirit to joy, but also acts itself as a call to devotion. Singing the poetry of worship in *Verses*, Rossetti seeks to provide her readers with the complementary benefits of soulful release.

Profoundly disaffected by the inequities of temporal existence, Rossetti schooled herself to the achievement of humility. Nevertheless, the claim to distinction that she disavowed as a Christian she earns as a poet. Experimenting with a plurality of discrete voices and forms throughout her career, she demonstrates an abiding interest in recovering and relating the processes of feminine consciousness. In her final lyrics, however, she seeks to construct an authoritative center from fragmented experience. Relying on scripture to provide comfort to the anxious spirit, she unites each and all and all in all in the universal speaker of *Verses*. Because she ultimately abstracts personality from the circumstances of class and gender, she ultimately creates a poetry that, for all its confessional intensity, is curiously impersonal. In the process, she not only consolidates all points of view in the perspective of the representative Christian, but also makes tormented self-consciousness the prelude to an exalted appreciation of Self.

Conclusion

"The voice which charms one generation is inaccessible to the next," says Christina Rossetti. "Words cannot describe it, notes cannot register it; it remains as a tradition, it lingers only as a regret" (*TF,* 30). Nevertheless, in the years immediately following her death, Rossetti's contemporaries chose to convey their impressions of her by describing the charm of her voice. As the vicissitudes affecting her poetic reputation over the last century suggest, however, her voice was indeed lost to succeeding generations. Only recently has Rossetti's work once more found an appreciative audience.

A mere child when she first met the poet in 1863, Grace Gilchrist fondly remembered her as a slender fairy princess who, when she spoke, enthralled her listeners. "She possessed . . . the beautiful Italian voice all the Rossettis were gifted with—a voice made up of strange, sweet inflections, which rippled into silvery modulations in sustained conversation, making ordinary English words and phrases fall upon the ear with a soft, foreign, musical intonation, though she pronounced the words themselves with the purest of English accents."[1] Similarly, when William Sharp met an older Rossetti in the autumn of 1880, he, too, fell under the spell of her voice. For Sharp, the "singularly clear, rippling laugh" that broke suddenly upon a drawing-room discussion of Holiday Charity, a program enabling impoverished children to experience rural life, acted not so much as a disruption as a diversion: "The voice had a bell-like sound, like that of resonant crystal. . . . Though so exquisitely distinct, the voice was not in the least mannered or affected; and except for a peculiar lift in the intonation, more suggestive of Edinburgh than of London, there was no reason to suppose it was not that of an Englishwoman."[2] Although Sharp, describing Rossetti's "muse" as "cloistral" (736), provides a portrait of the poet quite different from that of the woman who, according to Gilchrist, enjoyed travel and took pleasure in the delights of the Surrey countryside, both writers gradually elide the distinctions between her speaking voice and her poetic voice. But while Rossetti's contemporaries admired her work for its musicality and apparent spontaneity, these qualities failed to sustain her reputation among serious readers after the turn of the century.

Recognized by the Victorians as among the finest of living poets, Rossetti received little attention until the centenary of her birth in 1930. Even then, her life proved more fascinating than her art, which, despite New Criticism's emphasis on the autonomy of the text, went virtually unnoticed. Yet in "'I am Christina Rossetti,'" an essay first written in review of Mary Sandars's *Life of Christina Rossetti* and later collected in *The Second Common Reader* (1932), Virginia Woolf had warned readers not to allow the seductions of biography to force the poetry into obscurity. Turning from the life to the work, she thus addresses the dead poet directly and praises her verse for its complexity, its austerity, and its wit. Although Woolf, like Sharp and others, believed Rossetti to be a writer who did not develop much over the course of her career, she admired her esthetic control. Indeed, in *A Room of One's Own* (1929) she identifies Rossetti, with Tennyson, as one of the defining voices of Victorian poetry. But Woolf, separated from Rossetti and Tennyson by the events of August 1914, also found the rapture that their work inspired to be at odds with the temper of modern times. For whereas "the living poets express a feeling that is actually being made and torn out of us at the moment," the poet of the past "celebrates some feeling that one used to have (at luncheon parties before the war perhaps), so that one responds easily, familiarly, without troubling to check the feeling, or to compare it with any that one has now."[3]

The voice that had, for Woolf, lingered as a regretful reminder of lost innocence was heard sporadically after World War II when scholarly interest began slowly to revive. Even when its strengths received recognition, however, Rossetti's work frequently suffered from critical prejudices against women's poetry. C. M. Bowra, for instance, ascribes the intensity of her lyricism to the influence of personal experience rather than to the exercise of conscious artistry. "In perfect innocence," says Bowra, "she would write poems which are to all appearance dramatic lyrics about imaginary situations, but which none the less show unmistakable traces of her own feelings and sufferings."[4] Citing "Twice," he asserts that "no woman could write with this terrible directness if she did not to some degree know the experience which she describes" (Bowra, 261). Writing some 20 years later, Stuart Curran identifies Rossetti as a poet of limited range who, though she reveals genuine technical ability, lacks intellectual rigor. In his view, "she has the not inconsiderable gift of felicitous music," but "she falls back on pretty language, the bane of so many women poets," and fails to develop "her stock of images . . . in striking or suggestive ways."[5] Curran's point is a commonplace of

Rossetti criticism. Indeed, his ambiguous testament to the poet's achievement bears an odd resemblance to some Victorian estimates. Thus Edmund Gosse, arguing "that women, in order to succeed in poetry, must be brief, personal, and concentrated" (1896, 136), judges Rossetti as "one of the most perfect poets of the age—not one of the most powerful, of course, nor one of the most epoch-making, but . . . one of the most perfect" (1896, 138). She is, however, no more personal than Tennyson or Browning or Arnold. Moreover, although she, unlike Barrett Browning, wrote no epics, her published oeuvre features several dramatic works—"Under the Rose," "The Convent Threshold," "From House to Home," and "A Royal Princess"—that are anything but brief. In addition, such compound works as "Monna Innominata" and "Later Life" overcome generic constraints to provide a treatment of the soul that challenges readers intellectually and esthetically.

The formal and conceptual deliberation that informs Rossetti's work has received fuller acknowledgment since 1980. Whereas Woolf, after reviewing Sandars's biography, urged "the Common Reader" to consider the work rather than the life, Jerome McGann used his evaluation of Rebecca Crump's *The Complete Poems of Christina Rossetti,* the first volume of which appeared in 1979, to call for a new and "advanced criticism of her poetry" (1980, 240). Although Crump's variorum edition, finished in 1990, has helped facilitate an explosion of interest in Rossetti during the last decade and a half, the poet's other writings—her prose (fictional as well as devotional) and her correspondence—are not yet readily or completely accessible to interested readers. As recent criticism has shown, however, a better understanding of Rossetti's achievement depends on a familiarity with the entire scope of her writing. Now, in the wake of the centenary of her death, biography remains a significant area of research and speculation; but by allying close textual analysis to a recovery of the literary and cultural contexts for her work, feminist and New Historicist critics have done much to dispel the pervasive image of the writer as a saintly and reclusive neurotic. Consequently, even though the voice of the past is always, to some extent, inaccessible to the present, Rossetti has begun to emerge not merely as a regret but as a tradition.

Notes and References

Chapter One

1. *The Family Letters of Christina Georgina Rossetti*, ed. William Michael Rossetti (1908; New York: Haskell House, 1968), 176 and 177; hereafter cited in text as *FL*.

2. William Michael Rossetti, *Selected Letters of William Michael Rossetti*, ed. Roger W. Peattie (University Park: Pennsylvania State University Press, 1990), 578; hereafter cited in text. William gladly passed the obligation of a life to Mackenzie Bell. *Christina Rossetti: A Biographical and Critical Study* (London: Thomas Burleigh, 1898 [hereafter cited in text]) cannot, however, really be called an authorized biography. Against William's wishes, Bell named Rossetti's two suitors (see W. Rossetti 1990, 600–601). Moreover, he did not subscribe to William's view of her insularity (see Bell, 111 and 156). Along with William's accounts, Bell's biography provides the substance for most subsequent readings of Rossetti until 1963.

3. *The Poetical Works of Christina Georgina Rossetti*, ed. William Michael Rossetti (London: Macmillan, 1904), liii; hereafter cited in text as *PW*.

4. Modern biographical studies took a rather different turn with Lona Mosk Packer's *Christina Rossetti* (Berkeley: University of California Press, 1963). The untenability of Packer's thesis that Rossetti had a secret romance with W. B. Scott spoils otherwise sound scholarship. Published nearly 20 years later, Georgina Battiscombe's *Christina Rossetti: A Divided Life* (New York: Holt, Rinehart & Winston, 1981) offers a corrective balance to Packer's work. More recently, Kathleen Jones's emphasis on the maiming of Rossetti's character in *Learning Not to Be First: The Life of Christina Rossetti* (New York: St. Martin's Press, 1992) is disappointingly retrograde. Written partly in opposition to "Bell's careful hagiography" (xiv), Jones's work is less sympathetic to Rossetti's chosen life than its Introduction suggests. Frances Thomas, on the other hand, speculates that Rossetti suffered from clinical depression and suggests that a fear of insanity dictated her refusal to marry (*Christina Rossetti* [Hanley Swan, Worcs.: Self-Publishing Association, 1992]). Subsequent references to these works are cited in the text. I regret that Jan Marsh's *Christina Rossetti: A Literary Biography* (London: Jonathan Cape, 1994) appeared too late for consultation during the writing of this book.

5. Quoted in Ellen A. Proctor, *A Brief Memoir of Christina G. Rossetti* (London: Society for Promoting Christian Knowledge, 1895), 70.

6. *The Rossetti-Macmillan Letters: Some 133 Unpublished Letters Written to Alexander Macmillan, F. S. Ellis, and Others, by Dante Gabriel, Christina, and William Michael Rossetti, 1861–1889*, ed. Lona Mosk Packer (Berkeley:

University of California Press, 1963), 123; hereafter cited in text.

7. Gabriel translated the *Vita Nuova* for his *Early Italian Poets* (1861); William translated the *Inferno* (1865); Maria wrote *A Shadow of Dante* (1871). Christina published "Dante, an English Classic" in *Churchman's Shilling Magazine and Family Treasury* in October 1867 and "Dante: The Poet Illustrated Out of the Poem" in *Century Illustrated Monthly Magazine* in February 1884.

8. John O. Waller explores Dodsworth's significance for Rossetti's verse in "Christ's Second Coming: Christina Rossetti and the Premillenialist William Dodsworth," *Bulletin of the New York Public Library* 73 (1969): 465–82.

9. William Michael Rossetti, *Some Reminiscences of William Michael Rossetti*, 2 vols. (1906; New York: AMS Press, 1970), 1:21; hereafter cited in text.

10. James A. Kohl provides evidence, albeit secondhand, that Rossetti suffered "from a form of insanity, . . . a kind of religious mania" in the late 1840s ("A Medical Comment on Christina Rossetti," *Notes and Queries* 213 [November 1968]: 423). Taken in context of the period, her "mania" is not altogether exceptional.

11. Dante Gabriel Rossetti, *Letters of Dante Gabriel Rossetti*, 4 vols., ed. Oswald Doughty and John Robert Wahl (Oxford: Clarendon Press, 1965–67), 1:45; hereafter cited in text.

12. William Michael Rossetti, *The P.R.B. Journal: William Michael Rossetti's Diary of the Pre-Raphaelite Brotherhood, 1849–1853*, ed. William E. Fredeman (Oxford: Clarendon Press, 1975), 23; hereafter cited in text.

13. Dante Gabriel Rossetti, quoted in *The Pre-Raphaelites*, Tate Gallery (London: Penguin Books, 1984), 16.

14. George Price Boyce, *The Diaries of George Price Boyce*, ed. Virginia Surtees (Norwich: Real World, 1980), 10.

15. Dante Gabriel Rossetti, quoted in *The Paintings and Drawings of Dante Gabriel Rossetti (1828–1882): A Catalogue Raisonné*, 2 vols., ed. Virginia Surtees (Oxford: Clarendon Press, 1971), 1:14.

16. Ford Madox Brown, *Ruskin: Rossetti: PreRaphaelitism. Papers 1854 to 1862*, ed. W. M. Rossetti (1899; New York: AMS Press, 1971), 45–46; hereafter cited in text.

17. *Rossetti Papers, 1862 to 1870*, ed. W. M. Rossetti (1903; New York: AMS Press, 1970), 78; hereafter cited in text.

18. Quoted in Antony H. Harrison, "Eighteen Early Letters by Christina Rossetti," in *The Achievement of Christina Rossetti*, ed. David A. Kent (Ithaca, N.Y.: Cornell University Press, 1987), 205.

19. "Maude Clare" and "The Round Tower at Jhansi, June 8, 1857" appeared in *Once a Week*. Jan Marsh discusses the latter in "The Indian Mutiny and Christina Rossetti's First Appearance in *Once a Week*," *Journal of Pre-Raphaelite Studies* n.s. 1 (Spring 1992): 16–19.

20. M., "A Poetic Trio," *Athenaeum* (7 August 1897): 193–94.

21. See Martha Vicinus, *Independent Women: Work and Community for*

Single Women, 1850–1920 (London: Virago Press, 1985), 74–84; hereafter cited in text. Vicinus mentions that All Saints, the order to which Maria Rossetti became attached, had developed a reputation as one of the "fashionable sisterhoods" since its inception in 1851 (55).

22.   Although it is generally assumed that Rossetti was an associate of All Saints Sisterhood, Thomas notes that "the records show no trace of her" (182).

23.   Letitia Scott, quoted in *Autobiographical Notes of the Life of William Bell Scott*, 2 vols., ed. W. Minto (1892; New York: AMS Press, 1970), 2:59.

24.   *Three Rossettis: Unpublished Letters to and from Dante Gabriel, Christina, and William*, ed. Janet Camp Troxell (Cambridge: Harvard University Press, 1937), 143; hereafter cited in text.

25.   See Diane D'Amico, "Christina Rossetti and *The English Woman's Journal*," *Journal of Pre-Raphaelite Studies* n.s. 3 (Spring 1994): 20–23.

26.   Levy wrote about "The Poetry of Christina Rossetti" for *Woman's World* 1 (February 1888): 178–80. Also on the staff of Oscar Wilde's *Woman's World,* Tynan met Rossetti early in 1886 and was, as the elder poet observed, "deferential enough to puff me up like puff-paste" (*FL,* 149). For her part, Rossetti had a sincere, though quiet, regard for Tynan's verse.

27.   Diane D'Amico conveniently summarizes Rossetti's views on wifehood in her devotional writings ("Eve, Mary, and Mary Magdalene: Christina Rossetti's Feminine Triptych," in *The Achievement of Christina Rossetti,* 180–81).

28.   This action, performed by a woman who revered books, suggests intense hostility. Interestingly, William mentions that his sister, when on her deathbed, was "less prepared than myself to regard our mother's life as happy" (W. Rossetti 1906, 2:541). Sharing those exclusively feminine pursuits, Rossetti lived with her mother until the latter's death. Because she had therefore lived with Frances not only more constantly than William ever had, but more thoroughly than he ever could, she is an exceedingly credible authority on her mother's happiness.

29.   As evidence of William's perplexity, Rossetti seems to die twice in *Some Reminiscences*: once as he narrates the close of her affair with Cayley (2:314–15), and once as he talks of her illnesses (2:530–34).

Chapter Two

1.   [F. A. Rudd], "Christina G. Rossetti," *Catholic World* 4 (March 1867): 842; hereafter cited in text.

2.   Review of *Goblin Market and Other Poems, Athenaeum* (26 April 1862), 557; hereafter cited in text. Another contemporary critic similarly notes the volume's "very decided character and originality, both in theme and treatment" ("Miss Rossetti's Goblin Market," *Eclectic Review* n.s. 2 [1862]: 493).

3.   "Christina Rossetti's Poems," *Catholic World* 24 (October 1877): 122.

4. Edmund Gosse, *The Life of Algernon Charles Swinburne* (London: Macmillan, 1917), 137.

5. *Maude: Prose and Verse,* ed. R. W. Crump (Hamden, Conn.: Archon Books, 1976), 79; hereafter cited in text as *MPV.*

6. Because R. W. Crump, like William, believes Rossetti's "novella deserves study as one of her most autobiographical compositions" (*MPV,* 7), she introduces her edition by discussing the resemblances between the author and Maude. By claiming attention for *Maude's* literary qualities, I follow Diane D'Amico's discussion of theme and structure in "Christina Rossetti's *Maude*: A Reconsideration," *University of Dayton Review* 15 (Spring 1981): 129–42.

7. For further discussion of the sonnets written in competition with her brothers, see R. W. Crump, "Eighteen Moments' Monuments: Christina Rossetti's *Bouts-Rimés* Sonnets in the Troxell Collection," *Princeton University Library Chronicle* 33 (Spring 1972): 210–29.

8. Sandra M. Gilbert and Susan Gubar, *The Madwoman in the Attic: The Woman Writer and the Nineteenth-Century Literary Imagination* (New Haven: Yale University Press, 1979), 551 and 552; hereafter cited in text.

9. In an important article, Joanne Feit Diehl considers the relevance of Harold Bloom's theory of influence for women poets and argues that a "composite male figure" derived from a "succession of fathers" becomes their "main adversary" ("'Come Slowly—Eden': An Exploration of Women Poets and Their Muse," *Signs* 3 [Spring 1978]: 574). As "Goblin Market" suggests, her paradigm needs to be amended to admit the possibility that women's verse might posit a double muse combining male and female influences.

10. *The Complete Poems of Christina Rossetti,* 3 vols., ed. R. W. Crump (Baton Rouge: Louisiana State University Press, 1979–90), 1:234. When quoting from Rossetti's verse, I have used line numbers for citation.

11. Ellen Moers, *Literary Women* (London: Women's Press, 1978), 105.

12. William T. Going, "'Goblin Market' and the Pre-Raphaelite Brotherhood," *Pre-Raphaelite Review* 3 (November 1979): 6.

13. *Time Flies: A Reading Diary* (London: Society for Promoting Christian Knowledge, 1885), 26; hereafter cited in text as *TF.*

14. The poem's economies of sexual, commercial, and linguistic exchange have received attention from recent critics: Elizabeth Campbell, "Of Mothers and Merchants: Female Economics in Christina Rossetti's 'Goblin Market,'" *Victorian Studies* 33 (Spring 1990): 393–410; Mary Wilson Carpenter, "'Eat me, drink me, love me': The Consumable Female Body in Christina Rossetti's *Goblin Market,*" *Victorian Poetry* 29 (Winter 1991): 415–34; Terrence Holt, "'Men sell not such in any town': Exchange in *Goblin Market,*" *Victorian Poetry* 28 (Spring 1990): 51–67. While Carpenter and Campbell see "Goblin Market" as positing productive alternatives to women's commodification or marginalization within the Victorian marketplace, Holt believes the poem's language colludes in a commerce disempowering to women.

15. Mary Arseneau, "Incarnation and Interpretation: Christina Rossetti,

the Oxford Movement, and *Goblin Market," Victorian Poetry* 31 (Spring 1993), 84. Although Arseneau limits her discussion to Rossetti's treatment of the physical world, her emphasis on interpretation as a moral act has wider implications for an understanding of the poet's use of language. Katherine J. Mayberry also notes the importance of a "moral interpretative system" to "Goblin Market" (*Christina Rossetti and the Poetry of Discovery* [Baton Rouge: Louisiana State University Press, 1989], 95).

16. For the Miltonic resonances of "Goblin Market," see Gilbert and Gubar, 567–68. For a broader treatment of the poem's Christian allusions, see Sylvia Bailey Shurbutt, "Revisionist Mythmaking in Christina Rossetti's 'Goblin Market': Eve's Apple and Other Questions Revised and Reconsidered," *Victorian Newsletter* 82 (Fall 1992): 40–44.

17. D. M. R. Bentley uses these clues to read "Goblin Market" in light of "a possible intended audience of fallen women and Anglican sisters" ("The Meretricious and the Meritorious in *Goblin Market*: A Conjecture and an Analysis," in *The Achievement of Christina Rossetti,* 58). Less interested in intention than influence, Mary Wilson Carpenter suggests that the Anglican Sisterhoods "gave the poet access to a uniquely feminocentric view of women's sexuality and simultaneously opened her eyes to its problematic position in Victorian culture" (417).

18. *The Germ: The Literary Magazine of the Pre-Raphaelites* (Ashmolean Museum, Oxford, and Birmingham Museums and Art Gallery, 1984), [xxvii]; John Ruskin, *The Works of John Ruskin,* 39 vols., ed. E. T. Cook and A. Wedderburn (London: George Allen, 1903–12), 12:157; hereafter cited in text. Jerome Bump observes that Rossetti's "Judeo-Christian suspicion of nature" tempers her Pre-Raphaelite "love of nature," but he stops short of suggesting that she used this suspicion to disturb Pre-Raphaelitism's one truth ("Christina Rossetti and the Pre-Raphaelite Brotherhood," *The Achievement of Christina Rossetti,* 328).

19. Jerome J. McGann, "Christina Rossetti's Poems: A New Edition and a Revaluation," *Victorian Studies* 23 (Winter 1980): 251; hereafter cited in text. By following McGann, I differ from those critics who see the sisters as aspects of a single self rather than as individuals. See Winston Weathers, "Christina Rossetti: The Sisterhood of Self," *Victorian Poetry* 3 (Spring 1965): 81–89.

20. For a discussion of Lizzie as a female savior, see Marian Shalkhauser, "The Feminine Christ," *Victorian Newsletter* 10 (Autumn 1956): 19–20. Germaine Greer, on the other hand, argues that Laura's "salvation is literally that she makes love to her sister" (*Goblin Market* [New York: Stonehill, 1975], xxxv). Also rendering "Goblin Market" as lesbian fantasy, Kinuko Craft's illustrations for *Playboy* (September 1973) make female homoeroticism a subject for male voyeurism.

21. Dorothy Mermin, "Heroic Sisterhood in *Goblin Market," Victorian Poetry* 21 (Summer 1983): 116, 118. For an opposing view of the poem as priv-

ileging a "universal emotional kinship" that includes both sexes, see Janet Galligani Casey, "The Potential of Sisterhood: Christina Rossetti's *Goblin Market,*" *Victorian Poetry* 29 (Spring 1991): 70.

22.   I am indebted to the fine discussion Gail Lynn Goldberg provides in "Dante Gabriel Rossetti's 'Revising Hand': His Illustrations for Christina Rossetti's Poems," *Victorian Poetry* 20 (Autumn–Winter 1982): 145–59; hereafter cited in text. Unlike Goldberg, however, I feel the illustrations are coercive.

23.   As for Laurence Housman's illustrations, Rossetti "did not exactly take to them as carrying out her own notion of her own goblins" (*PW,* 460). Forwarding a copy of *Goblin Market* (1893) to William, "she wrote on the wrapper the single word 'Alas'" (*FL,* 190).

24.   Helena Michie, "'There Is No Friend like a Sister': Sisterhood as Sexual Difference," *ELH* 56 (Summer 1989), 404.

25.   William Michael Rossetti, in *Poems of Christina Rossetti* (London: Macmillan, 1905), ix.

26.   Helena Michie, "The Battle for Sisterhood: Christina Rossetti's Strategies for Control in Her Sister Poems," *Journal of Pre-Raphaelite Studies* 3 (May 1983): 42. Jeanie Watson also speculates "that the second sister is simply jealous of both her sister's marriage and her lover"—a motive she also imputes to Sister Maude ("'Eat Me, Drink Me, Love Me': The Dilemma of Sisterly Self-Sacrifice," *Journal of Pre-Raphaelite Studies* 7 [November 1986]: 56).

27.   Dolores Rosenblum, *Christina Rossetti: The Poetry of Endurance* (Carbondale and Edwardsville: Southern Illinois University Press, 1986), 161; hereafter cited in text.

28.   John Kucich, *Repression in Victorian Fiction* (Berkeley: University of California Press, 1987), 17.

29.   Alice Meynell, *Prose and Poetry,* ed. Frederick Page et al. (1947; Freeport, N.Y.: Books for Libraries Press, 1970), 146.

30.   Angela Leighton, *Victorian Women Poets: Writing against the Heart* (Charlottesville: University Press of Virginia, 1992), 159. On the doctrinal context for Rossetti's treatment of death, see Jerome J. McGann's discussion of soul sleep ("The Religious Poetry of Christina Rossetti," *Critical Inquiry* 10 [September 1983]: 134–36). On the other hand, Linda E. Marshall convincingly argues that the Anglican concept of Hades informs the varieties of Rossetti's posthumous awareness ("What the Dead Are Doing Underground: Hades and Heaven in the Writings of Christina Rossetti," *Victorian Newsletter* 72 [Fall 1987]: 55–60).

31.   Constance W. Hassett, "Christina Rossetti and the Poetry of Reticence," *Philological Quarterly* 65 (Fall 1986): 498. Mentioning the way "Arnoldian values and an Arnoldian view of culture" shaped her education, Isobel Armstrong comes to a similar point about the inadequacy of certain approaches to reading Rossetti's poetry ("Christina Rossetti: Diary of a Feminist Reading," *Women Reading Women's Writing,* ed. Sue Roe [Brighton: Harvester Press, 1987], 123).

32. Thomas Burnett Swann, *Wonder and Whimsy: The Fantastic World of Christina Rossetti* (Francestown, N.H.: Marshall Jones, 1960), 45.

Chapter Three

1. Harold Bloom, *The Anxiety of Influence: A Theory of Poetry* (New York: Oxford University Press, 1973). Dolores Rosenblum also observes the applicability of "the Bloomian concept of poetic belatedness" to "The Prince's Progress" ("Christina Rossetti and Poetic Sequence," in *The Achievement of Christina Rossetti,* 140).

2. Antony H. Harrison, *Christina Rossetti in Context* (Chapel Hill: University of North Carolina Press, 1988), 120; hereafter cited in text.

3. Joan Rees, "Christina Rossetti: Poet," *Critical Quarterly* 26, no. 3 (Autumn 1984): 69.

4. Luce Irigaray, *This Sex Which Is Not One,* trans. Catherine Porter with Carolyn Burke (Ithaca, N.Y.: Cornell University Press, 1985), 78; hereafter cited in text.

5. Walter E. Houghton, *The Victorian Frame of Mind, 1830–1870* (New Haven: Yale University Press, 1957), 243.

6. Elizabeth Barrett Browning, *The Letters of Elizabeth Barrett Browning,* 2 vols., ed. Frederic G. Kenyon (London: John Murray, 1898), 2:445.

7. For a discussion of "Under the Rose" in the context of the poet's rescue work, see Diane D'Amico, "'Equal before God': Christina Rossetti and the Fallen Women of Highgate Penitentiary," *Gender and Discourse in Victorian Literature and Art,* ed. Antony H. Harrison et al. (Dekalb: Northern Illinois University Press, 1992), 67–83.

8. By contrast, Mary E. Finn argues that the poem's anxiety has more to do with psychological guilt—that is, Margaret's predisposition to sin—than sociological circumstance. See *Writing the Incommensurable: Kierkegaard, Rossetti, and Hopkins* (University Park: Pennsylvania State University Press, 1992), 23–34; hereafter cited in text.

9. *The Face of the Deep: A Devotional Commentary on the Apocalypse* (London: Society for Promoting Christian Knowledge, 1892), 501; hereafter cited in text as *FD.*

10. Sharon Leder and Andrea Abbott, *The Language of Exclusion: The Poetry of Emily Dickinson and Christina Rossetti* (Westport, Conn.: Greenwood Press, 1987), 124.

11. Arguably, Rossetti makes a case for systemic change in "A Royal Princess." Privately, however, she expressed cynicism about the effectiveness of her heroine's action. "I do not," she told Gabriel, "fight for the R.P.'s heroism; though it seems to me that the royal soldiers might yet have succeeded in averting *roasting*. A *yell* is one thing, and a *fait accompli* quite another" (W. Rossetti, ed., 1903, 99). Because the poem ends before the princess acts on her personal decision, the political outcome remains, as Rossetti's comments here affirm, doubtful.

12. Review of *The Prince's Progress and Other Poems, Athenaeum* 2017 (23 June 1866): 825.

13. See Diane D'Amico, "Christina Rossetti's 'Maiden-Song': The Regal Power of Humility and Patience," *Journal of Pre-Raphaelite Studies* 6 (November 1985): 24–33. and "Fair Margaret of 'Maiden-Song': Rossetti's Response to the Romantic Nightingale," *Victorian Newsletter* 80 (Fall 1991): 8–13.

14. See, for example, *The Language and Poetry of Flowers, and Poetic Handbook of Wedding Anniversary Pieces, Album Verses, and Valentines* (New York: Hurst & Co., n.d.). As Gisela Hönnighausen points out, the Victorian vogue for floral poesy informs Rossetti's use of such imagery ("Emblematic Tendencies in the Works of Christina Rossetti," *Victorian Poetry* 10 [Spring 1972]: 9–10).

15. Review of *The Prince's Progress and Other Poems, Saturday Review,* 23 June 1866, 762.

16. Kathy Alexis Psomiades, "Feminine and Poetic Privacy in Christina Rossetti's 'Autumn' and 'A Royal Princess,'" *Victorian Poetry* 31 (Summer 1993), 188.

17. According to Edna Kotin Charles, Rossetti's reviewers generally inclined to judgments based on "contemporary Christian social ethics" (*Christina Rossetti: Critical Perspectives, 1862–1982* [Selinsgrove, Pa.: Susquehanna University Press, 1985], 66).

18. Christina Rossetti, quoted in Edmund Gosse, *Critical Kit-Kats* (New York: Dodd, Mead & Co., 1896), 159; hereafter cited in text.

19. Oscar Wilde, *The Picture of Dorian Gray* (1891; Harmondsworth: Penguin, 1949), 5.

20. Virginia Woolf, *The Second Common Reader* (New York: Harcourt Brace Jovanovich, 1932), 220.

21. Nina Auerbach, *Woman and the Demon: The Life of a Victorian Myth* (Cambridge: Harvard University Press, 1982), 129.

22. Ronald D. Morrison, "'One droned in sweetness like a fattened bee': Christina Rossetti's View of Marriage in Her Early Poetry," *Kentucky Philological Review* 5 (1990): 20. Morrison discusses essentially the same group of poems that I have isolated, but he incorrectly includes "Maude Clare" among the suppressed lyrics (25n9).

23. Harrison makes Rossetti's remark here central to his discussion of "The Poetics of 'Conciseness'" in *Christina Rossetti in Context*.

24. Diane D'Amico, "Christina Rossetti's 'From Sunset to Star Rise': A New Reading," *Victorian Poetry* 27 (Spring 1989): 95.

25. The fate of "Margery," once a candidate for publication in 1866, shows how rigorously Rossetti aimed at conciseness to avoid moral censure. Although the poem was never published in its entirety during her lifetime, she did use five of its original 55 lines for the first half of the lyric "The sinner's own fault? So it was." First published in *Time Flies,* the poem stands as the entry between the feasts of Saint Margaret, the Virgin Martyr (20 July), and Saint Mary Magdalene (22 July). The position of the erstwhile "Margery," now

severely cannibalized, allows Rossetti to point elliptically toward the issue of feminine vice and virtue.

Chapter Four

1. Review of *Commonplace and Other Short Stories, Spectator,* 29 October 1870, 1292. Even favorable reviews failed to communicate enthusiasm. For example, the contention that Rossetti's "homely fiction" is "more absorbing in its interest than any sensational novel" seems hardly calculated to stimulate a prospective audience (review of *Commonplace and Other Short Stories, Athenaeum* 2223 [4 June 1870]: 734).

2. *Commonplace and Other Short Stories* (London: F. S. Ellis, 1870), 4: hereafter cited in text as *CSS.*

3. *Seek and Find: A Double Series of Short Studies of the Benedicite* (London: Society for Promoting Christian Knowledge, 1879), 309; hereafter cited in text as *SF.*

4. Pamela K. Gilbert provides a more comprehensive discussion of the father's role in "'A Horrid Game': Woman as Social Entity in Christina Rossetti's Prose," *English* 41 (Spring 1992): 15–16; hereafter cited in text.

5. *Letter and Spirit: Notes on the Commandments* (London: Society for Promoting Christian Knowledge, 1883), 43; hereafter cited in text as *LS.*

6. Algernon Charles Swinburne, *The Swinburne Letters,* 6 vols., ed. Cecil Y. Lang (New Haven: Yale University Press, 1959), 2:116.

7. As a result, children's literature circumvents the contradiction between motherhood and authorship that Margaret Homans describes in *Bearing the Word: Language and Female Experience in Nineteenth-Century Women's Writing* (Chicago: University of Chicago Press, 1986). See especially her discussion of "The Author as Mother: Bearing the Word as Nineteenth-Century Ideology" (153–88).

8. I discuss the importance of the volume's arrangement at greater length in "Sound, Sense, and Structure in Christina Rossetti's *Sing-Song,*" *Children's Literature* 22 (1994): 3–26.

9. Lila Hanft, "The Politics of Maternal Ambivalence in Christina Rossetti's *Sing-Song,*" *Victorian Literature and Culture* 19 (1991): 217.

10. Virginia Sickbert argues for the egalitarianism of the mother-child relationship in "Christina Rossetti and Victorian Children's Poetry: A Maternal Challenge to the Patriarchal Family," *Victorian Poetry* 31 (Winter 1993): 389.

11. James R. Kincaid, *Child-Loving: The Erotic Child and Victorian Culture* (New York: Routledge, 1992), 12.

12. Sidney Colvin, review of *Sing-Song, The Princess and the Goblin, Through the Looking-Glass,* and *More Nonsense, Academy* 3 (15 January 1872): 23; hereafter cited in text. R. Loring Taylor is one modern critic who confesses discomfort with Rossetti's allusions to death (*Sing-Song, Speaking Likenesses, Goblin Market* [New York: Garland Publishing, 1976], xi).

13. Review of *Sing-Song, Nation* 14 (2 May 1872): 295.

14. Review of *Sing-Song, Scribner's Monthly* 3 (1872): 629.

15. The average number of live births for marriages lasting 20 years or longer dropped from 6.16 in the 1860s to 5.8 in the 1870s (Pat Jalland, *Women, Marriage and Politics: 1860–1914* [Oxford: Clarendon, 1986], 175).

16. For a discussion of women's fears in childbirth, see Jalland, 159–85. Also helpful is Patricia Branca, *Silent Sisterhood: Middle Class Women in the Victorian Home* (London: Croom Helm, 1975), 74–113.

17. Ann and Jane Taylor, *Original Poems for Infant Minds and Rhymes for the Nursery* (New York: Garland Publishing, 1976), 3:19–20; hereafter cited in text.

18. Barbara Garlitz uses these terms in her discussion of "Christina Rossetti's *Sing-Song* and Nineteenth-Century Children's Poetry," *PMLA* 70 (1955): 542.

19. Roderick McGillis, "Simple Surfaces: Christina Rossetti's Work for Children," *The Achievement of Christina Rossetti,* 222.

20. G. B. Tennyson outlines these doctrines in *Victorian Devotional Poetry: The Tractarian Mode* (Cambridge: Harvard University Press, 1981), 44–56; hereafter cited in text.

21. *Speaking Likenesses,* (London: Macmillan, 1874), [v]; hereafter cited in text as *SL*.

22. Wendy R. Katz discusses the relationship between these two traditions in "Muse from Nowhere: Christina Rossetti's Fantasy World in *Speaking Likenesses,*" *Journal of Pre-Raphaelite Studies* 5 (November 1984): 14–35.

23. Review of *Speaking Likenesses, Athenaeum* 2461 (26 December 1874): 877.

24. U. C. Knoepflmacher, "Avenging Alice: Christina Rossetti and Lewis Carroll," *Nineteenth-Century Literature* 41 (December 1986), 310 and 314; hereafter cited in text.

25. Nina Auerbach and U. C. Knoepflmacher make a similar point in their introduction to *Speaking Likenesses* in *Forbidden Journeys: Fairy Tales and Fantasies by Victorian Women Writers* (Chicago: University of Chicago Press, 1992), 320.

26. Kathleen Blake, *Love and the Woman Question in Victorian Literature: The Art of Self-Postponement* (Brighton, England: Harvester Press, 1983), vii; hereafter cited in text. Blake's fine discussion of self-postponement in Rossetti's work does not examine the contradictions in her treatment of motherhood (3–25).

Chapter Five

1. Dante Gabriel Rossetti, *The Works of Dante Gabriel Rossetti,* ed. William Michael Rossetti (London: Ellis, 1911), 296; hereafter cited in text.

2. Sarah Ellis, *The Daughters of England: Their Position in Society, Character, and Responsibilities* (London: Fisher, 1843), 126.

3. William Whitla, "Questioning the Convention: Christina Rossetti's Sonnet Sequence 'Monna Innominata,'" in *The Achievement of Christina Rossetti,* 86; hereafter cited in text. Whitla provides the best essay-length discussion of the Petrarchan conventions that Rossetti challenges in her sequence.

4. Marya Zaturenska, *Christina Rossetti: A Portrait with Background* (1949; New York: Kraus, 1970), 155.

5. Margaret Homans, "'Syllables of Velvet': Dickinson, Rossetti, and the Rhetorics of Sexuality," *Feminist Studies* 11 (Fall 1985): 574; hereafter cited in text.

6. Betty S. Flowers, "'Had Such a Lady Spoken for Herself': Christina Rossetti's 'Monna Innominata,'" *Library Chronicle of the University of Texas at Austin* 22 (1992): 18.

7. Incidentally, in the same year that Rossetti published "Monna Innominata," Julia Fletcher, writing under the name George Fleming, brought out a translation of Gaspara Stampa's *Rime d'amore,* which had originally appeared just after her death in 1554. Noting the coincidence, one reviewer says that the Venetian woman's sonnets provide "the actual thing which Miss Rossetti had imagined" and are, by comparison, "less deliberate, more intense and direct" ("New Poetry of the Rossettis and Others," *Atlantic Monthly* 49 [January 1882]: 121–22).

8. Although Rossetti probably sought to deflect rather than invite comparison between "Monna Innominata" and *Sonnets from the Portuguese,* critics have quite naturally examined the two sequences in tandem. See Antony H. Harrison, "In the Shadow of E. B. B.: Christina Rossetti and Ideological Estrangement," *Victorian Poets and Romantic Poems: Intertextuality and Ideology* (Charlottesville: University Press of Virginia, 1990), 108–43; Joan Rees, *The Poetry of Dante Gabriel Rossetti: Modes of Self-Expression* (Cambridge: Cambridge University Press, 1981), 146–60.

9. T. Hall Caine, review of *A Pageant and Other Poems, Academy* (27 August 1881): 152. Caine later wrote that he esteemed "Monna Innominata" above *Sonnets from the Portuguese* "in purity of lyric medium"; however, he found the two sequences "on a level . . . in points of tenderness and resignation" (*Sonnets of Three Centuries: A Selection* [London: Elliot Stock, 1882], 311).

10. Helen H. Wenger, "The Influence of the Bible in Christina Rossetti's 'Monna Innominata,'" *Christian Scholar's Review* 3 (1973): 15.

11. Quoted in Dorothy Margaret Stuart, *Christina Rossetti* (London: Macmillan, 1930), 106.

12. Betty S. Flowers, "The Kingly Self: Rossetti as Woman Artist," in *The Achievement of Christina Rossetti,* 167.

13. Linda Schofield, "Being and Understanding: Devotional Poetry of Christina Rossetti and the Tractarians," in *The Achievement of Christina Rossetti,* 309, 321.

14. Interested in the structure of the series, Diane d'Amico is one of the few critics to examine "Christina Rossetti's 'Later Life': The Neglected Sonnet Sequence," *Victorians Institute Journal* 9 (1980–81): 21–28.

15. *Called to Be Saints: The Minor Festivals Devotionally Studied* (London: Society for Promoting Christian Knowledge, 1881), 435.

16. Catherine Musello Cantalupo, "Christina Rossetti: The Devotional Poet and the Rejection of Romantic Nature," in *The Achievement of Christina Rossetti*, 292–93.

17. David A. Kent, "Sequence and Meaning in Christina Rossetti's *Verses* (1893)," *Victorian Poetry* 17 (Autumn 1979): 261. Kent also notes that the subsequent dismantling of *Verses* for the *Poetical Works* destroys the integrity of the sequence ("W. M. Rossetti and the Editing of Christina Rossetti's Religious Poetry," *Pre-Raphaelite Review* 1 [May 1978]: 18–26).

Conclusion

1. Grace Gilchrist, "Christina Rossetti," *Good Words* 37 (1896): 823.

2. William Sharp, "Some Reminiscences of Christina Rossetti," *Atlantic Monthly* 75 (June 1895): 737; hereafter cited in text.

3. Virginia Woolf, *A Room of One's Own* (1929; London: Grafton, 1977), 19.

4. C. M. Bowra, *The Romantic Imagination* (1949; New York: Oxford University Press, 1961), 261; hereafter cited in text.

5. Stuart Curran, "The Lyric Voice of Christina Rossetti," *Victorian Poetry* 9 (Autumn 1971): 298, 291.

Selected Bibliography

PRIMARY WORKS

Poetry

Verses. London: Privately printed by G. Polidori, 1847.
Goblin Market and Other Poems. Illustrated by D. G. Rossetti. London: Macmillan, 1862.
The Prince's Progress and Other Poems. Illustrated by D. G. Rossetti. London: Macmillan, 1866.
Sing-Song: A Nursery Rhyme Book. Illustrated by Arthur Hughes. London: George Routledge and Sons, 1872.
Goblin Market, The Prince's Progress, and Other Poems. Illustrated by D. G. Rossetti. London: Macmillan, 1875.
A Pageant and Other Poems. London: Macmillan, 1881.
Poems. New and enlarged edition. Illustrated by D. G. Rossetti. London: Macmillan, 1890.
Goblin Market. Illustrated by Laurence Housman. London: Macmillan, 1893.
Verses. Reprinted from *Called to Be Saints, Time Flies,* and *The Face of the Deep*. London: Society for Promoting Christian Knowledge, 1893.
New Poems, Hitherto Unpublished or Uncollected. Edited by William Michael Rossetti. London: Macmillan, 1896.

Prose Fiction

Commonplace and Other Short Stories. London: F. S. Ellis, 1870.
Speaking Likenesses. Illustrated by Arthur Hughes. London: Macmillan, 1874.
Maude: A Story for Girls. Edited by William Michael Rossetti. London: James Bowden, 1897. Because of copyright restrictions, William had to omit several poems from the English edition of his sister's 1850 tale. R. W. Crump provides the complete text in *Maude: Prose and Verse* (Hamden, Conn.: Archon Books, 1976).

Devotional Prose

Annus Domini: A Prayer for Each Day of the Year, Founded on a Text of Holy Scripture. Oxford and London: James Parker, 1874.
Seek and Find: A Double Series of Short Studies of the Benedicite. London: Society for Promoting Christian Knowledge, 1879.

Called to Be Saints: The Minor Festivals Devotionally Studied. London: Society for Promoting Christian Knowledge, 1881.

Letter and Spirit: Notes on the Commandments. London: Society for Promoting Christian Knowledge, 1883.

Time Flies: A Reading Diary. London: Society for Promoting Christian Knowledge, 1885.

The Face of the Deep: A Devotional Commentary on the Apocalypse. London: Society for Promoting Christian Knowledge, 1892.

Collected Works

The Poetical Works of Christina Georgina Rossetti. Edited by William Michael Rossetti. London: Macmillan, 1904. Still useful for memoir and notes.

Sing-Song; Speaking Likenesses; Goblin Market. Introduction by R. Loring Taylor. New York and London: Garland Publishing, 1976. Brings together facsimile reprints of Rossetti's work for children.

The Complete Poems of Christina Rossetti. A Variorum Edition. 3 vols. Edited by R. W. Crump. Baton Rouge and London: Louisiana State University Press, 1979–90. The standard edition.

Christina Rossetti: Poems and Prose. An Everyman Edition. Edited by Jan Marsh. London: J. M. Dent; Vermont: Charles E. Tuttle, 1994. A selection featuring several short stories as well as useful explanatory notes.

Letters and Rossettiana

Cline, C. L., ed. *The Owl and the Rossettis: Letters of Charles A. Howell and Dante Gabriel, Christina, and William Michael Rossetti.* University Park: Pennsylvania State University Press, 1978. Contains six letters by Christina Rossetti.

Doughty, Oswald, and John Robert Wahl, eds. *Letters of Dante Gabriel Rossetti.* 4 vols. Oxford: Clarendon Press, 1965–67. Includes many letters and references to his sister.

Fredeman, William E., ed. *The P.R.B. Journal: William Michael Rossetti's Diary of the Pre-Raphaelite Brotherhood, 1849–1853.* Oxford: Clarendon Press, 1975. Provides essential contextual material.

Harrison, Antony H., ed. *The Collected Letters of Christina Rossetti.* 2 vols. Charlottesville: University Press of Virginia, 1997–. Promises to fill the gap in Rossetti scholarship.

Maser, Mary Louise Jarden, and Frederick E. Maser. *Christina Rossetti in the Maser Collection.* Bryn Mawr, Pa.: Bryn Mawr College Library, 1991. Short study of manuscript collection plus 45 letters to friends and acquaintances.

Packer, Lona Mosk, ed. *The Rossetti-Macmillan Letters: Some 133 Unpublished Letters Written to Alexander Macmillan, F. S. Ellis, and Others, by Dante Gabriel, Christina, and William Michael Rossetti.* Berkeley: University of

California Press, 1963. Contains 96 letters demonstrating Christina
Rossetti's interest in the business of publication.

Peattie, Roger W., ed. *Selected Letters of William Michael Rossetti*. University Park:
Pennsylvania State University Press, 1990. Includes letters and references
to his sister.

Rossetti, William Michael, ed. *The Family Letters of Christina Georgina Rossetti*.
London: Brown, Langham, 1908; reprinted, New York: Haskell House,
1968. Also valuable for notes and appendices.

———, ed. *Rossetti Papers, 1862–1870*. London: Sands, 1903; reprinted, New
York: AMS Press, 1970. Includes several important letters concerning
poems for the 1866 volume.

———, ed. *Ruskin: Rossetti: Preraphaelitism. Papers 1854 to 1862*. London:
Allen, 1899; reprinted, New York: AMS Press, 1971. Contextual material plus two items by Christina Rossetti.

———. *Some Reminiscences of William Michael Rossetti*. 2 vols. London: Brown,
Langham, 1906; reprinted, New York: AMS Press, 1970. William's
autobiography, containing many references to his sister.

Troxell, Janet Camp, ed. *Three Rossettis: Unpublished Letters to and from Dante
Gabriel, Christina, and William*. Cambridge: Harvard University Press,
1937. Devotes two chapters to Christina Rossetti's correspondence.

SECONDARY WORKS

Bibliographies

Crump, R. W. *Christina Rossetti: A Reference Guide*. Boston: G. K. Hall, 1976.

Fredeman, William E. "Christina Rossetti." In *The Victorian Poets: A Guide to
Research,* edited by Frederic E. Faverty, 284–93. Cambridge: Harvard
University Press, 1968.

———. *Pre-Raphaelitism: A Bibliocritical Study*. Cambridge: Harvard University
Press, 1965.

Books and Parts of Books

Battiscombe, Georgina. *Christina Rossetti: A Divided Life*. New York: Holt,
Rinehart & Winston, 1981. Sees conflict between passion and restraint in
Rossetti's character as internalized aspects of her Anglo-Italian heritage.

Bell, Mackenzie. *Christina Rossetti: A Biographical and Critical Study*. London:
Thomas Burleigh, 1898. First full-length study. Indispensable for presentation of generous excerpts from letters and other materials as yet
unavailable elsewhere.

Blake, Kathleen. *Love and the Woman Question: The Art of Self-Postponement.* Brighton, England: Harvester Press, 1983. Opening chapter provides a discussion of the feminine strategies of deferral and suspension that Rossetti uses to embody Christian consciousness.

Charles, Edna Kotin. *Christina Rossetti: Critical Perspectives, 1862–1982.* Selinsgrove, Pa.: Susquehanna University Press, 1985. Reviews three periods in Rossetti scholarship since 1862, but falls short of rigorous metacritical analysis.

D'Amico, Diane. "'Equal before God': Christina Rossetti and the Fallen Women of Highgate Penitentiary." In *Gender and Discourse in Victorian Literature and Art,* edited by Antony Harrison et al., 67–83. Dekalb: Northern Illinois University Press, 1992. Valuable discussion of contexts for Rossetti's "fallen woman" poems.

Finn, Mary E. *Writing the Incommensurable: Kierkegaard, Rossetti, and Hopkins.* University Park: Pennsylvania State University Press, 1992. Uses Kierkegaardian rhetoric to explore paradox between religious belief and poetic expression in Rossetti and Hopkins.

Gilbert, Sandra M., and Susan Gubar. *The Madwoman in the Attic: The Woman Writer and the Nineteenth-Century Literary Imagination.* New Haven: Yale University Press, 1979. Includes a discussion of the esthetics of renunciation as operative in *Maude* and "Goblin Market."

Harrison, Antony H. *Christina Rossetti in Context.* Chapel Hill: University of North Carolina Press, 1988. Describes Rossetti as a highly self-conscious writer within an intellectual milieu defined by Tractarianism, Pre-Raphaelitism, and estheticism. New Historicist approach yields sophisticated insight into her revisions of Dante and Petrarch.

———. *Victorian Poets and Romantic Poems: Intertextuality and Ideology.* Charlottesville: University Press of Virginia, 1990. Important for one chapter on Rossetti's corrections of Barrett Browning.

Hickok, Kathleen. *Representations of Women: Nineteenth-Century British Women's Poetry.* Westport, Conn.: Greenwood Press, 1984. Wide-ranging survey ends with an evaluation of Rossetti's use of common female types.

Jiménez, Nilda. *The Bible and the Poetry of Christina Rossetti: A Concordance.* Westport, Conn.: Greenwood Press, 1979. A reference tool clumsy to use partly because the *Poetical Works* has since been superseded as the standard edition of Rossetti's verse.

Jones, Kathleen. *Learning Not to Be First: The Life of Christina Rossetti.* New York: St. Martin's Press, 1992. Portrays the poet as "a passionate, angry woman" who stifled her inner life in conformance with an external rule of religious belief.

Jurlaro, Felicita. *Christina Georgina Rossetti: The True Story.* London: Excalibur Press, 1991. Draws on recollections of the poet's niece, Olivia Rossetti Agresti.

Kaplan, Cora. "The Indefinite Disclosed: Christina Rossetti and Emily Dickinson." In *Women Writing and Writing about Women,* edited by Mary

Jacobus, 61–79. London: Croom Helm, 1979. A discussion of elliptical strategies in the dream lyrics and fantasy poems. Attempts to resolve the problem of "the recalcitrant female psyche" for the feminist critic.

Kent, David A., ed. *The Achievement of Christina Rossetti*. Ithaca, N.Y.: Cornell University Press, 1987. Invaluable collection of essays.

Leder, Sharon, with Andrea Abbott. *The Language of Exclusion: The Poetry of Emily Dickinson and Christina Rossetti*. Westport, Conn.: Greenwood Press, 1987. Considers Rossetti as a public poet engaged in a feminist critique of her society but oversimplifies contradictions posed by her conservatism.

Leighton, Angela. *Victorian Women Poets: Writing against the Heart*. Charlottesville: University Press of Virginia, 1992. Devotes one chapter to Rossetti's self-invention as a poet of mystic melancholy.

Marsh, Jan. *Christina Rossetti: A Literary Biography*. London: Jonathan Cape, 1994. Speculates that Rossetti was a victim of paternal incest. Destined to become the standard biography.

Mayberry, Katherine J. *Christina Rossetti and the Poetry of Discovery*. Baton Rouge: Louisiana State University Press, 1989. A readable introduction to Rossetti's poetry.

Packer, Lona Mosk. *Christina Rossetti*. Berkeley: University of California Press, 1963. Mistakenly discovers a clue to Rossetti's impassioned verse in her unrequited love for a married man. Patient documentation of much previously unpublished material only partially redeems damage done by indefensibility of author's key premise.

Rees, Joan. *The Poetry of Dante Gabriel Rossetti: Modes of Self-Expression*. Cambridge: Cambridge University Press, 1981. Provides a solid discussion of rhetorical strategies in "Monna Innominata."

Rosenblum, Dolores. *Christina Rossetti: The Poetry of Endurance*. Carbondale and Edwardsville: Southern Illinois University Press, 1986. Argues that the esthetic of renunciation enables the woman poet to survive discontinuities between lived and literary experience. Important feminist analysis.

Tennyson, G. B. *Victorian Devotional Poetry: The Tractarian Mode*. Cambridge: Harvard University Press, 1981. Concluding chapter discusses influence of Oxford Movement on Rossetti and Hopkins.

Thomas, Frances. *Christina Rossetti*. Hanley Swan, England: Self-Publishing Association, 1992. Depicts Rossetti as a woman who, despite bouts of severe depression, engaged in a range of religious and philanthropic activities.

Articles

Bump, Jerome. "Hopkins, Christina Rossetti, and Pre-Raphaelitism." *Victorian Newsletter* 57 (Spring 1980): 1–6. Identifies Rossetti as primary Pre-Raphaelite influence on Hopkins.

Connor, Steven. "'Speaking Likenesses': Language and Repetition in Christina Rossetti's *Goblin Market*." *Victorian Poetry* 22 (Winter 1984): 439–48.

Reads "Goblin Market" in light of the verbal techniques used in nursery rhyme and fairy tale.

D'Amico, Diane. "Christina Rossetti's *Maude*: A Reconsideration." *University of Dayton Review* 15 (Spring 1981): 129–42. Emphasizes esthetic elements of *Maude* to counter view of the young Rossetti's overscrupulous religiosity.

Fass, Barbara. "Christina Rossetti and St. Agnes' Eve." *Victorian Poetry* 14 (Spring 1976): 33–46. Examines Rossetti's attraction to the motif of the waiting woman in Keats's work.

Flowers, Betty S. "'Had such a lady spoken for herself': Christina Rossetti's 'Monna Innominata.'" *Library Chronicle of the University of Texas* 22 (1992): 12–29. Argues that "Monna Innominata" corrects "patterns of emotion" found in the conventional amatory sonnet.

Gilbert, Pamela K. "'A Horrid Game': Woman as Social Entity in Christina Rossetti's Prose." *English* 41 (Spring 1992): 1–23. Explores the ambivalence toward contemporary constructs of femininity evident in Rossetti's fiction.

Goldberg, Gail Lynn. "Dante Gabriel Rossetti's 'Revising Hand': His Illustrations for Christina Rossetti's Poems." *Victorian Poetry* 20 (Autumn–Winter 1982): 145–59. Argues that the designs for "Goblin Market" and "The Prince's Progress" offer sensitive interpretations of the text.

Hanft, Lila. "The Politics of Maternal Ambivalence in Christina Rossetti's *Sing-Song*." *Victorian Literature and Culture* 19 (1991): 213–32. Views infanticidal impulses in Rossetti's nursery rhymes as indicative of contradictions in domestic ideology.

Hassett, Constance W. "Christina Rossetti and the Poetry of Reticence." *Philological Quarterly* 65 (Fall 1986): 495–514. An analysis of stylistic features focusing on Rossetti's evasiveness as a poet.

Helsinger, Elizabeth K. "Consumer Power and the Utopia of Desire: Christina Rossetti's 'Goblin Market.'" *ELH* 58 (Winter 1991): 903–33. Interesting account of economies of sexual and mercantile exchange in "Goblin Market" as well as Rossetti's rural ballads.

Homans, Margaret. "'Syllables of Velvet': Dickinson, Rossetti, and the Rhetorics of Sexuality." *Feminist Studies* 11 (Fall 1985): 569–93. Contends that masculine plots of heterosexual desire defeat Rossetti's effort to privilege the female voice in "Monna Innominata."

Hönnighausen, Gisela. "Emblematic Tendencies in the Works of Christina Rossetti." *Victorian Poetry* 10 (Spring 1972): 1–15. Classic article on Rossetti's floral symbolism.

Kent, David A. "Sequence and Meaning in Christina Rossetti's *Verses*." *Victorian Poetry* 17 (Autumn 1979): 259–64. Points out the importance of the principle of arrangement in Rossetti's volumes of verse.

Knoepflmacher, U. C. "Avenging Alice: Christina Rossetti and Lewis Carroll." *Nineteenth-Century Literature* 41 (December 1986): 299–328. Provocative discussion of *Speaking Likenesses* as an ironic repudiation of Carroll's idealized female child.

Kooistra, Lorraine Janzen. "The Representation of Violence / The Violence of Representation: Housman's Illustrations to Rossetti's *Goblin Market*." *English Studies in Canada* 19 (September 1993): 305–28. Argues that pictorial (and critical) interpretations of "Goblin Market" master the text by misreading it.

Leighton, Angela. "'Because Men Made the Laws': The Fallen Woman and the Woman Poet." *Victorian Poetry* 27 (Summer 1989): 109–27. Locates "The Convent Threshold" in a tradition that also includes work by Elizabeth Barrett Browning, Augusta Webster, Amy Levy, and Charlotte Mew.

McGann, Jerome J. "Christina Rossetti's Poems: A New Edition and a Revaluation." *Victorian Studies* 23 (Winter 1980): 237–58. Influential review that broadens into an analysis of Rossetti's use of symbol to approach social issues.

―――. "The Religious Poetry of Christina Rossetti." *Critical Inquiry* 10 (September 1983): 127–44. Brings a historicist awareness to the doctrinal features of Rossetti's art.

Marshall, Linda E. "What the Dead Are Doing Underground: Hades and Heaven in the Writings of Christina Rossetti." *Victorian Newsletter* 72 (Fall 1987): 55–60. Fine discussion of the religious prose and verse. Puts Rossetti's Adventism firmly in the context of Anglican eschatology.

Mermin, Dorothy. "The Damsel, the Knight, and the Victorian Woman Poet." *Critical Inquiry* 13 (Autumn 1986): 64–80. Considers attempts by Rossetti, Barrett Browning, and Dickinson to deal with paradox of the woman poet by taking the role of both subject and object in verse.

―――. "Heroic Sisterhood in *Goblin Market*." *Victorian Poetry* 21 (Summer 1983): 107–18. Discusses "Goblin Market" as a fantasy of feminine fulfillment that ultimately excludes men.

Michie, Helena. "The Battle for Sisterhood: Christina Rossetti's Strategies for Control in Her Sister Poems." *Journal of Pre-Raphaelite Studies* 3 (May 1983): 38–55. Sees the "rhetorical combat" between women in Rossetti's verse as the means she chose to define her poetic voice.

Morrill, David F. "'Twilight Is Not Good for Maidens': Uncle Polidori and the Psychodynamics of Vampirism in *Goblin Market*." *Victorian Poetry* 28 (Spring 1990): 1–16. Reads "Goblin Market" as a corrective response to treatment of adolescent desire in *The Vampyre*.

Psomiades, Kathy Alexis. "Feminine and Poetic Privacy in Christina Rossetti's 'Autumn' and 'A Royal Princess.'" *Victorian Poetry* 31 (Summer 1993): 187–202. Concerns mediation of Tennysonian myth of esthetic autonomy.

Rees, Joan. "Christina Rossetti: Poet." *Critical Quarterly* 26.3 (Autumn 1984): 59–72. Uses a "traditional" reading of "The Prince's Progress" to dispute feminist approaches to Rossetti's work.

Ricks, Christopher. "Christina Rossetti and Commonplace Books." *Grand Street* 9 (Spring 1990): 190–98. Makes a case for a reappreciation of Rossetti as a sophisticated prose stylist.

Sickbert, Virginia. "Christina Rossetti and Victorian Children's Poetry: A Maternal Challenge to the Patriarchal Family." *Victorian Poetry* 31 (Winter 1993): 385–410. A reading of *Sing-Song* stressing the reciprocity between mother and daughter.

Smulders, Sharon. "'A Form That Differences': Vocational Metaphors in the Poetry of Christina Rossetti and Gerard Manley Hopkins." *Victorian Poetry* 29 (Summer 1991): 161–73. Examines the figure of the nun as a means to relate concomitant spiritual and esthetic goals.

Thompson, Deborah Ann. "Anorexia as a Lived Trope: Christina Rossetti's 'Goblin Market.'" *Mosaic* 24 (Summer–Fall 1991): 89–106. Uses images of feast and fast to consider the link between eating disorders and "widespread cultural gender-orders."

Victorian Poetry 32 (Winter 1994). This issue, edited by Antony H. Harrison, brings together essays written to celebrate the centenary of Rossetti's death.

Watson, Jeanie. "'Men Sell Not Such in Any Town': Christina Rossetti's Goblin Fruit of Fairy Tale." *Children's Literature* 12 (1984): 61–77. Argues that the combination of fairy tale and moral tale in "Goblin Market" leads to the exaltation of imagination over convention.

Weathers, Winston. "Christina Rossetti: The Sisterhood of Self." *Victorian Poetry* 3 (Spring 1965): 81–89. Seminal discussion of Rossetti's presentation of the divided self.

Westerholm, Joel. "'I Magnify Mine Office': Christina Rossetti's Authoritative Voice in Her Devotional Prose." *Victorian Newsletter* 84 (Fall 1993): 11–17. Posits that Rossetti's theological writings implicitly contradict orthodox Anglican position on women preachers.

Zasadinski, Eugene. "Christina Rossetti's 'A Better Resurrection' and 'Up-Hill': Self-Reliance and Its Limitations." *Journal of Pre-Raphaelite and Aesthetic Studies* 4 (May 1984): 93–99. Focuses on issue of works and faith to pose double reading of religious verse as simultaneously orthodox (Anglican) and heterodox (Roman Catholic).

Index

The Author

Sharon Smulders was born in London, Ontario, and received her D.Phil. from the University of Sussex in 1988. She teaches in the English Department at Mount Royal College, Calgary. Her interest in nineteenth-century poetry has led to articles on Elizabeth Barrett Browning, Alice Meynell, Christina Rossetti, and Dante Gabriel Rossetti.